TRACKING DOWN STEAM

← Looking through a window to the past days of steam. Two enthusiasts 'spot' BR Standard Class 5MT 4-6-0 No 73037 from the carriage window as they pass Basingstoke shed. This was a typical view of the time, in this case the train on which we were travelling was being hauled by preserved A4 Pacific No 4498 *Sir Nigel Gresley* and was en route to Weymouth, on 4 June 1967.

First published in June 2013

A catalogue record for this book is available from the British Library

ISBN 978 0 85733 236 3

Library of Congress control card no 2013932255

Published by Haynes Publishing,
Sparkford, Yeovil, Somerset BA22 7JJ, UK
Tel: 01963 442030 Fax: 01963 440001
Int. tel: +44 1963 442030 Int. fax: +44 1963 440001
E-mail: sales@haynes.co.uk
Website: www.haynes.co.uk

Haynes North America Inc.,
861 Lawrence Drive, Newbury Park, California 91320, USA

Designed and typeset by Austin Taylor
Project managed by Sophie Blackman

Printed and bound in the USA by Odcombe Press LP,
1299 Bridgestone Parkway, La Vergne, TN 37086

All photographs were taken by the author unless specified.

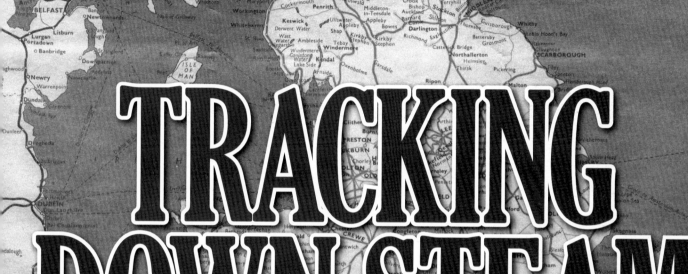

TRACKING DOWN STEAM

BR STEAM IN ACTION AND ON SHED, IN WORKS, INDUSTRY AND PRESERVATION, AND AWAITING SCRAP

PETER NICHOLSON

Haynes Publishing

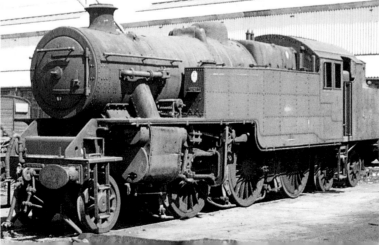

CONTENTS

FOREWORD

THERE ARE ALWAYS some people who seem to be in the background all the time, although every now and again you might bump into them at some function or other and are reminded about how knowledgeable they are. The author of this fabulous book is one such person. A true rail enthusiast par excellence – as evidenced in this work.

Peter Nicholson is someone who understands both the necessity and the need for modernisation in the railway and who grasps the importance of these changes. I have to confess that the major change from steam to the new locos largely passed me by at the time since I loved both! The bonus for me was that I could travel by rail every day to London so I watched the transformation from a carriage window.

It is thanks to Peter and others like him that I was able to return to steam with so much enthusiasm. For the past 25 years I have had the honour of saving many engines and I have relished the magnificent steam era.

This book is full of previously unseen photographs, taken by someone who had the foresight to recognise a changing world and the need to create a record for the rest of us – a record that had nothing to do with the music business!

Put the kettle on, and 'all aboard' with your cuppa in a quiet room with sufficient time to allow this book to take you back through a time machine of memories.

Pete Waterman

Photograph courtesy of Jack Boskett

INTRODUCTION

THIS BOOK IS DEVOTED to my pursuit of the steam locomotives of British Railways and its predecessor companies. Initially, my railway interest was solely inspired by the Ian Allan *abc* locomotive books. Simply, if a locomotive was listed therein, it needed to be seen; if it was not in there it was clearly of no importance.

This was a view shared by others I'm sure, and I well remember our arrival at Swindon Works on a special in 1960, when one of the first locos we saw in the sidings was a rusty-looking Dean Goods carrying the number 2516. Someone shouted out: 'What's that? It doesn't exist!' as he quickly looked it up in his *abc*, and found it was not listed in there, having been withdrawn. That pretty well summed up the attitude at that time for many of us.

Later, my railway interest changed or perhaps developed, to encompass locos that were not in the book but today, although still confined to those to be found within the British Isles, it now embraces steam, diesel, petrol and electric traction, from 7¼in to 7ft ¼in gauge. My passion for narrow gauge Lister and 'Planet' petrol and diesel locos is perhaps as far as you can get from chasing magnificent Bulleid Pacifics, even though the latter are still top of my favourites list, along with some types in between, such as the English Electric Class 37s.

I still regard 'locospotting' as an important aspect to the railway hobby. To me, it has never been the collection of numbers for its own sake, as is so often portrayed by the media and non-enthusiasts, but a means of maintaining a record of those locomotives seen and photographed.

A knowledge of locos and their numbering (their identities) seems to me to be a basic way of keeping a check on which locos are extant today, the quantity of each type that existed in the past (and therefore their importance), and where they can and could have been seen. This is surely an important aspect of any interest in locomotives, which have all been produced to fulfil a certain purpose, and not simply for someone's

entertainment, although perhaps this is changing with some of the 21st century 'new-builds' proposed.

In fact, I have a certain suspicion of so-called 'railway enthusiasts' who proudly proclaim, 'of course, I was *never* a train spotter'. I find it difficult to accept that they have the same passion, commitment or depth of basic railway knowledge say, of the old companies and their locos as someone who was or is a methodical observer of the railway scene. For example, Pete Waterman, a self-confessed 'spotter', is clearly the 'real thing' when it comes to being a railway enthusiast, whereas those such as the lovely Julia Bradbury, Michael 'Bradshaw' Portillo, or Dan 'Pistol packing' Snow, as good and enthusiastic presenters as they are, perhaps are not.

Today, you get those who spend an inordinate amount of time volunteering on a heritage railway, and to whom we should all be grateful for their commitment, but who are happy to boast they 'are not railway enthusiasts' at all. Who are they kidding, and more importantly why?

Over the years I have taken many railway photos, quite a lot in fact, but I have never classed myself as a 'railway photographer' as such, but as an enthusiast who takes photos for record purposes. More or less as soon as I became interested in railways from the age of four or five, I started to use a basic camera, a Hawkeye – nothing so elaborate as a Box Brownie!

The 'view finder' was a piece of wire bent to form a rectangle the size of the back of the camera, that was pulled up to look through. The main problem, but only one of many with it, was that the very wide-angle lens gave a totally different image

← My first railway photo – taken from platform 10 at King's Cross, using a 'state-of-the-ark' Hawkeye camera. The photo is undated but almost certainly 1959, showing a pair of B17 class 4-6-0s, No 61623 *Lambton Castle* (withdrawn in September that year), and No 61653 *Huddersfield Town* to the right. This was my only ever sighting of any of these wonderful engines apart from one B2, No 61607 *Blickling*, at Liverpool Street. This photo at least survives, unlike my uncle's effort.

to that seen with the eye. Combined with a slow shutter speed, the first attempts at approaching trains were not too successful. In fact, the loco was sometimes so small within the image that you could not really see it, although at the time of taking the photo the loco appeared to be bearing down on me. My father even accused my once of taking the photo when I heard the loco rather than waiting to see it! It is perhaps fortunate that it took only eight pictures on a 127 film, of which I could not afford to buy too many, otherwise there would have been even more useless snaps. I was, if nothing else, persistent.

Nevertheless, all were kept as they were my record of the occasion, which is all I ever considered my photos to be. As time went by better cameras were acquired, but it has to be said, not much better, and I have always worked with those from the cheaper end of the scale, as finances have inevitably been somewhat limited. The obvious thing, to others perhaps, would have been to have spent less on film and travel, and get better equipped, but I decided to wait until income picked up rather than cut down on the trips.

Even though I have used digital with all its advantages for nearly a decade, I have continued to carry a loaded film camera in the bag as a back-up and a 'just in case'. I am still not completely convinced by digital photography and have concerns about its long-term archival qualities. In a way, I am pleased it did not come along earlier in my life. On the other hand, I would have loved to have had such a camera when going on those shed trips as far as quantity of pictures was concerned!

When questioned about my film camera I have replied that I will stop using it when I run out of film. As Jessops have always supplied a replacement film when returning the processed one, I thought this meant I had quite an assured future with film. The demise of this company means that 2013 will indeed probably be my last year for using the old, but dependable format.

I was inspired and encouraged to become interested in railways and to take photos by my father. His interest was more in photography in itself, and he took photographs of many different subjects, ranging from portraits to village scenes, but surprisingly few railway photos, leaving that mainly to me I suppose. The DIY approach to photography obviously ran in the family as we always developed and printed our own black and whites, while my uncle was even more adventurous in this respect. He was, if anything, more interested in the chemical side of it all than actually taking the photos. He was taking colour slides in the 1950s, more often than not, of bowls of fruit on the table, but on one occasion my father and I persuaded him to meet us at the end of platform 10 at King's Cross station, one of our favourite spotting spots.

Uncle Bill took a few shots including, at my prompting, a pair of B17s, in a perfect sunny position in the station sidings, amongst other more common locos there. His colour shots were superb. A few years later, I asked if there was any chance of him letting me have these photos for my collection, but he was very cagey about them. It was not until he died a few years ago and I had the opportunity of sorting through his photos that I got very excited when I found a slide box with 'King' Cross engines' marked on it. Can you imagine my disappointment when, on extracting the slides, I found they had turned completely black!

He was an experimenter all right. Not content with doing his own developing and printing with Johnson's chemicals as we did, he enjoyed concocting the developer and fixer from the basic chemicals. On top of that, he had been making his own film, a habit he had picked up just after the war. He bought ex-aircraft camera gun film from shops in Charing Cross Road, cleaned off the images and then recoated it with his patent mix. All very clever and satisfying for him at the time no doubt, but evidently its archival qualities left something to be desired. It would be no exaggeration to say that the arsenal of toxic chemicals he kept in his tiny under-

⬇ An early spotting place on the South Western main line within cycling distance that I often used on a sunny summer's evening was the public golf course at Esher. This view, dated 10 October 1964, shows rebuilt 'West Country' 4-6-2 No 34100 *Appledore* on an up train. Many of my early 'cops' were seen from this pleasant vantage point. Lineside tree growth makes such a view impossible today, as it does for so many places throughout the country. Hence 'leaves on the line'...

stairs darkroom would today result in the bomb squad sealing off the property!

The family thought it a health hazard if only because amongst the bottles of chemicals stored in the cubby hole, lit only by a dull red light, there was always one with beer in, which he swigged from time to time. He assured us he always knew which one it was!

Early days

Like many, my introduction to railways was by means of the Ian Allan *abc* books, which in my case, was a late 1940s Southern Region edition. It was not until 1955/56 that my parents accepted that I needed those for other regions and these were bought one at a time, to avoiding the big outlay for a combined volume.

The first outing I was taken on was specifically to tick off some locos – I did not underline in these books as everyone else did, but preferred to tick in pencil each loco every time I saw it – was a cycle ride to the nearest steam location. This was on the South Western main line at Berrylands, were there was a children's play area, in case I got bored after a while. (I never did.)

First up and thus my first ever 'cop' was 'Merchant Navy' No 35017 *Belgian Marine*. This was viewed from the approach road to the station where I stood my ground while father went into

the corner shop for his 'baccy'. He came out to find me agitated as I wanted to make a note of this number before I forgot it. Perhaps it should not have been such a concern as I clearly remember it, more than half a century later. We marked it off in what had been his, previously unused, *abc*, that he had bought from a shop next to Thornton Heath station, purely as a reference for his railway modelling activities. He had not then expected it to be used for its intended purpose. The carefully preserved remains of that precious little booklet, long without its cover, lies on my desk here as I write. Father was obviously a railway enthusiast,

but never himself a spotter and therefore never showed the same passion for the subject as I did.

We then went round to the sports field and waited for trains to pass. A couple more Bulleid Pacifics went by, as did a 'King Arthur' and a 'Lord Nelson', and all were ticked off in the book; so far so good. By looking at the pictures I was soon getting to know what each class looked like, and was getting the hang of it, or so I thought.

The next engine to pass on a down train, was an immaculate No 35020. 'Hang on a minute! That was 35020 wasn't it?' I asked dad. 'Yes. That's right,' he replied. 'But 35020 is a streamlined 'Merchant Navy' and that certainly wasn't,' I exclaimed. 'It looked like an *ordinary* loco.' We went home puzzled. Perhaps it was not that simple after all, and you could have two different types of loco carrying the same number. How confusing.

Of course, all was revealed when father came home one evening a short while later with a copy of the latest *Trains Illustrated* which featured details of the 'Merchant Navy' rebuilding programme. I regret now that I did not always distinguish in my notebooks between Bulleid Pacifics seen in their original form, and the Ron Jarvis rebuilds. *

Having sorted out that little puzzle, a study of the *abc*s showed how methodical loco numbering

←↗ The homemade cover for the much-used Ian Allan *abc Locoshed Book* of Summer 1961 and a spread, but not all were so well marked up as this was I am afraid. The pencilled 'C' means the loco had been 'cabbed' (usually when the engine was in steam), and 'H' indicates I had been on a train hauled by the loco.

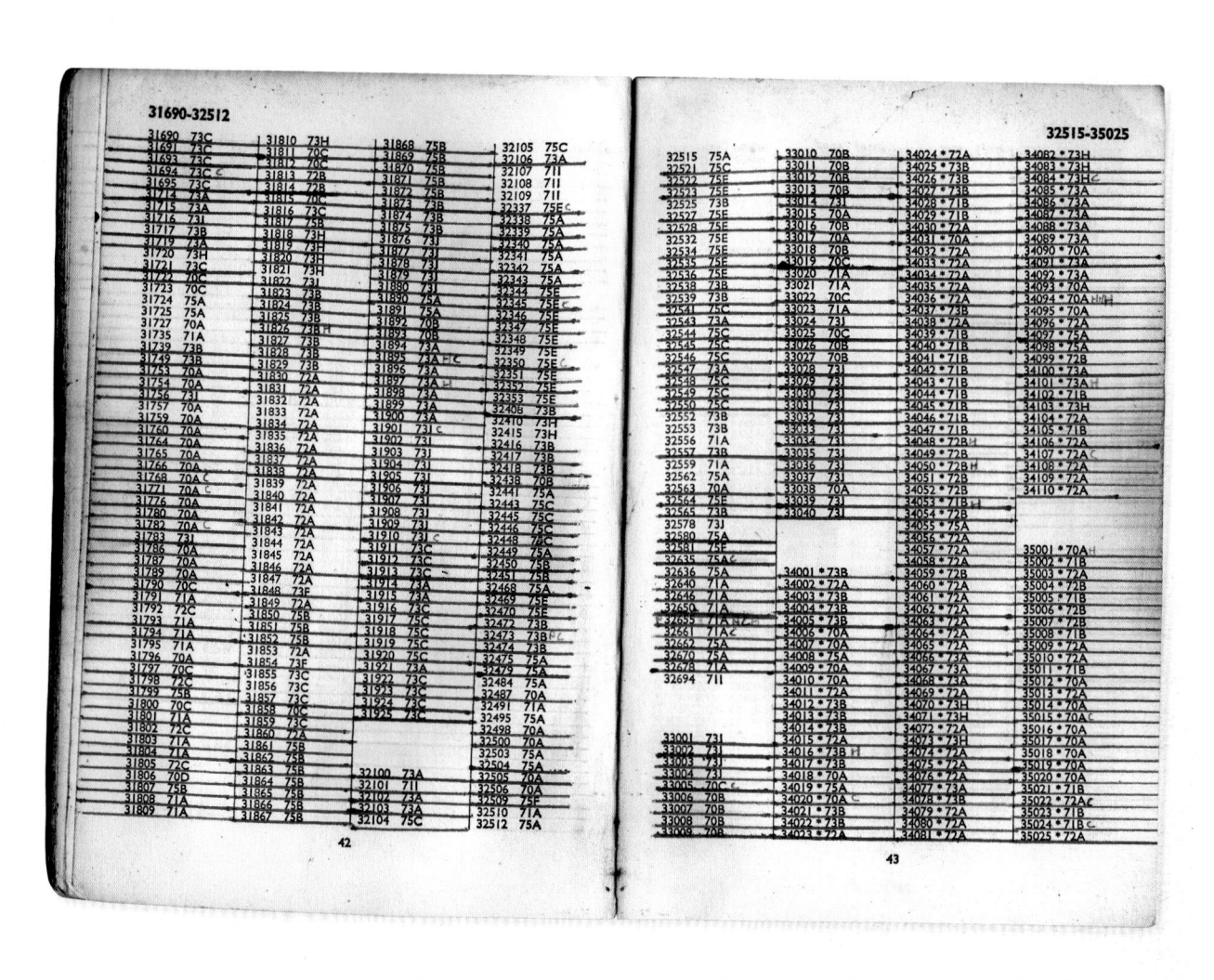

was generally, with the exception of the pre-Grouping Southern types, with former LSWR and SECR locos very much all over the place in their respective 30000 and 31000 series. Looking back now on those times, everything appeared to be so much more straightforward and orderly in fact.

My other interest, which actually started before locospotting, was aircraft, thanks to the Farnborough Air Show, which I attended every year from 1953 until about 2004. In that case, each country had a national airline and bought aircraft in consecutively registered blocks. Gas was supplied by the gas board, electricity came from the electricity company, and telephone calls were through the GPO. Car makers each had their own distinctive designs, there were just the two TV channels to choose from, and cinema films were simply rated as U, A or X. Everything seemed to be so logical and methodical. When the diesel and

electric classes started being delivered to BR they were all in neatly numbered blocks enabling you to see exactly what was what. These days, nothing seems so straightforward or presented so logically, but that's probably just me, and I digress…

Although I had always taken the odd photo or two, this was never really of prime concern on railway trips. I went out to see steam locos and enjoy the experience, appreciating the sight, sound and smell of steam, even if it were of locos seen before. Likewise, although I was keen to see as many locos as I could, and was desperate to mark off all the Bulleid Pacifics and the other main classes, I never pursued all BR's locos at all costs, as others did. As time went by, more and more photos were taken, but it was only in later years that the present policy was adopted, *ie* try to photograph everything railway-wise, which is now easier and cheaper with digital photography.

GOING SPOTTING

My father and I shared the colour camera for a few years, so it is not now possible to determine who took some of these photos, but the majority would have been by me. There were a few occasions when it is obvious dad took the photo, such as this one at Ryde shed, Isle of Wight on 21 July 1964.

I was unaware of this photo being taken, but see my version in Chapter 4, of O2 class 0-4-4Ts Nos W26 *Whitwell* left, and W33 *Bembridge.*

I never went on a railway expedition without the trusty duffle bag, or 'crazy bag' as we called them after school pal Peter Munday became dangerously entangled in its ropes while trying to get his off his back one time when in a hurry to get his camera out at Clapham Junction.

My bag did not normally hang so limply as seen here. On a typical day out it would have contained the camera (initially a Korelle, but later, two Olympus Pen half-frames (one for black and white, one for colour), a pair of 8x30 Imperator binoculars, Aidan Fuller's Shed Directory, Ian Allan's *abc Locoshed Book* Summer 1960 (in which all my cops were underlined, but only when I got home), a notebook and spare pens, Pacamac and refreshments. These became pretty standardised over time: cheese and pickle sandwiches (after I made the mistake of telling mother once how much I had enjoyed them, so was condemned to cheese and pickle for ever more), Lyons individual fruit pie (square), home-made custard trifle in a Tupperware

bowl, Kit Kat, 6d Mars Bar, and the ubiquitous bottle of Tizer. Later, this was replaced by a Corona drink as their bottles were ergonomically designed and slipped into and came out of the well-loaded bag much more easily. Despite the rest of the 'healthy-living' diet, Smith's crisps were never included as these simply became crushed to dust before they could be eaten.

There was a good reason for using the Summer 1960 *Locoshed abc.* It was the first edition to include all steam locos and their allocations up to and including No 92220 *Evening Star* (86C Cardiff Canton), so was never going to become out of date in that respect, as well as containing nearly all the locos I had seen previously. This was the year when my spotting really got going in earnest.

The shed book gave all the locos without the unnecessary photos which got in the way of looking up the numbers, and the other information which did not need to be carried around all the time. This booklet was used right through to the end of steam. It lost its cover and I made a new one for it, but it soldiered on and is still my main, instant reference as to which BR steam locos I saw. As such it is one of my most-treasured possessions. Older, individual regional *abcs* were also marked up to maintain a full record of all locos seen, including those withdrawn prior to 1960, as did exercise books written up with all the locos seen on every day of spotting. I have always liked writing out lists.

The makings of this book

Although I had built up quite an extensive collection of photos, both black and white and colour slides taken during the BR steam era, I did not think I had sufficient of any one area or topic to make up a book. Looking through the photos they appeared to be a rather a haphazard collection. It was certainly not possible to theme a book such as *Double-headed Great Western Steam on the Devon Banks* or anything like it.

On the other hand, such books have been done already and perhaps it was the very variety of locations where I had seen steam which was the interesting aspect of my collection. I had chosen to go looking for locos whereever they were, hence the title *Tracking Down Steam*. Otherwise a book of lineside photos of trains passing would have to be called *Waiting for Steam*, but I have never really had the patience for that. In fact, I have spent little time linesiding since I decided that standing on a platform waiting for the trains to come was not the best way of seeing lots of locos.

So, instead of the traditional lineside scenes of trains passing by, there are photos of locos in many different settings, some from the platform, which is where my interest started, to shed scenes, in works, in scrapyards awaiting their demise or a new life, then in preservation on display in parks, stored in works, on show in museums, and on preserved railways waiting their opportunity to steam again. Also, there is a selection of locomotives given a new lease of life in industry, and the narrow gauge engines owned by main line railway companies.

To keep some sort of parameter on the subject covered, I decided to confine it to the period up to what is always regarded as the end of BR steam, August 1968, as it was to be 'main line' steam locos to be featured, and that was the end of the era.

To fill in what would otherwise be some glaring gaps in the loco coverage, a few shots taken shortly after that date have been included, but only where I had not had time to previously capture a particular scene. No doubt my final shot, taken on the significant date of 11 August, will come as a surprise to many-a-reader, but I have never been one to comply with expectations or convention!

This perhaps eclectic mix of railway scenes is presented in the hope it will be found interesting and above all, entertaining, as that's how it was when visiting all these places – great fun.

⬇ All my railway journeys started from Ewell West station on the Epsom to Waterloo line, where the 13 milepost was mounted on the platform. All trains then were the ubiquitous 4-SUB EMUs, and steam was a great rarity, other than the midnight shunters of the goods yard, but that had closed on 1 May 1961. The last wagons were not cleared until 4 June, by U1 class 2-6-0 No 31910 which we were incredibly lucky to see, albeit in failing light. We arrived at Ewell West having returned from a railtour to Doncaster Works hauled by A4 No 60022 *Mallard* to find the loco standing in the goods yard. We were invited onto the footplate while the loco pulled the short train out on to the main line and ran round, before heading north; a memorable end to an already outstanding day.

Occasional railtours were seen however, including the LCGB's 'Wealdsman Rail Tour' on 13 June 1965, which passed through on its outward journey, a few minutes past 10.00 en route from London Waterloo to Horsham. Headed by rebuilt 'Battle of Britain' No 34050 *Royal Observer Corps*, it passes the former goods yard site. The excursion continued on to Hastings and Eastbourne, the return run including the 19¼-mile Cranleigh Line, Horsham to Guildford, which I had travelled on only the day before on the 'last day' of services (see Chapter 8); its official closing date being 14 June.

ACKNOWLEDGEMENTS

FIRST, I WOULD LIKE TO THANK all those who have regularly accompanied me on railway trips over the years. I shall always be grateful to my father for introducing me to railways, taking me lineside at Berrylands and Esher, and then around the London termini when I was quite small. Also, he took me on my first shed visit to 75C and later 70A, and then on the first railtour to Swindon, but my interest expanded far beyond anything he imagined!

From the earliest days until the end of BR steam, my school pal and life-long friend Brian Davis was a frequent travelling companion. We got into some scrapes at times, but he always kept our spirits up when we were out and about on the BR network, in all weathers. I have lost contact with other school pals, but I shall always remember them, mainly from the London shed bashes, these being Richard and Robert Burr, John Hattom and Peter Munday. Then there were John Bennett and Brian Small whom I got to know through the Epsom & Ewell Model Railway Club. I only had a few trips with them, but these included perhaps the most important of all, the epic Rail Rover tour in August–September 1966, to which a whole chapter is devoted.

Later trips, in search of the more obscure industrial and narrow gauge locomotives were with Rich Morris (now of monorail fame), Stan Robinson, Andrew Wilson and the much-missed Doug Semmens. They showed me there was a whole new world of railways after BR steam, some of it not far from home, but not known to me previously.

Later still, I met up with Francis Blake who deserves the utmost credit in ensuring Woodham Bros did not scrap all their locos, but held on to them while suitable buyers were found. Dai was becoming inundated with enthusiasts all telling him they wanted this and wanted that; some had the money, many did not, some were telling tales about others, and he was getting bogged down by all these people. Fortunately, Francis was able to come along and take all that off Dai's shoulders and keep him informed as to who was genuine, and who were time-wasters.

Without that valuable assistance Woodhams was on the brink of cutting everything up simply to solve the problem. This is perhaps an aspect of the Barry story not actually stated anywhere previously. Anyway, Francis and I have remained in contact since those interesting days of the Barry Steam Locomotive Action Group (BSLAG), and he has now once again provided an invaluable service by carefully reading through each chapter as completed and picking up many things that I would otherwise have missed. Sincere thanks therefore, to Francis for his thoroughness in reading the manuscript but as authors always tend to say, any errors are mine alone.

Others who have helped with snippets of information include Rory Cook, Collections Information Officer, The Science Museum; Antony Coulls of The National Railway Museum; and Gavin Morrison, whose photo collection I am fully aware is in a totally different league to mine.

Over the years I have built quite an extensive library, of which a few titles have proved invaluable references and have been much used in putting these notes together. I therefore thank the various authors for making such information available through their books, as detailed in the Bibliography.

The internet provides many answers these days, but as I have found, not all of them, particularly with regard to precise opening (and closing) dates of museums and preserved railways. One invaluable and highly recommended website has to be Gary Thornton's Six Bells Junction, which includes a section called the Railtour Files. The amount of information contained therein on railtours, from 1841 to the most recent tour to be run, is phenomenal. I learnt a lot about the trains I travelled on the 1960s, but did find one I went on that had missed the net until now. It is well worth checking www.sixbellsjunction.co.uk, whether you are looking for railtour information or have further details and photos that could fill in some of the gaps.

At the publishers, I would like to thank Mark Hughes for kindly and bravely taking me on as an author and having faith in this title, and to Sophie Blackman for her patience and understanding in seeing it all through the editorial process so smoothly. Also, to Nick Ewers for his expert scanning, which ensured the best has been obtained from some rather variable photos. Grateful thanks, too, to Pete Waterman for kindly supplying the Foreword.

Finally, thanks go to my wife Pauline who has had to live with my railway interest for more than 30 years. She has become used to living in a library, visiting a railway or two whenever we go out, and accepting that railways will crop up in the conversation on occasions. Of late, she has also become my driver on most of our more local railway trips, often now accompanied by our young grandson Joshua, who is clearly something of an enthusiast too. Her support in pursuing my railway hobby and publishing involvements during this time has been invaluable and is fully appreciated.

AUTHOR'S NOTES

Locomotive withdrawal and scrapping dates

Unfortunately, published information on when BR locomotives were withdrawn and broken up can vary considerably, depending on which reference is used. To be consistent, and hopefully accurate, I have based nearly all such dates on Hugh Longworth's magnificent book *British Railway Steam Locomotives 1948–1968*.

Locomotive names

In many cases, a loco is depicted after it had lost its nameplates, these often being removed in latter days for safe keeping. However, these are still quoted in the caption as I consider that they formed part of the locomotive's permanent identity. For example, A3 Pacific LNER No. 4472/BR No 60103 is *Flying Scotsman*, even when its nameplates are removed.

Since steam days, loco names have become much more transitory, either being carried for just a small part of the loco's life, and even swapped from loco to loco. They therefore do not have the same importance as say that of a 'Royal Scot', 'Duchess', 'Castle', 'King', 'Hall' or 'Grange', a Bulleid Pacific, 'Britannia' or the LNER Pacifics. Names were changed on some of these, but it was always with good reason and intended to be permanent thereafter.

Irish Railways

In this survey of British main line steam in the 1960s, Northern Ireland should of course have been included. However, I did not visit the Emerald Isle until 1973, well past the book's cut-off date, and the only remaining steam by then was preserved. As the British Government took control of all Irish railways from December 1916 until August 1921, surviving locos operated on the Irish main line during that period would have been eligible for inclusion. I regret this oversight on my part, but all too often, Irish railways are unfortunately ignored by the UK rail enthusiast.

Tickets

Nearly all the tickets illustrated are the actual ones purchased and used by the author at the time the accompanying photographs were taken.

Contact

Anyone wishing to get in touch with the author is welcome to do so by email: trackingdownsteam@btinternet.com

Abbreviations

BPGVR	Burry Port & Gwendraeth Valley Railway	GWR	Great Western Railway	NBR	North British Railway
		HCRC/S	Home Counties Railway Club/Society	NCB	National Coal Board
BR	British Railways	HR	Highland Railway	NER	North Eastern Railway/ North Eastern Region (BR)
BR (LMR)	British Railway (London Midland Region)	IWSR	Isle of Wight Steam Railway		
		KESR	Kent & East Sussex Railway	NRM	National Railway Museum
BSLAG	Barry Steam Locomotive Action Group	KWVR	Keighley & Worth Valley Railway	NSR	North Staffordshire Railway
		LBSCR	London, Brighton & South Coast Railway	NYMR	North Yorkshire Moors Railway
BTC	British Transport Commission			RAF	Royal Air Force
CR	Caledonian Railway	LCGB	Locomotive Club of Great Britain	RPS	Railway Preservation Society
CSP	Cotswold Steam Preservation Ltd	LMR	Longmoor Military Railway	S&DR	Stockton & Darlington Railway
DMU	diesel multiple unit	LMS/LMSR	London Midland & Scottish Railway	ScR	Scottish Region (BR)
DVR	Dart Valley Railway	LNER	London & North Eastern Railway	SDR	South Devon Railway
ECS	empty carriage stock	LNWR	London & North Western Railway	SECR	South Eastern & Chatham Railway
EMU	electric multiple unit	LRC	London Railfans' Club	SLS	Stephenson Locomotive Society
ER	Eastern Region (BR)	LSWR	London & South Western Railway	SMLR	Shropshire & Montgomeryshire Light Railway
ERS	Epsom Railway Society	LTSR	London, Tilbury & Southend Railway		
FR	Furness Railway	LYR	Lancashire & Yorkshire Railway	SPR	Sandy & Potton Railway
GCR	Great Central Railway	M&GNJR	Midland & Great Northern Joint Railway	SR	Southern Railway/ Southern Region (BR)
GER	Great Eastern Railway				
GJR	Grand Junction Railway	MPD	motive power depot	TPO	Travelling Post Office
GNR	Great Northern Railway	MR	Midland Railway	TR	Talyllyn Railway
GNSR	Great North of Scotland Railway	MR-NCC	Midland Railway – Northern Counties Committee	USAF	United States Air Force
GPO	General Post Office			VofR	Vale of Rheidol Railway
G&SWR	Glasgow & South Western Railway	MRT	Midland Railway Trust	WR	Western Region (BR)

CHAPTER 1

FROM THE PLATFORM END

On Southern lines – from the beginning to the end

HAVING BEEN INTRODUCED to loco spotting at Berrylands, for a while we were quite happy waiting about for the trains to pass by, 'picking up' locos as they went through the station. As well as Berrylands, the other usual station for me initially was Surbiton on the South Western main line, as these two were the easiest to cycle to or reach by bus. Brian Davis, a school pal who became a great spotting companion and lifelong friend, favoured Raynes Park, which was a train ride on a 4-SUB EMU from our local station, Ewell West.

The busiest station, and one on which we liked to spend time, was Clapham Junction, but even in those days, 'spotters', certainly of our young age, were usually asked to leave after a short while.

Things soon progressed to travelling all the way to Waterloo, although our parents presumably thought we were safely just a few stations away at Raynes Park. We perhaps forgot to mention that we were going *through* there, on the way to London.

Once in London the underground enabled us to get to all the main termini: Paddington, Euston, King's Cross, St Pancras, Liverpool Street and Victoria. Sometimes, but only very rarely, we looked in for a few minutes at Marylebone, Charing Cross, Cannon Street, Fenchurch Street or Broad Street to see what was around.

After just a short while at these fantastic stations our notebooks were filled with locos from all regions – where else could you do that? I really loved the time we spent at these 'cathedrals of steam', but we spent little time or money taking photos. There was partly the matter of 'why photograph something you can come back and see any time?' That's how London was, and had been for so long, and probably would be all the time we would remain as spotters.

Surbiton was still visited on occasions as it was always such a thrill to see the Bulleids and BR Standards passing through at speed, and we realised that such delights as the T9s, H15s

HAYLING ISLAND STATION

The first time I remember being taken by my father to a station to see steam was when we went for a week's holiday to Hayling Island. This must have been 1953, the year I started school and so I am wearing my brand-new cap. We did not go by train but by coach as it was cheaper. I have a distinct recollection that when we arrived at the island we had to get off the coach and walk across the toll bridge because of a weight restriction. It was a weight restriction on Langstone railway bridge that had ensured the use of the Brighton 'Terriers' on this branch for so long too.

On just one occasion while we were there, I was taken to the station as father knew the line was still worked by the 'Terriers'. Here, I am standing on a platform barrow with No 32646 behind. I suppose this was my first 'cop' although it was not marked off as such until a few years later when I referred to the photo, not having jotted it down at the time. I remember all the people getting off the train and crowding the platform, which prevented me from getting a better view, hence I took refuge on the barrow.

and 'King Arthurs' were being seen less and less frequently. I well remember one very brief visit to the footpath that slopes down to the station, on the down side. I arrived on my bike and asked a spotter there if he had seen No 34080 *74 Squadron*. 'No,' he replied, but as he spoke, there was the shriek of a whistle and it went thundering past on a down train. 'That's it!' I cried, 'Cleared the lot!' and got on my bike and rode straight off home again, much to his surprise at such a brief visit, no doubt. But what else was there to do that day, having now seen all the Bulleid Pacifics?

Earlier, the last 'Merchant Navy' was becoming something of an irritation as I kept missing it, even after it was transferred to the South Western Division from the Central. Today's enthusiast with so much technology to hand won't understand the lack of information we had about where locos were in those days.

Eventually, another school mate and spotting pal, Peter Munday, phoned me up one Saturday lunchtime to say he'd seen this loco going down in the morning so it was almost certain to be working back up to Waterloo that afternoon. I promptly made my way up to Clapham Junction and after waiting patiently for an hour or so it duly came through, and that cleared the 'Merchants'. Now, whatever happened, nothing could take away the fact that I had seen all 30 'Merchant Navys'; what a relief. There were several of the important classes where I did miss just the one, such as the GWR 'Kings', Southern 'Schools' and BR 'Britannias' – something one has to live with for the rest of one's life…

I didn't know it at the time of course, but I need not have had any fears regarding the 'Merchant Navys' as the last two needed were ex-Stewarts Lane locos, No 35027 *Port Line*, and that actual last one, none other than No 35028 *Clan Line*. For a while though, *Clan Line* seemed to me to be almost as rare as those other 'Clans', the Scottish BR Standard Pacifics.

A similar thing happened many years later with my last 'Western' diesel-hydraulic. If I had known that No D1023 *Western Fusilier* was going to become part of the National Collection, I perhaps would not have spent such a desperate weekend chasing round the West Country specifically to track it down! I had already missed one Class 52 however.

It was not long before our trips to Raynes Park and on to London took us even further into the world of steam – the London sheds.

Before that though, after starting with the first station visit specifically to see a loco, here are some shots I did get of locos from the stations visited in our area, and slightly further afield on the Southern Region. These work up the line from Surbiton to the terminus, just as we progressed when we started spotting, as well as some scenes from the last days of Southern steam when old haunts were revisited.

STATIONS TO WATERLOO

When we took up loco spotting in earnest, it was a matter of varying our viewing points along the South Western main line from Waterloo, from our nearest point at Surbiton station to nearly all those in between there and the terminus.

Surbiton 12 MILES 3 CHAINS FROM WATERLOO

This was where most of my childhood Southern main line spotting was done. Although many hours were spent there, I took hardly any photos, so there is little to show for all that time apart from the marked-off numbers in the Southern Region edition of Ian Allan's *abc of British Railways Locomotives*. Plenty of happy memories though, such as watching a 700 class 0-6-0 blowing huge smoke rings as it shunted the station yard one summer's evening. Another time, on a Saturday morning, a couple of down trains headed by 'air-smoothed' 'Battle of Britains' stopped, from

which lots of troops alighted. One I recall was No 34055 *Fighter Pilot*, giving a rare chance to stand by the loco and admire it as it waited at the platform end. This was one of the occasions that really affirmed my interest, awe and devotion for steam locos in general, and Bulleids in particular.

It was because steam-hauled trains rarely stopped at Surbiton when we were there, but went rushing through at high speed, that early photography was restricted. Much better to save the film for shed visits where the locos were not moving so much!

↑ The view from a much-favoured spot, the footpath on the down side of the line at Surbiton, leading from Ewell Road to the station. This location is clearly featured, showing three boys spotting, in a marvellous painting by David Charlesworth, *Sir Lamiel at Surbiton,* produced as a Christmas card in 2012 by the Railway Children charity.

This was the closest place to home we could reach by bicycle and in the summer months we would go there after school for an hour or so. During this time there was a constant procession of Southern locos and BR Standards. Just occasionally, one would stop at the up main line platform as here, with rebuilt 'Battle of Britain' No 34071 *601 Squadron* in August 1961.

→ I am not able to produce many photos from my numerous visits to Surbiton station, but this one shows 'West Country' No 34108 *Wincanton,* which stopped on an up train to Waterloo. This is undated, but is probably 1959, and was the third photo I took, using the very primitive Hawkeye camera, the first two shots being at King's Cross. This was the only photo I ever obtained of a Bulleid Pacific in its original form that was later rebuilt (No 34108 was rebuilt in May 1961).

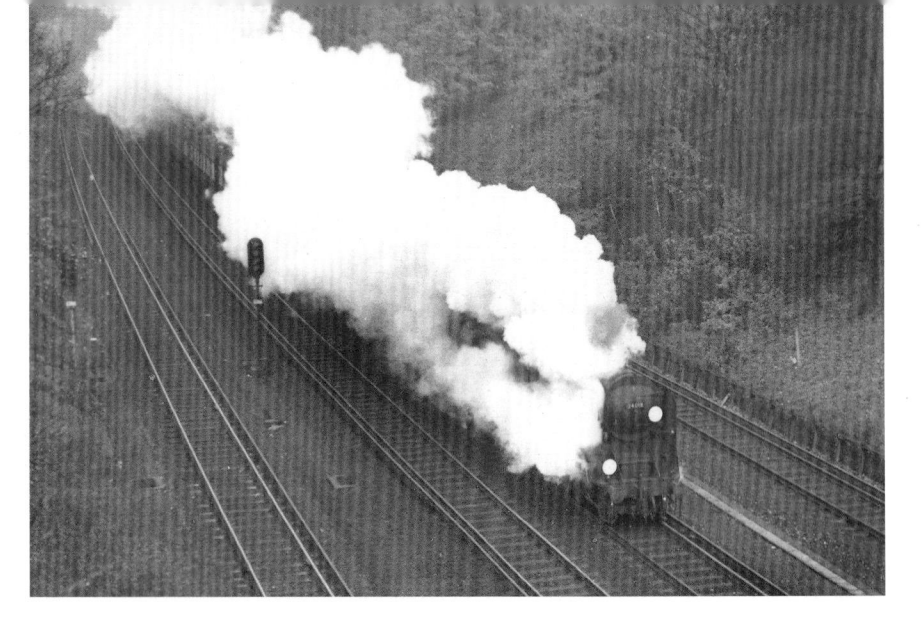

➔ A visit to Surbiton specially to photograph the 'Bournemouth Belle' Pullman train before the expected take-over by Brush Type 4s, did not quite get the desired result! Viewed from Ewell Road bridge, rebuilt 'West Country' No 34018 *Axminster* put up a spectacular display of smoke and steam on the down working, on 19 November 1966.

Berrylands 10 MILES 78 CHAINS FROM WATERLOO

This was the first station I was taken to specifically for noting the numbers of passing locos. It provided a clear view of trains on a long straight stretch of track which could be seen all the way from New Malden Junction in the up direction.

The station was not opened until 16 October 1933 and was named after the housing development that had built up near the line.

🡇 The back of the ticket shows this was issued on 8 October 1966 for a charge of 3d, not 2d as printed on the front.

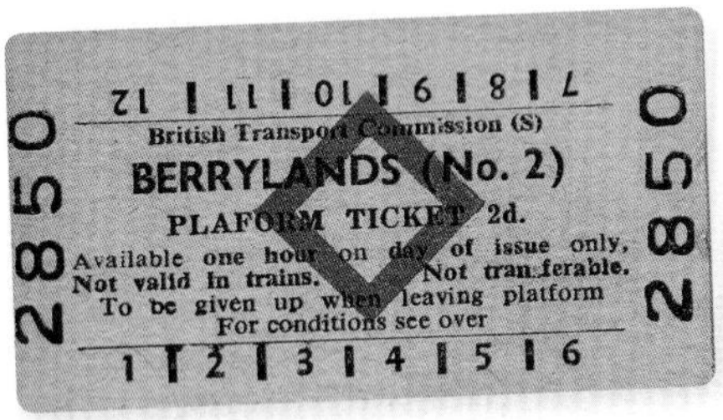
0582
7 8 9 10 11 12
British Transport Commission (S)
BERRYLANDS (No. 2)
PLATFORM TICKET 2d.
Available one hour on day of issue only. Not valid in trains. Not transferable. To be given up when leaving platform
For conditions see over
1 2 3 4 5 6
2850

🡇 The down platform at Berrylands was a regular viewing spot from the earliest days of watching locos go by. Here, 'Battle of Britain' No. 34057 *Biggin Hill* heads a down train at 11.50 on 15 October 1966, when I returned to the station to capture some scenes from my first spotting days in the late 1950s.

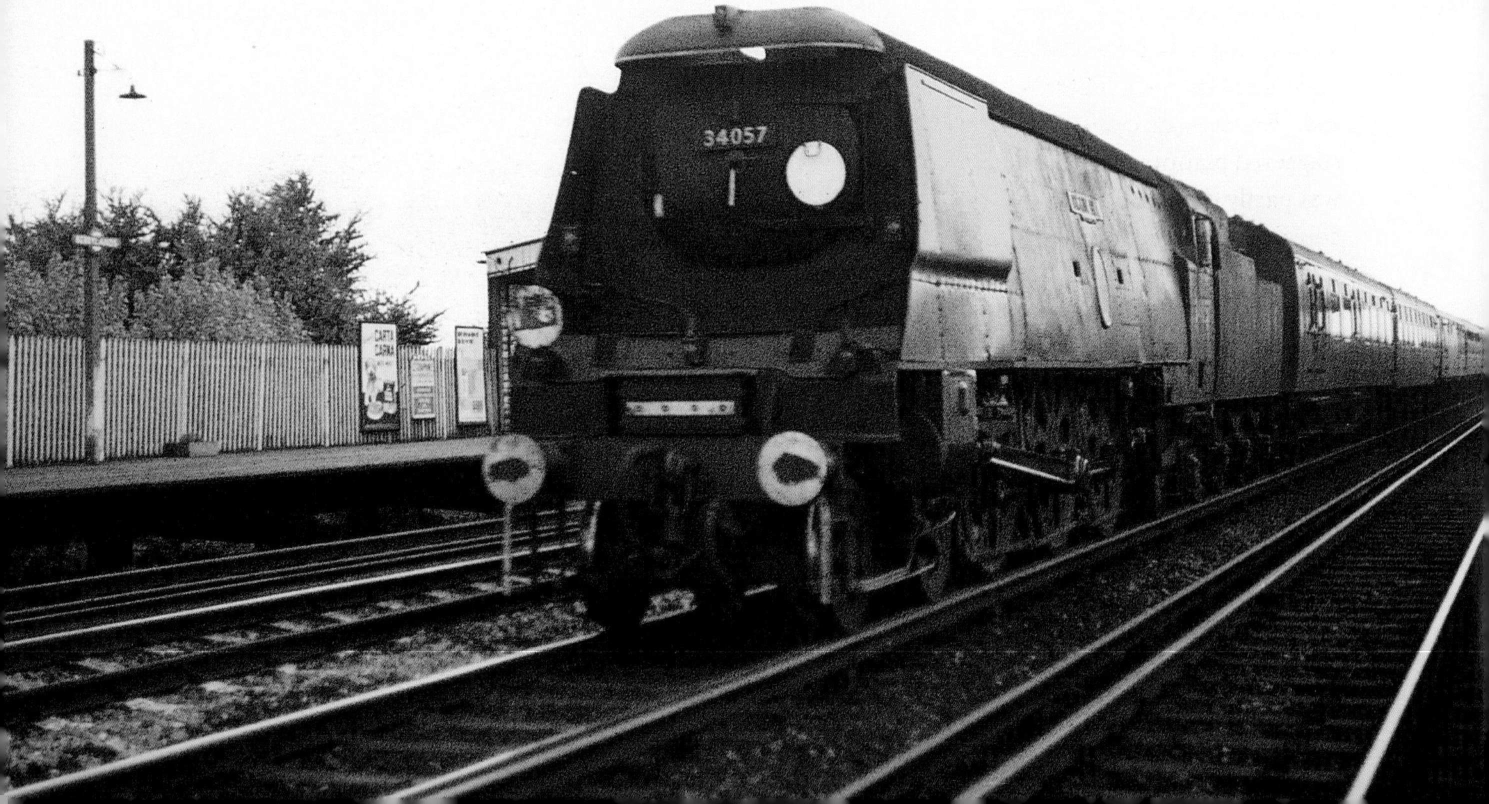
34057

← A distinctive feature of Berrylands station was the long, unsurfaced wooden platforms, seen here. Access to the raised platforms was up steep flights of steps and from one platform to the other by means of a footpath under the lines. The old track-level wooden station buildings were replaced by a ground-level Clasp structure in 1969. BR Standard Class 5MT 4-6-0 No 73020 heads a short train of vans on the down fast line on 15 October 1966.

Raynes Park 8 MILES 51 CHAINS FROM WATERLOO

We travelled to London from our local station at Ewell West on the Epsom line, which merged with the Chessington South branch at Motspur Park. The two lines then joined the South Western main line at Raynes Park, making this the first station where we could see steam passing through. Hence it was a popular station for local spotters. It has been said that the late Richard Briers, the well-known comedy actor, was sometimes among them, but whether this is true or not I don't know.

There was a serious accident here on 28 November 1967 when a short-wheelbase van, restricted to 45mph, running in a train hauled by an electro-diesel at about 60mph, became derailed and struck the long footbridge that connects the up and down staggered platforms. The bridge was partly demolished and of course, caused major disruption. I remember father arriving home late and disgruntled that night from his daily commute to London, just as he had done on 10 May 1965, when Clapham Junction 'A' signalbox had partly collapsed. No doubt things returned to normal far more quickly then than they would do after similar incidents today.

↓ Like Berrylands, Raynes Park afforded a good clear view of the steam-hauled trains that passed through non-stop, in between the electrified suburban lines. Here, rebuilt 'Merchant Navy' No 35023 *Holland-Afrika Line* heads a down train on 3 June 1967 at 09.40. Unfortunately, I made little effort to record the train working details, mainly due to ignorance at the time, but did occasionally note down passing times. Neither was the study of headcodes given any priority, hence the lack of such detail in these captions.

Wimbledon

7 MILES 19 CHAINS FROM WATERLOO

➜ Only occasionally was Wimbledon station used as an observation point, but some time was spent there on 10 March 1967, as the end of Southern steam approached. Rebuilt 'West Country' No 34093 *Saunton* heads an up train. On the right is a London Transport District Line train, Wimbledon being the terminus of the line from Earls Court. Today, the station is also a terminus for London Tramlink, providing an interchange for all three rail systems.

← This ticket is dated 28 July 1960, so at age 12, going on to Wimbledon was thought more adventurous than to Raynes Park, but not yet going quite as far as 'up the Junction'.

⬇ BR Standard 5MT 4-6-0 No 73065 heads an up train through Raynes Park on 10 March 1967, passing under the footbridge which was nearly brought down by a derailed van later that year.

→ Having just experienced steam haulage between Clapham Junction and Kensington Olympia on 10 March 1967, I stopped off at Wimbledon for a few shots on the way into work. We did not have to wait long before rebuilt 'West Country' No 34104 *Bere Alston* rushed through at 09.45 with a down working of the 'Union-Castle Express' boat train to Southampton. The photographer on the right is John Bennett, of Rail Rover fame (see Chapter 5).

→ The sole member of the BR Standard Class 3MT 2-6-0s allocated to the Southern, No 77014, was caught on camera from a north-bound train, while heading an engineer's train alongside Wimbledon EMU depot. This was a major track-relaying programme on 19 March 1967.

Clapham Junction

3 MILES 74 CHAINS FROM WATERLOO

Having what has often been referred to as Britain's, Europe's or even the world's 'busiest station' en route to London was obviously something of a magnet for us spotters. Such a claim is based on the number of trains passing through rather than the number of passengers using the station, which was, after all, what we wanted. However, the majority of these trains were Southern EMUs (electric multiple units), so not all were really what we wanted, although the set numbers of these were always collected.

When we were younger this was the only station on our line where staff could be a bit difficult, asking us to move on as 'the station had a no-trainspotter policy', as they would word it today. As we got older, and nearer the last days of Southern steam in 1967, I do not recall any such problems.

What was interesting was the constant coming and going of the empty stock trains between here and Waterloo. When we first went there it was all M7 0-4-4Ts, but these were later replaced, much to our surprise and disappointment, by ex-GWR pannier tanks. Latterly, it was BR Standard 2-6-2 and 2-6-4 tanks that performed this duty.

I have always been proud of my railway interest, but when I was asked once by a non-railway person what I was reading at the time, and I replied it was a book on Clapham Junction, they just said: 'You've bought a book on Clapham Junction?' It did make me sound rather nerdish I admit, but they did not know or appreciate this marvellous place as well as I did.

← A little-known feature on Clapham Junction's Platforms 11 (South Western Division, Down main local) and 12 (Central Division, Up through) were two bricks marking the boundary between the LSWR and LBSCR. Prior to the Grouping these were Platforms 6 (LSWR, Down main local) and 7 (LBSCR, Up main). Photographed on 22 October 1966, I would imagine these were later covered over when the platform was resurfaced.

→ BR Standard Class 4MT 2-6-4T No 80143 pulls the ECS (empty coaching stock) for the 'Bournemouth Belle' all-Pullman train out from the carriage sidings at Clapham Junction on 11 September 1966.

↑ One of the currently extinct BR Standard Class 3MT 2-6-2Ts, No 82028 heads a rake of milk tanks at Clapham Junction on 10 April 1966. I say currently extinct as there is a new-build project reaching an advanced stage at Bridgnorth on the Severn Valley Railway, which will create the 46th member of the class to be completed, No 82045.

West London Extension Railway

The three-mile line from Clapham Junction to Kensington (Olympia) via Latchmere Junction had become something of a forgotten route by the mid-1960s. Its attraction was that it was virtually the last steam-hauled suburban service anywhere in the country. Although not strictly true as it was a connecting line, it was often referred to as BR's 'last steam branch'. Services were not advertised in the public timetables but we learnt there were two return trips each weekday morning (08.16 and 08.46). Evening trains departed Kensington at 16.36 and 17.06 or 17.36, depending which weekday it was.

This was a must to travel before it lost its steam haulage, but it meant making the journey on a working day and leaving home quite early. Fortunately, two of the three partners in the firm of accountants I was articled to at that time were railway enthusiasts. So, when I asked if it was OK to come in late one morning, and gave the reason, they were only too happy to give their blessing as it was a 'good cause'.

The last steam working of the service took place on 7 July 1967, with BR 2-6-2T No 82019. Now electrified, the line is part of the London Overground system.

↑ Dated 1 March 1967, this was booked separately to my tickets from Ewell West to Clapham Junction and back to Epsom, as I specifically wanted this one, showing 'Clapham Junction to Kensington (Olympia)' and return, never thinking it would one day be published in a book.

⬇ BR Standard Class 3MT 2-6-2T No 82029 runs round the train at Clapham Junction before taking it through to Kensington (Olympia) on 1 March 1967.

A shot obviously taken in the excitement of the occasion, but an interesting view nevertheless. It shows the scene from the front compartment window as the 08.16 Clapham Junction to Kensington (Olympia) train, headed by No 82029, crossed the River Thames by means of Battersea Railway Bridge. More correctly called Cremorne Bridge, this was designed by William Baker and was opened in March 1863. It is now Grade II* listed.

↑ No 82029 waits at Kensington (Olympia) ready to return to Clapham Junction on 10 March 1967.

→ Having run round, No 82029 heads the train at Clapham Junction for its second hop round to Kensington (Olympia) at 08.46.

➜ The locos running light through Vauxhall, between Waterloo and Nine Elms shed, were often in pairs, but I never remember seeing more than two locos coupled together. Here, rebuilt Bulleid Pacifics work up to the terminus, freshly coaled, on 13 August 1966. Nearest the camera is 'West Country' No 34040 *Crewkerne* with 'Merchant Navy' No 35013 *Blue Funnel*. Unlike in later days, both still have their nameplates in place.

Vauxhall 1 MILE 29 CHAINS FROM WATERLOO

The first station out from Waterloo was another good vantage point for down trains, and for light engines working between Nine Elms shed and the terminus, creating a non-stop flow of locos at all times.

⬇ A short while later, dead on cue, No 35013 *Blue Funnel Certum Pete Finem*, to quote its full name as per the nameplates, reappeared at Vauxhall, heading the 'Bournemouth Belle' all-Pullman train. Although it became noted for some high-speed runs in the last days of Southern steam, this is one of the MN class that did not survive, it being broken up by Buttigieg's at Newport, but not until March 1968. It had been one of the last seven members of the class to remain in traffic until the last day of Southern steam, 9 July 1967.

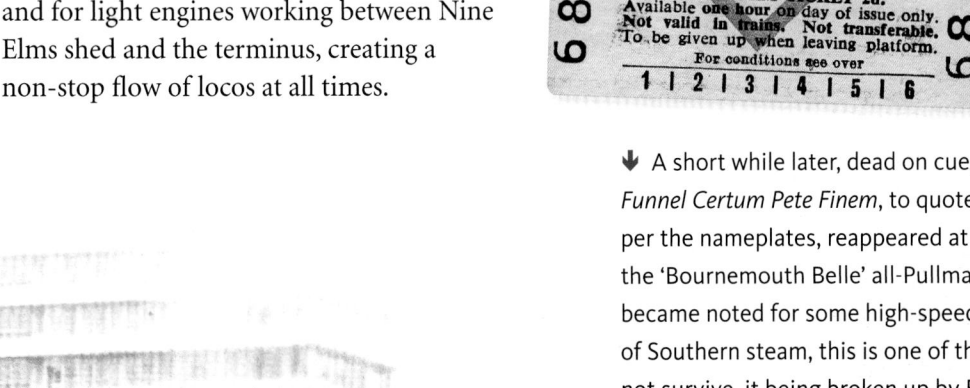

↑ Another Bulleid Pacific in the constant procession plying to and from Waterloo all day, every day. Rebuilt 'West Country' No 34024 *Tamar Valley*, minus nameplates, approaches Vauxhall with the down 'Bournemouth Belle' on 22 October 1966.

→ As the end grew nigh every opportunity to observe Southern steam in action was taken. The weather was probably not quite this murky when I left home to spend some time at Vauxhall, but I decided to stick it out and experience steam in the fog. Rebuilt 'West Country' No 34093 *Saunton* emerges from the mists with a down train on 9 October 1966, its exhaust adding to the atmosphere.

← Then just another Ivatt 2-6-2T, No 41312, heads towards Waterloo for use on ECS back down to Clapham Junction, on 22 April 1967. Today, this loco is one of four survivors of the class of 130 examples built between 1946 and 1962, having been rescued from Barry scrapyard. It is now resident on the Mid-Hants Railway.

← I was always ready with my camera on the approach to Waterloo as the door windows on the 4-SUB EMU could be let right down for a good clear view. This was particularly lucky positioning of BR Standard Class 5MT 4-6-0 No 73065 on 21 January 1967.

↓ The fireman attends to the front end of rebuilt 'Merchant Navy' No 35003 *Royal Mail* at Waterloo on 21 January 1967, sweeping off an accumulation of coal dust from under the smokebox door.

Waterloo

The big one – the Southern Region's busiest station, judged by the number of passengers passing through each day. This was, and is, a wonderful light and airy station and was one of the reasons we lived where we did. When my parents were looking for a house soon after the war, father decided that as he had to travel to and from London, passing through a terminus twice a day, every weekday for the next quarter-century, our house had to be on a line served by trains from Waterloo. Hence we moved from Thornton Heath to West Ewell, or Ewell West as the station is known, on the Epsom line.

When it became the last London terminus with a steam service he regarded this as a bonus. Although he loved seeing the locos arriving and departing as he passed through in his clean and efficient EMU, he does not appear to have taken any railway photos during his journeys, for reasons I never discovered. Perhaps he thought I was taking enough for both of us!

↓ There was always a tank engine waiting at the end of the platforms at Waterloo, ready to take empty stock to the carriage sidings at Clapham Junction. Latterly, these were BR Standard tanks, 2-6-4Ts and 2-6-2Ts, as well as Ivatt Class 2MT 2-6-2Ts, a number of which were supplied new, direct to the Southern Region. While many have regarded these as ex-LMS, only the first ten were built prior to Nationalisation, at Crewe Works. The next 110 were completed by BR at Crewe, and the last ten at Derby. They were numbered 41200 to 41329, which gave rise to the LMS myth.

No 41298, seen here at Waterloo on 26 March 1967, was bought for preservation direct from BR following withdrawal in July 1967. Restoration to working order has only now been completed, with entry into service on the Isle of Wight Steam Railway due in October 2013.

← A tender-end view of rebuilt 'Merchant Navy' No 35023 *Holland-Afrika Line* on 15 April 1967. Waterloo's distinctive signalbox is on the right.

I always feel that enthusiasts do not devote enough attention to the study and record of the all-important loco tender. For instance, of all the listings of preserved steam locos published, these never quote tender details such as the number, date of build, or capacity. Nor is there a listing of surviving tenders currently available, even on the Internet.

The study of Bulleid Pacific tenders and their variations is a particularly fascinating topic. It is remarkable that this loco, which entered service with BR in November 1948 and was rebuilt in February 1957, retained the same 6,000-gallon tender, No 3341, throughout its life until withdrawal in July 1967. The tender was scrapped with the loco in April 1968 at Buttigieg's, Newport, one of six 'Merchant Navys' broken up there.

← A typical Waterloo scene in the latter days of steam when grubby Bulleid Pacifics worked Britain's last main line passenger steam services to Southampton, Bournemouth and Weymouth. Rebuilt 'West Country' No 34018 *Axminster* is ready for departure at 08.35 on 22 April 1967.

↑ BR Standard Class 3MT Prairie tank No 82019 takes water at Waterloo while on ECS duties, on 20 May 1967.

↑ Rebuilt Bulleid Light Pacific No 34025 *Whimple* is seen at the bufferstop end of Waterloo, in the marvellous, light and airy train shed, on 1 July 1967 – just another week to go before such a scene was to become a thing of the past.

← Rebuilt 'Merchant Navy' – No 35028 *Clan Line* is, today, probably the best-known member of the class, but this former Stewarts Lane loco, which worked out of Victoria, was the one that eluded me the longest. In fact, I was getting concerned at one time it would be whisked off for scrap before I had a chance to see it! Never any fear of this though, as it was transferred to Nine Elms well before it or any of its class mates were in danger. It became a frequently seen loco thereafter but its first sighting at Clapham Junction one Saturday afternoon nevertheless gave a great feeling of achievement and satisfaction.

It is seen here at Waterloo on 2 May 1967 nearing the end of its BR career, and minus its nameplates. Alongside is a 'Crompton' diesel-electric.

↓ A regular sight at Waterloo, but one of which I never tired – two rebuilt Bulleid Light Pacifics, as seen on 12 May 1967. Even at that late stage I could not really

imagine such a scene was something that would soon be gone for ever. On the left is No 34090 *Sir Eustace Missenden, Southern Railway* and on the right, No 34052 *Lord Dowding*, but by now most, if not all, had their nameplates removed. However, locos such as these, which had been named for so long were still those engines to me, unlike modern traction units. Nowadays, nameplates come and go and change so frequently that they have lost all meaning and are only a transitory identification of the loco concerned. Earlier diesel classes, such as the 'Warships', 'Westerns'. 'Peaks' and 'Deltics' were allowed to perpetuate the tradition of properly named locos, however.

SOUTHERN STATIONS

In addition to spending many hours on the platforms of the nearest stations where steam could be seen, we visited a number of other Southern stations.

Bournemouth Central

108 MILES 2 CHAINS FROM WATERLOO

↑ Not a bit like Hayling Island – BR Standard Class 4MT 2-6-0 No 76062 waits to depart from Bournemouth with an up train on 26 August 1963. I left home that day with the idea of travelling down to the Hayling Island branch, which I had only ever visited as a five-year-old. Inexplicably, when the booking clerk at Ewell West station asked me where I wanted to go, I answered 'Bournemouth', rather than Hayling Island. This must have been a last-second change of mind because I decided to go for some steam haulage down the main line that day, rather than electric to Havant. I have no idea why I made such a decision at that moment. I never did get to the Hayling Island branch again.

← Also at Bournemouth on 26 August 1963, rebuilt 'West Country' No 34042 *Dorchester* was seen on an up departure. This was of particular interest as it was the loco Hornby had released as their three-rail model in October 1961, and of which I was, and am, a proud owner.

Guildford 30 MILES 27 CHAINS FROM WATERLOO

This was another favourite station as there was always plenty of loco variety here and the shed yard was clearly visible from the platform. It was almost mid-way on the all-steam route from Reading to Redhill, a line the family used to travel on for the novelty of steam haulage.

However, most spotting visits to the station were made by London Transport Country bus as a Green Rover ticket costing 2s 6d (12p) allowed all-day travel so, with careful planning, we could take in Guildford, Horsham, Redhill and Tonbridge sheds. Tunbridge Wells was just a bit too much to add to all these others in one day and besides, the Rover ticket was not valid that far and the conductor would insist we paid a few pence more. Therefore, that shed was never visited so often as the others.

↓ A favourite class at a favourite location: Maunsell Mogul, U class No 31619 at Guildford on 21 July 1964 with a Redhill to Reading train. It was the sight of sister No 1618 fully restored in Southern Railway olive-green livery at Sheffield Park a few years later that so impressed me, I returned my attention (partly) from 'rusty little industrial locos', back to main line engines again. This led to life membership of the Maunsell Locomotive Society and a big involvement with the Barry loco phenomenon.

↑ Representing the other main Maunsell Mogul class, N (with 5ft 6in driving wheels compared with the U's 6ft), No 31817 enters Guildford from the west with a Redhill train on 1 October 1963. In order to distinguish the Ns from the Us when seeing them, I used to remember the former had 'no' splashers above the footplate. The shed can be seen, right, beyond the road bridge.

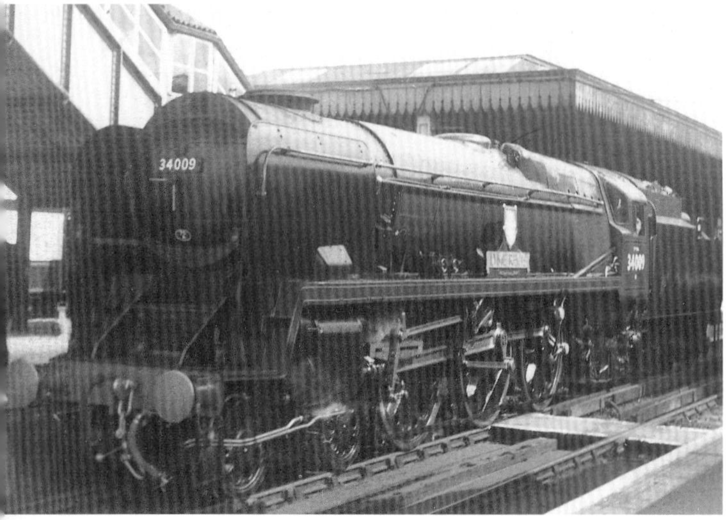

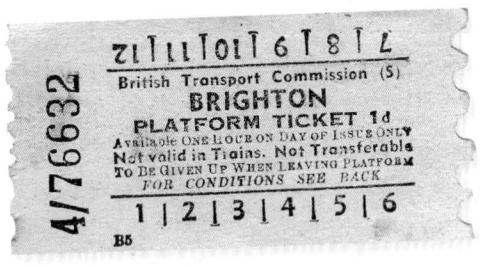

↑ A visit to Guildford was made midweek on 17 May 1961, in the hope of finding a quiet moment which might enable a sneak visit into the shed. Unbeknown to me until I got there, this was totally the wrong day for such a trip. The streets were lined with hundreds of people and police everywhere, including the road bridge over the line from where the shed was entered. HM the Queen and other members of the Royal Family were visiting the new Guildford Cathedral for its consecration. Motive power for the Royal Train was provided by rebuilt 'West Country' No 34009 *Lyme Regis*.

Brighton 50 MILES 61 CHAINS FROM VICTORIA, VIA QUARRY LINE

In my younger days most station visits were on the Southern Region's South Western Division, but news that a school pal had just found his way to Brighton on the Central Division one Saturday afternoon was the spur to do likewise as soon as possible. I ventured to the south coast on 29 July 1963, having a marvellous day out by myself, as many spotting trips have been, through choice.

7 | 8 | 9 | 10 | 11 | 12
4/76632
British Transport Commission (S)
BRIGHTON
PLATFORM TICKET 1d
Available One Hour on Day of Issue Only
Not valid in Trains. Not Transferable
To Be Given Up When Leaving Platform
FOR CONDITIONS SEE BACK
1 | 2 | 3 | 4 | 5 | 6
B5

↓ The beauty of Guildford station was that, like the West Somerset Railway's Minehead station today, it afforded an excellent view of the shed yard from the platform. The shed itself was the other side of the road overbridge on the south end, and was never the most welcoming of Southern depots. Coaling facilities, however, were in full view from the station, and there were always locos on display, such as U class 2-6-0, No 31800 in early 1965.

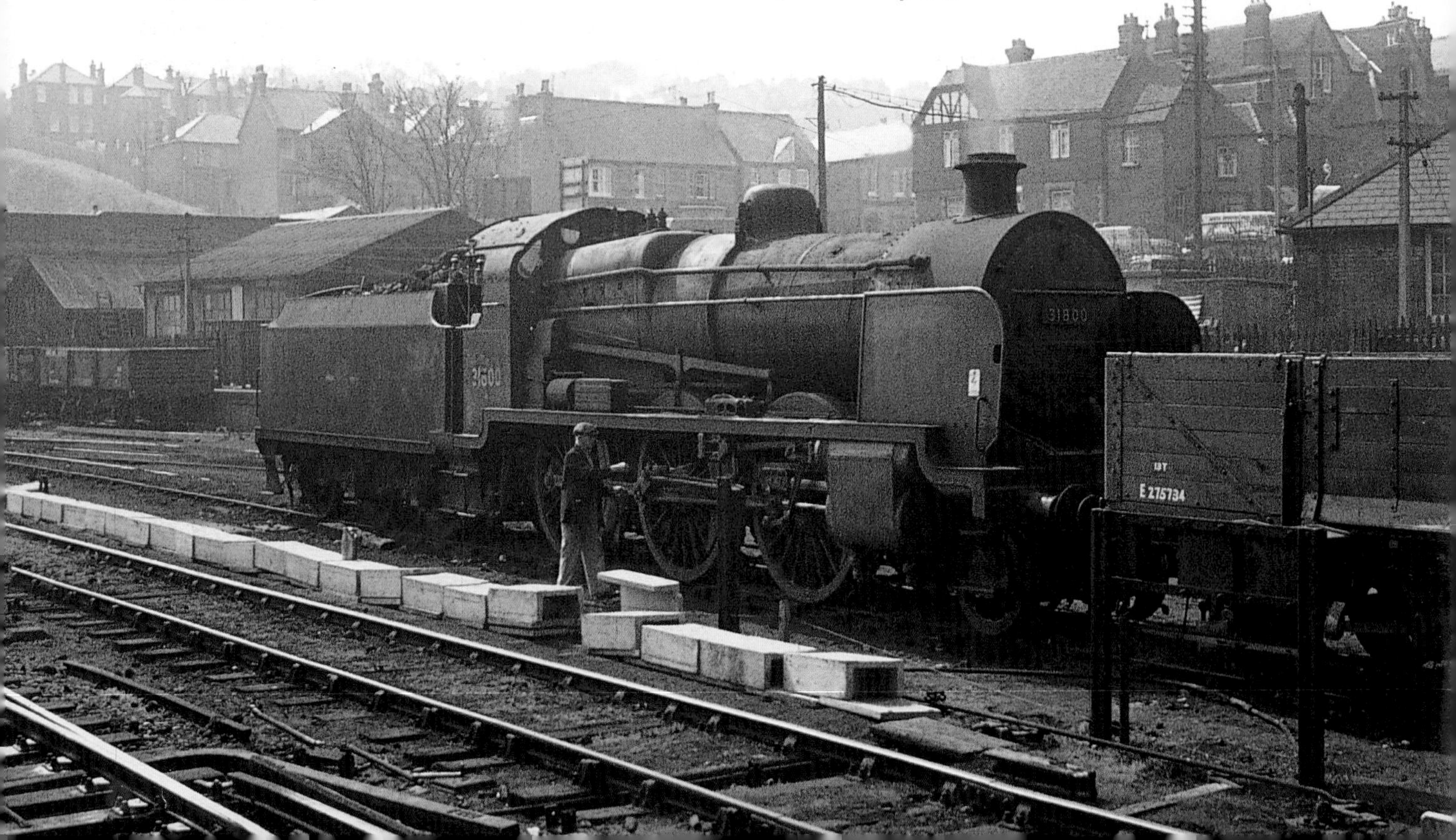

➔ I was always pleased to see No 34057 *Biggin Hill*, which became one of my most-photographed original Bulleids. Never rebuilt, it is seen from Brighton station platform, the sun revealing that the 'air-smoothed' casing was not all that smooth. The reason I favoured this loco was that every September, without fail, I attended the Battle of Britain day at the famous Biggin Hill RAF airfield in Kent where a superb air show was held, quite unlike anything that can be experienced in the UK today. Jets, such as the USAF's 'Skyblazers' F-100 Super Sabre aerobatic team, flew just a few feet directly above the crowd, with full reheat on – the kids screamed, dogs barked, and the ground shook – fantastic!

← This 29 July 1963 view from the platform at Brighton station looks across to the large loco shed water tower, with the water softener to the right. To the left of Ivatt 2-6-2T No 41300 is the wheel drop.

The last scene of southern steam

↘ With the end of regular steam working on the Southern Region set for the weekend of 8/9 July 1967, I had to make sure I experienced it on Friday 7 July. The next day I was setting off for a week in Wales in pursuit of the narrow gauge – a 'new life' beckoned.

After a final visit to Nine Elms MPD (Motive Power Depot), I stopped off at Clapham Junction for one last look at some steam action. A few trains passed through, then rebuilt 'West Country' No 34037 *Clovelly* ran light, very slowly puffing through the carriage sidings and heading sedately, almost symbolically, towards Nine Elms. As it went off into the distance under the distinctive Clapham Junction 'A' signalbox I took this parting shot to mark the end of an era, and a chapter of my life.

Built in 1907 and closed in 1990, and later demolished, it hit the headlines on 10 May 1965 when it threatened to collapse on to the tracks. One corner had suddenly subsided about 3½ft resulting in the closure of all services to Waterloo. The reason for this was that since the Second World War the structure had carried a 40-ton steel roof as air raid protection, on the framework visible here. Metal corrosion had led to the partial collapse and in the course of repairs the roof was removed, but the structure remained an iconic feature of Clapham Junction for another 25 years.

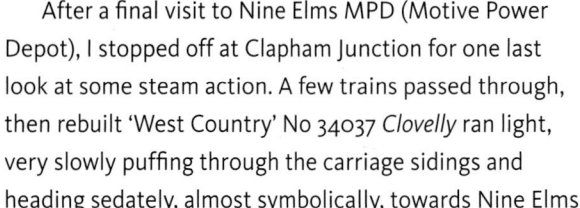

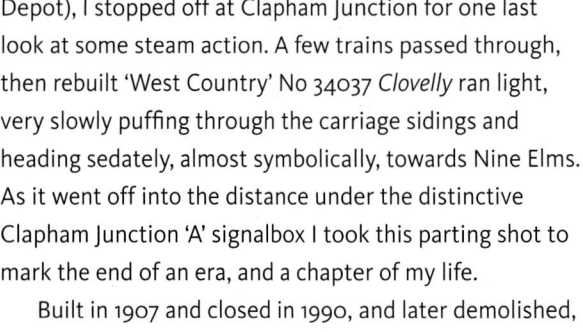

CHAPTER 2

STEAM ON SHED

*Making tracks to where
the locos lived*

THE NEXT STEP after spending time on platforms waiting for the trains to go by, was to make tracks to where the locos 'lived', the engine sheds. At first these appeared to be totally out of bounds, but the restrictions were nothing like today, and many sheds were fairly easily visited, either with or without an official permit.

The first shed to be visited was one I was particularly interested in, this being 75C Norwood Junction. Not only was this located a short distance from where I lived for the first three years of my life, but I knew it would be packed full of ex-LBSCR locos as well as other Southern types. A visit became possible when I was 11 years old due to a lucky opportunity. Rather tenuous perhaps, but it came to be known that my uncle's business partner's father-in-law was shedmaster there. News of my interest had been passed on and my uncle mentioned to my father that if he were to take me along one Sunday morning we would be made most welcome.

A date was soon arranged and we duly reported to the office a couple of weeks later where we met shedmaster Mr Shepherd. He was very kind and after a chat in his office about the dangers and potential pitfalls inside the shed, he let us have a wander around. I was overwhelmed to find K

↑ A general view of Norwood Junction shed from the footbridge on a brief visit in 1960. The shed closed on 5 January 1964 and was demolished in 1966.

class 2-6-0s, C2X 0-6-0s, E4 and E6 0-6-2Ts and others I had only really seen in photos up until that time, and so close up. We climbed into a number of cabs and generally had a good, leisurely look round. Photography was very limited at that time as all I had was the basic Hawkeye camera which took eight photos on a 127 roll film, but I did use a whole film that morning. Also, being with my father and younger sister, these were all expected to include each other standing in front of a loco. Even then, this was not something I really wanted, as these would only be of interest in the family album.

Later visits, or attempted ones with pals, were not so successful as the layout of the shed, completely surrounded by electrified lines and approached by a footbridge in full view of the shedmaster's office, made it a very difficult one to penetrate. Needless to say, Mr Shepherd had retired shortly after a second family visit.

Once we started visiting the big London engine sheds we soon found that nothing could ever equal the thrill and excitement, sometimes coupled with fear, of such fantastic places. Nothing in railway preservation can ever recapture the atmosphere of sheds such as Old Oak Common, Willesden, Camden, Cricklewood, Kentish Town, King's Cross 'Top Shed', Stratford, Nine Elms or Stewarts Lane.

↑ The only photo from my first shed visit to Norwood Junction of any general interest is this view. It shows shedmaster Mr Shepherd, left, outside his office, together with my father, Don, and shy sister. Beyond is ex-SECR C class 0-6-0 No 31297, which was withdrawn in September

The nearest we can get to that is Didcot and Barrow Hill roundhouse, two marvellous railway centres, which I always very much enjoy visiting as they do present a flavour of what it was like to go round a real, working engine shed in the days of steam. (The one aspect that is recreated so authentically throughout the country these days at heritage railway engine sheds, it has to be said, is the over-officious 'shed foreman' barring access.)

If I could be transported back in time to just one place, I would have difficulty in deciding whether it would be 81A Old Common, 34A King's Cross, or 70A Nine Elms, but like all sheds each was very different. While 81A was always an easy shed to get round and 1A Willesden just down the road was variable, depending who was on duty, 34A was definitely one of the 'fear' sheds. Like most Eastern Region depots, it was never an easy shed to enter or walk round without being quickly ejected.

I have heard artist David Shepherd say how much he enjoyed being in the absolute squalor and dereliction of Nine Elms in its last days, where he produced some of his finest paintings. Pete Waterman has also stated he actually liked the muck and filth of the last days of steam, and I very much agree with both of them. Nine Elms really had become a dreadful place, so far removed from today's sanitised environment, that it was fantastic! I really would love the opportunity to walk (carefully) round it again, with a modern camera!

The roofless building, with piles of coal dust and hot ashes scattered everywhere making it hazardous to walk between the tracks, the filthy engines and the smell of sulphury smoke all added to the general state of dereliction, and yet, amongst all this were locos in steam, living and breathing and awaiting their next call to duty. Once released they would head a train from London, down to the clean and clear country air of the West Country. As was obvious at the time, such an environment was soon to disappear, never to be experienced again.

The last days of Southern steam in 1967 happened to coincide with the only time I ever worked in London, albeit just for a few weeks on an audit, and I made a point of stopping off at

Vauxhall and heading for Nine Elms on several occasions on the way home from work. It was by then far more readily accessible than it had been in previous years, when a walk along Wandsworth Road and down the Brooklands Road cul-de-sac leading to the entrance so often met with disappointing results when access was denied.

We had Flt Lt Aidan L F Fuller's *British Locomotive Shed Directory* as our invaluable guide, but this was of no help when it came to King's Cross shed. There was just no way in, or so it seemed. The approach road had an office at the shed end, so as soon as you started walking down it the foreman would step outside, with arms folded so that his body language alone said 'no entry', and that was it. Similar in fact to Norwood Junction, once the friendly foreman there had retired.

We thought we would glean some local knowledge, so early one evening after we had been to all the other main London sheds, we walked down York Road beside King's Cross station and around the roads leading towards the shed until we saw a couple of likely looking spotters. 'How do we get in?' we asked. 'Easy,' was their surprise reply, 'we've just been round and seen everything.' They said, 'Follow us,' and they showed us the way, which we used several times subsequently, including once,

bravely I suppose, for a 14-year-old, by myself. This was the early 1960s remember, not 21st-century 'nanny-state' Britain.

The local lads took us to the coal yard and we walked along the staithes where lorries were loaded with coal dropped from the wagons on the tracks above, until we saw one where the wagon above had discharged its coal below. We clambered onto the pile of coal and climbed up until we got underneath the wagon. We then squeezed out between the wheels and hey presto, we were in the yard, well away from the foreman's office. The lads said: 'Well, off you go then – you only need to duck under about half a dozen wagons or so and you'll be in the shed yard. Good luck and goodbye,' and they were gone. That's right, 'all' we had to do now was clamber under and through about eight rows of coal wagons which did indeed bring us to the front of the main shed building. It was a Sunday evening and there did not appear to be any train movements so it seemed safe enough, at least it got us into the otherwise impossible shed.

On that first occasion we did not relish going back the same way, so we walked along the top of the staithes at their ends above the canal, where we saw some lads fishing. We thought this a safer way of leaving the premises, but how wrong we were. One of the four of us inadvertently kicked a piece of coal as he walked along. It went down off the edge and hit one of the lads. They immediately thought we had thrown it at them. We did not know a quick way down from there, but they certainly knew a quick way up! As they came up towards us we spotted they were wielding flick knives and our shouts of 'sorry' did not seem to have much effect.

We just ran towards the main entrance of the goods yard where there was a watchman on duty, the very place we had been trying to avoid, but this suddenly seemed the lesser of two evils. We 'gave ourselves up' and explained we were being chased by some 'thugs' and we had not wanted to be in his goods yard!

He seemed to accept this and showed us out though the gateway. He said he knew who we meant and that they were not really all that dangerous,

adding they would not have killed us, just cut us up a bit probably. His acceptance of normality seemed a bit different to ours. After that, 34A was dropped from the itinerary for a few months. When we did return we were even more careful how we went in and out, but what a fantastic shed – well worth all the effort, but definitely no time ever for standing about taking snaps!

As good as the London sheds were, with locos of all regions being present, it was not long before we wanted to go a bit further afield. Every month, *Modern Railways* and *The Railway Magazine* carried what now seems quite an unbelievable number of advertisements for clubs organising shed visits. One that caught my eye, and which I replied to, was the London Railfans' Club, and this probably turned out to be one of my best decisions, ever.

THE LONDON RAILFANS' CLUB caters for all Railway Spotters. Regular week-end visits to Motive Power Depots, Works, etc. All tours start from London and normally terminate before 9 p.m. Forthcoming trips for 1963 will include: Swindon, Crewe, Derby, Doncaster, Leeds, Manchester, all London Depots, and many more. Membership costs only 3/3 for first 6 months (badge included); thereafter 1/6 per half-year. Badges available in following colours: Green (S.R.), Maroon (L.M.R.), Brown (Western) and Blue (Eastern). Details (enclose 3d S.A.E.) to: Potter, 18 Hilltop Road, West Hampstead, N.W.6.

The first trip I went on was a modest one, visiting just one shed on a Sunday morning. The only major London shed I had never managed to get in was the biggest, 30A Stratford, so I jumped at the chance of visiting it at last. We met at Liverpool Street and bought our tickets to Stratford and the group slowly gathered together, about 20 in number. It was to be the first of very many trips with this club which enabled me to visit sheds in England, Scotland and South Wales, which I would not have been able to do otherwise. Day trips from London were often by coach, but those further afield meant an overnight train journey and then having a coach waiting for us first thing in the morning at out destination station.

Obviously, I wished later I had gone on even more trips as lots of sheds never did get visited, but at the time I went on all those I could afford, in time and money. And if only I'd taken more photos, but that would have meant more expense.

A decision had to be made: was it to be more trips and fewer photos, or fewer trips and more photos? I balanced it as best I could, but time was running out as sheds started to close and locos were consigned to scrap. Our world was changing, and quicker than we liked to think.

Although it is often said when looking back to those days that there was no health and safety culture, people were much more personally aware of potential danger, and how to avoid it, than they are today.

On all those trips, making our way round loco sheds and yards from quite a young age, the only accident of any sort I can recall was on a later visit to Stratford. We were walking through the long shed which was really dark, making it difficult to write down the numbers. As I picked my way through and over the many obstacles on the ground, a kid just behind me stepped forward to say something and walked straight into a water column between the tracks. He simply had not seen it in the pitch dark and knocked himself out. We had to stop to carry him outside and left him beside a track. By the time we had finished the shed he had come to and was then really put out that the party would not wait while he went back into the shed to see what he had missed. We needed to get on to the next shed and could not spare the time for someone to do the shed again. Needless to say, he was told that if anyone asked him what he had done over the weekend, he would have to say he had been on a 'shed bash'.

I have wondered what happened to other LRC members. Are they still enthusiasts? The only person I have since met who was a member, not that I recall seeing him on any of the trips I went on, is railway author Richard Derry. I see him from time to time as he too now lives in Somerset and can often be found on duty on the West Somerset Railway. I also had a nice letter in late 1971 from someone I only knew as 'Gilbert' when on the trips, from which I learnt this was not his Christian name, which was Barry. An LRC reunion was being organised, but whether I got the date or venue wrong I don't know, but where I went no-one else turned up.

The leader of the London Railfans gained

a certain amount of notoriety when an article appeared in a Sunday paper stating he was more interested in boys than steam locos, and only organised railway days out to attract them. I was certainly never aware of any problems with him in that respect, other than to feel sorry for him on occasions because of the lack of respect shown to him by some of the participants. He obviously went to a lot a trouble to organise so many trips, week after week for years, booking the transport, accommodation when necessary, and of course obtaining the shed permits whenever possible.

This publicity resulted in some trips having their departure arrangements altered to avoid further press harassment, so while the leaflets and adverts may have said 'departing from King's Cross' we regulars knew this actually meant Waterloo.

We did find a bit of a dodge at one time though. I turned up at Waterloo without having booked in advance and so had not paid. I asked if there were any places left on the coach and Potter (never 'Mr' or 'David') said there was just one place, and that as I had booked so many trips, and this was now all paid for, I was welcome to come along.

Someone else tried this again successfully on the next trip. Then, on the following coach tour, hardly any of the regulars had booked in advance, but they all turned up on the day as usual, resulting in far more spotters than places on the coach. Each was expecting a last-minute freebie as they thought it was their turn for such a trip. However, Potter said that he was now able to accept on-the-day payments and he could take fares there and then without problem. We ended up leaving with a couple of empty seats, as several then wandered off to do something else that day.

Membership of the London Railfans' Club enabled me to travel round a great deal of Great Britain at quite a young age, not only 'copping' locos but seeing many towns, villages, landmarks and the country in general, which many others never get to see at any age. This is one aspect that non-railway enthusiasts do not seem to grasp. They do not realise just how ignorant they are of British geography, or how few places in their own country they have visited, compared with any railway enthusiast who has studied and travelled the network.

Quite often, at the beginning or end of the day on these trips, sheds were visited in failing light or even the pitch dark. I well remember reporting to the office at Severn Tunnel Junction while it was still dark in the morning en route to the South Wales sheds. If there was a permit it was certainly not for that time of the day, but the foreman was persuaded to let us go round after a bit of discussion. However, he was fully aware of the 'health and safety' implications because as we all scattered into the total darkness looking for locos, each of us with a small torch, he shouted out after us: 'Mind how you go!'

LONDON MIDLAND REGION

3A Bescot

⬇ Membership of the London Railfans' Club enabled me to visit many more sheds than I would never have done by myself. A trip on 26 April 1964 took us to the Birmingham area depots. This included Bescot where this would have been a 'cop' for me that day: ex-LNWR G2 class Super D 0-8-0 No 49446. Built at Crewe in 1922 it only had a short time to live as it was withdrawn that month and broken up in July, but here it is fully coaled up.

3D Aston

⬆ Among the few photos from such trips was this one from Aston shed of 'Britannia' No 70052 *Firth of Tay*. Even if not a 'cop', I must have thought it looked good, standing there in the spring sunshine, on 26 April 1964.

5B Crewe South

⬇ Ex-Crosti boiler BR Standard 2-10-0 No 92025 is turned at Crewe South on 12 April 1967. Ten 9F class 2-10-0s were built at Crewe with Franco-Crosti boilers in 1955. The exhaust did not pass through the front chimney, which was only used when lighting up, but through a separate outlet on the boiler side. This system did not reduce coal consumption as much as hoped and all were rebuilt in 1959–60 with conventional boilers. These were smaller than on the normal 9Fs and so their power classification was lower (8F). They certainly suffered in appearance from this, not helped by the lack of smoke deflectors, as fitted to the other 241 members of the class. Most of the ex-Crostis remained in service until November 1967, but all were scrapped.

6A Chester (Midland)

← The London Railfans' outing on 24 May 1964 took in Chester (Midland) shed where this delightful scene, looking more like a model railway cameo, was captured. LMS 'Jinty' 0-6-0T No 47669, in steam, is posed on the end of a rake of 16-ton mineral wagons in the coaling yard.

9B Stockport (Edgeley)

→ The sun catches the tops of the boilers of locos stored in Stockport (Edgeley) shed on 12 April 1967. Left to right these are Class 5 4-6-0s No 45139 and 45225, and 8F 2-8-0 No 48373, the latter two with their chimneys capped off.

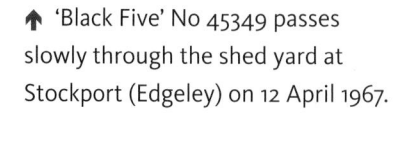

↑ 'Black Five' No 45349 passes slowly through the shed yard at Stockport (Edgeley) on 12 April 1967.

↓ The doyen of the class – Stanier 8F 2-8-0 No 48000 at Stockport (Edgeley) on 12 April 1967. Withdrawn the previous month, it appeared to have been set aside, as if earmarked for preservation. Alas no, and it was broken up in September. This first LMS 8F was completed at Crewe in June 1935 and total production amounted to 849. The most ever in BR stock was 666, from 1957 until 1959. The others mainly served on overseas railways following a military career.

8B Warrington (Dallam)

⬇ BR Standard Class 5 4-6-0 No 73011 stands in steam at Warrington (Dallam) on 12 April 1967.

9D Newton Heath

Two very interesting and rare locos were found on the visit to Newton Heath shed on 13 August 1967. In the process of being broken up in the shed yard were two ex-Lancashire & Yorkshire Railway 0-4-4Ts that I was not even aware existed. They had never been recorded in Ian Allan's *abc*, so this was something of a scoop – and in the nick of time! I was by now becoming familiar with the industrial railway scene as to what was what and where, but these particular locos did not show up in any such listings either. They had been withdrawn from traffic prior to the First World War but had survived all this time in use as stationary train heating boilers.

⬇ Boiler No 903 was LYR No 636 (Kitson 2224 of 1878) withdrawn in June 1908 and used for carriage heating at Queens Road, Manchester until October 1965. It was in an advanced stage of being dismembered when seen, but still recognisable as an LYR 0-4-4T.

⬆ Ivatt Class 2MT 2-6-0 No 46485 is viewed through the remains of a derelict building at Newton Heath on 13 August 1967. Built at Darlington in 1951, it had been withdrawn two months previously when seen here, and was broken up in May 1968.

⬇ With dismantling only just started, LYR No 925 (previously No 519, Sharp Stewart 3318 of 1886) was a lot more complete. Withdrawn in June 1910, it was used at Blackpool North and Cheetham Hill carriage sidings. It soon followed No 636 to oblivion.

14B Kentish Town

➜ This view of 'Jubilee' class 4-6-0 No 45667 *Jellicoe* was snatched as we hurried around Kentish Town shed yard on 6 May 1961. Considering we were aged only 13 at the time, I feel we did well to see and achieve as much as we did. This was probably my first daylight visit to this shed, the first time having been in darkness in an attempt to avoid being seen. We went through the Shand Kydd wallpaper factory, climbed over a wall and jumped into the shed yard. The drop on the other side was much greater than on the side we climbed, so we did not do that again. In fact, it turned out to be one of the easier London sheds to get into.

21A Saltley

➜ BR inherited more than 300 ex-Midland Railway 3F class 0-6-0s in 1948, some dating right back to 1888. Even in 1961, when we visited Saltley shed in August, there were still 54 left in stock, including No 43583, seen here in steam. Built by Kitson of Leeds in 1899, it was withdrawn in August 1962 and broken up in May 1963.

27B Aintree

⬇ The Liverpool area sheds were visited on 24 May 1964, including Aintree. Although this view, without any background, could be anywhere, I was later pleased to find that I had taken one of my few photos that day at this shed, of BR Standard Class 4MT 4-6-0 No 75043. I visited the shed again, about 20 years later when it was long abandoned and frequented by some of the less-desirable characters of the area for all sorts of illicit purposes. My visit was on a sunny Saturday afternoon when it was completely deserted and the buildings were eerily quiet.

When we visited my wife's parents in Bootle, we would go round in the evening and visit an old friend of hers. Then one day, we called round on a summer afternoon and I was amazed that looking down the short street (Ealing Road) from her doorstep I could see the old shed in a vast area of waste ground. We had been there so many times in the dark and had not realised it was still there and so close. While the ladies chatted I wandered off for a nostalgic look round the ancient ruins. It remained like that until early 1996 when it was demolished, nearly 20 years after abandonment and the tracks had been lifted.

EASTERN REGION

33B Plaistow (sub-shed of Tilbury)

➜ A lovely mucky shed, just the sort I liked to visit. Plaistow's main claim to fame was probably that it was where singer/guitarist Joe Brown was a fireman before he became a famous rock 'n' roller with his Bruvvers. Visited on 25 October 1961, we were delighted to find the last surviving LTSR loco in BR service, 3F 0-6-2T No 41981, but it was at the back of the shed, too dark to photograph. However, Fairburn 4MT class 2-6-4T No 42223 of 33C Shoeburyness was more prominent. Spotting pal John Hattom holds on to the grab rail with Burr brothers Robert (small) and Richard (tall) looking on.

34E New England

⬇ You never see a steam loco looking like this today. Perhaps even modellers do not 'weather' their locos to this extent. It is an Ivatt Class 4MT 2-6-0 No 43150 in steam on New England shed on 14 June 1964. Only the first three of these distinctive-looking Moguls were completed by the LMS at Horwich before Nationalisation, the remaining 158 being delivered to BR between then and 1952. Construction was shared between Horwich, Darlington and Doncaster works, so it was an appropriate loco for use on the Eastern Region, despite their number series being 43000 to 43161. Never regarded the most handsome of engines, it is pleasing that one example of the 'Flying Pigs', No 43106, is maintained in working order on the Severn Valley Railway. The BR Standard Class 4MT 2-6-0, 76000 series, also built at Doncaster and Horwich, was based on the Ivatt design, but with subtle detail differences which made it look much more handsome.

36A Doncaster

← Two typical-looking spotters hurry round Doncaster shed yard on 4 June 1961, passing Thompson B1 class 4-6-0 No 61270. Built by the North British Locomotive Co in 1947, it was one of a class of 409. Withdrawn in September 1963, it was cut up two months later. Two B1s remain today, Nos 61264 and 61306.

↑ LNER K3 class 2-6-0, No 61839 is seen at Doncaster shed on 4 June 1961. Although there were nearly 200 of these useful and attractive locos built, none has been preserved. They are said to have had the largest boiler ever used on a British loco, at 6ft in diameter.

↓ Two unknown boys, representing the thousands of loco spotters of the time, jot down the engine numbers in Doncaster shed yard on 9 June 1963. Behind is an equally anonymous ex-ROD (Railway Operating Division) LNER Class O4 2-8-0.

↑ Another type seen at Doncaster on 4 June 1961, which later became extinct, was Gresley's graceful Class O2 2-8-0. This is No 63941, one of 67 engines built between 1918 and 1943; it was scrapped in 1964.

→ Quite probably the loco number the boys on the facing page were writing in their notebooks: Class O4/8 No 63858, fitted with a 100A (B1-type) boiler and side-window cab. It was broken up in July 1966.

← An example of one of Gresley's masterpieces, V2 class 2-6-2 No 60921 at Doncaster shed on 9 June 1963, the month it was withdrawn and scrapped, but here it has a fully coaled tender. A total of 184 V2s were built between 1936 and 1944, mainly at Darlington but a few were completed at Doncaster. The first one, LNER No 4771 (BR No 60800) *Green Arrow* was chosen for the National Collection and was at one time a popular main line performer.

→ Although early preservation was good for LNER constituent company locos, many important LNER designs have been lost, including Gresley's J50 class 0-6-0Ts for the GNR. Between 1913 and 1939 102 were built, but all had gone by the end of 1965. Lined up at Doncaster on 9 June 1963 were Nos 68976, 68961 and Departmental No 10 (ex-68911).

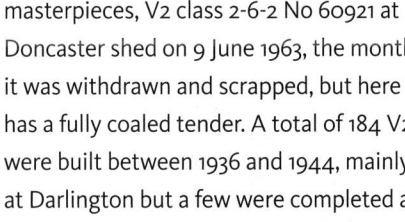
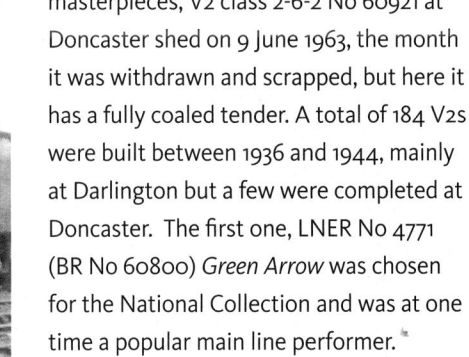

SCOTTISH REGION

65A Eastfield (Glasgow)

← My first visit to Scottish sheds was on 28 September 1963, having travelled north by train overnight. This meant the first shed was visited early in the day, just as the sun was rising. What delights I found there too – including a number of Caledonian Railway-design engines, which were definitely 'winners' for me, and among the first 50000 series numbers ever seen.

First up was 3F class 0-4-4T No 55269, an LMSR development of the CR's McIntosh Class 439. Built in 1925 it had been withdrawn in March 1962 and was broken up in November 1963. To the right is sister No 55263, which had been stored since November 1961 and was scrapped at the same time.

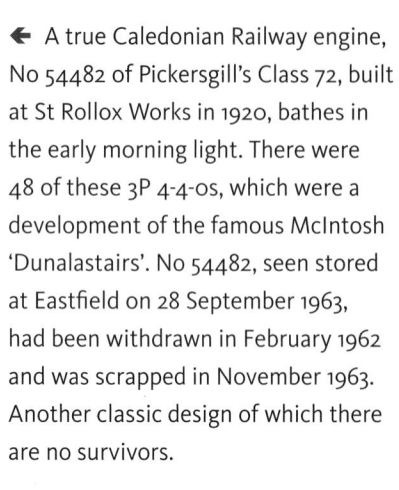

← A true Caledonian Railway engine, No 54482 of Pickersgill's Class 72, built at St Rollox Works in 1920, bathes in the early morning light. There were 48 of these 3P 4-4-0s, which were a development of the famous McIntosh 'Dunalastairs'. No 54482, seen stored at Eastfield on 28 September 1963, had been withdrawn in February 1962 and was scrapped in November 1963. Another classic design of which there are no survivors.

→ Also at Eastfield that morning, on 28 September 1963, was ex-LNER Gresley J38 class 0-6-0 No 65911. The 35 engines of this powerful class were all built in 1926 at Darlington Works and spent their working lives in Scotland. All were withdrawn and scrapped between 1963 and 1967. These were identical to the more numerous J38s apart from having 5ft 2in driving wheels compared with the latter's 4ft 8in.

Although 289 J39s were built, from 1926 to 1941, none of these survive either, but the J39 Locomotive Group was launched by some young enthusiasts in 2011 with the aim of creating a new-build loco.

65B St Rollox

↓ The aim of the visit to Scotland on 28 September 1963 was not just looking for rarities, but picking up previously unseen examples of the more common types which were based north of the border, and not seen down south. An example was this 'Black Five' 4-6-0, No 44998 of 63A Perth smartly turned out at St Rollox shed, and a welcome 'cop'.

↓ The shed yard at St Rollox, showing, left to right, a 'Black Five', BR Standard 4MT 2-6-4T No 80125 of 65J Stirling, and No 44998, as to the left.

64F Bathgate

➜ Ex-North British Railway Class S, LNER Class J37 No 64583, was an interesting find at Bathgate shed on 28 September 1963, as none of these 0-6-0s would have been seen before this trip. In total, 104 of this design by Reid were built, 1914–21, and it was an exceptionally long-lived type. The last examples were still at work until the end of 1966 and we saw the final four in traffic, Nos 64547, 64577, 64597 and 64608, at 62B Dundee Tay Bridge on 1 September 1966 on our Rail Rover holiday (described in Chapter 5). No 64583 was withdrawn in December 1963 and broken up in May 1964.

SOUTHERN REGION

70A Nine Elms

➜ A general view of Nine Elms from just inside the entrance at the end of Brooklands Road. The limited lighting in the shed can be seen, as can smoke coming from a couple of Battersea Power Station's iconic chimneys on the left. The huge coaling tower is on the right in this view, dated 13 November 1966.

⬇ Rebuilt Bulleid Pacific No 34040 *Crewkerne* has its tubes cleaned at Nine Elms on 26 March 1967.

⬇ A number of former LBSCR E4 class 0-6-2Ts were used for a while on Waterloo to Clapham Junction ECS turns having been transferred from the Central Division to 70A. No 32487 is seen at Nine Elms on 4 March 1961 in between such duties, and freshly coaled up including some on the cab roof. Known as the Radial Tanks, they were introduced in 1897 by R.J. Billinton. Originally No 487 *Fishergate,* it was withdrawn in December 1962 and scrapped the following August. One of the 70 locos built survives, the now well-known Bluebell Railway engine, No 2473 *Birch Grove.*

↑ Ivatt Class 2MT 2-6-2T No 41298 comes on shed at Nine Elms from one of its last BR duties, on 7 July 1967. It was to be another 46 years before it would be seen in steam again, with a return to traffic on the Isle of Wight due to take place in October 2013.

↑ The last days at Nine Elms saw large numbers of photographers capturing the scene, unhindered by authority and even artists were able to set up their easels and work undisturbed. This was the last weekday evening of Southern steam, 7 July 1967. Sitting on an oil drum, an artist works on his painting of BR Standard 2-6-4T No 80145. While he was doing this, David Shepherd was at work in the gloomiest part of the shed sketching 'West Country' No 34002 *Salisbury*, which became one of his best-known paintings of this period.

70B Feltham

➜ Feltham shed and yard was always full of interesting locos and was where the impressive Maunsell W class 2-6-4Ts could be found, such as No 31917 on 7 December 1963. Fifteen of these engines were built for freight work, mainly for use on inter-regional trains in the London area. This one was condemned the following month and broken up in August 1964. There are no survivors.

← Bulleid's distinctive Q1 class 0-6-0s were a common sight at Feltham and No 33003 was seen there on 7 December 1963. A total of 40 were built, all in 1942, the first 16 completed at Brighton Works and the rest at Ashford Works. Originally No C3, this loco was withdrawn in June 1964 and broken up six months later. Fortunately, the first, No C1 (later 33001), was claimed for the National Collection.

70C Guildford

➜ The view of Guildford shed as seen from the road bridge, with BR Standard Class 5 4-6-0 No 73119 *Elaine* on the turntable, sometime in spring 1965.

← A closer view of No 73119 *Elaine* at Guildford on the same occasion as the view above, and also looking down from the road bridge. This had been the first of the 20 'Standard Fives' I had seen with a name, one evening at Esher, prior to reading about them in the railway press, and I wondered how official it was.

➜ Guildford became noted for retaining old and rare locos as shed pilots. Latterly, a more modern loco was used, but nevertheless, an unusual one. This was one of the 14 USA 0-6-0Ts which had been acquired by the Southern Railway from the US Army Transportation Corps after the Second World War. These were purchased to replace the LSWR B4 class 0-4-0Ts for shunting within Southampton Docks. When the USAs were replaced by Ruston & Hornsby 0-6-0DEs (Class 07), several found other duties, mainly in departmental use as works shunters. No 30072 became a well-known pilot at Guildford, where it is seen outside the semi-roundhouse on 7 December 1963. Today, it is preserved on the Keighley & Worth Valley Railway.

70D Basingstoke

⬇ Even in 1967 these wheelbarrows neatly lined up inside the shed looked pretty antiquated, another aspect of the steam railway swept away by modernisation.

70G Weymouth

⬇ BR Standard 4MT 2-6-0 No 76053 was one of many withdrawn locos laid up at Weymouth shed seen by those who had arrived behind the immaculately restored A4 No 4498 *Sir Nigel Gresley* on 4 June 1967 (see also Chapter 10). The Mogul had been withdrawn that January and was reduced to scrap in August.

⬆ The first-built Bulleid Light Pacific, No 34001 *Exeter,* awaits its next duty at Basingstoke on 29 January 1967. Completed at Brighton Works in June 1945, it was rebuilt at Eastleigh in November 1957 and remained in traffic until the end of steam on the Southern, and was withdrawn in July 1967. It was broken up that October at Cashmore's yard, Newport, one of 38 of the type processed there.

Steaming slowly through the shed yard at Weymouth, which was full of visiting enthusiasts, was rebuilt 'Battle of Britain' No 34087 *145 Squadron*, looking fairly clean for the time.

71A Eastleigh

⬇ A visit to Eastleigh shed on 29 January 1967 gave an opportunity for some detail shots and to try something completely different. Steam is ejected from the cylinders of BR Standard Class 5MT 4-6-0 No 73020.

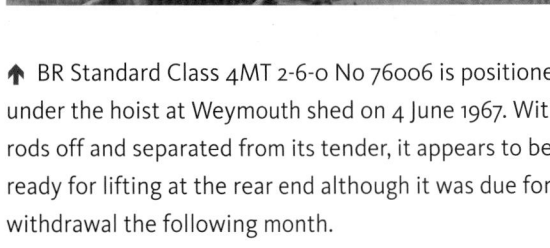

⬆ BR Standard Class 4MT 2-6-0 No 76006 is positioned under the hoist at Weymouth shed on 4 June 1967. With rods off and separated from its tender, it appears to be ready for lifting at the rear end although it was due for withdrawal the following month.

→ BR Standard Class 4MT 2-6-0 No 76016 had obviously not turned a wheel for some while when viewed in close-up on 29 January 1967. It had been withdrawn the previous October and was broken up the following June.

↓ Another BR Standard Mogul on Eastleigh shed, No 76066, but still in use on 4 June 1967 with a little over a month to go before withdrawal, along with the rest of the Southern Region steam fleet.

→ From when I first saw a Brighton 'Terrier' on Hayling Island in 1953 to the present time, they have been one of my favourite classes. It is therefore pleasing to see that no fewer than ten of the 50 locos built between 1872 and 1880 still exist. This is No 32670 (originally No 70 *Poplar*), at Eastleigh shed on 7 December 1963. It is now on the Kent & East Sussex Railway as it was from 1901–31, and is again running as No 3 *Bodiam*.

The second 'Terrier', behind No 32670, is No 32650 (LBSCR No 50 *Whitechapel*) now undergoing restoration on the Spa Valley Railway.

71B Bournemouth

↓ Something of a classic view, or at least a familiar one, of a rebuilt Bulleid Pacific outside Bournemouth shed. This is 'West Country' No 34098 *Templecombe* on 7 May 1967, approaching the last days of Southern steam and looking much neglected and minus nameplates.

↑ On shed at Bournemouth on 26 August 1963 was Drummond M7 class 0-4-4T No 30052. The LSWR built 105 of these very successful and useful locos between 1897 and 1911 for suburban and branch line services. Two survive today, Nos 30053 and 30245. When built in 1905, No 30052 was classified X14, one of 50 with slightly longer frames and other detail variations, but all were later reclassified M7. It was withdrawn in May 1964 and broken up in October.

WESTERN REGION

81C Southall

➔ I must admit that when visiting Southall shed in 1964 with the end of Western Region steam predicted for the following year, I would not have imagined it to still be an important steam depot nearly 50 years later! My few photos of 'Grange' class 4-6-0s became of greater interest when I realised none had survived. This is No 6831 *Bearley Grange* on 12 January 1964, with a bunch of London Railfans to the right.

81D Reading

➔ Collett 2251 class 0-6-0 No 2257 was seen later the same day, 12 January 1964, at Reading. Again, only one example survives of this useful class of locos, of which 120 were built to Collett's design, No 3205 on the South Devon Railway.

↑ I was particularly pleased to get a photo of 'Large Prairie' 2-6-2T No 6167 at Southall on 12 January 1964 as this was the subject of a Kitmaster oo gauge plastic kit, later re-released by Airfix. This was not considered sufficient justification for a loco of this type to be taken into the National Collection however, or even a 'Small' one come to that, but the 6100 class is represented at Didcot by No 6106.

87D Swansea East Dock

⬆ One of many highlights of the first trip to South Wales sheds was Kitson 0-4-0ST No 1338 at Swansea East Dock. Originally Cardiff Railway No 5, it had been withdrawn in September 1963, but was still present on 26 January 1964, along with Peckett 0-4-0ST ex-Powlesland & Mason (shunting contractors in Swansea docks), GWR/BR No 1151. The Kitson (3799 of 1898) was saved by the 1338 Trust and is now safely at Didcot, but the Peckett was sold and scrapped. One of P&M's nine locos has been preserved, No 6 (GWR No 921) at Snibston – see Chapter 12.

88B Cardiff Radyr

⬇ The 5600 class 0-6-2Ts always looked a bit ungainly to me, but I had not seen many of them until going to the South Wales valleys sheds, where they seemed to be everywhere. No 5624 was seen by Radyr's coaling

88L Cardiff East Dock

⬇ This shed closed in March 1958, but was reopened in September 1962 when Cardiff Canton was closed to steam, suddenly getting an allocation of 68 locos following its period of abandonment. It finally closed on 2 August 1965 becoming the last steam shed in South Wales. A visit on 26 January 1964 found a lot of activity including Churchward 2884 class 2-8-0 No 3840 at the coaling stage. There were 52 steam locos present; not bad for a shed we previously thought we had missed the opportunity to visit!

stage on 26 January 1964. A total of 200 of the Collett design were built from 1924–28 (Nos 5600–5699 and 6600–6699), of which nine are in preservation, all but one thanks to Woodham Bros, Barry.

CHAPTER 3

WORKS VISITS

To Ashford, Crewe, Derby, Doncaster,
Eastleigh and Swindon

FROM MY EARLIEST BR spotting trips, the most exciting and eagerly anticipated visits were to the big railway works. These were usually visited on special excursions, some running right into the works complex, such as at Crewe and Swindon (see Chapter 8). The fares for these trains often seemed cheap even at the time. My first visit to a major works was to Swindon when the half-fare from London Paddington was only 7s 6d (37.5p) and the full, adult fare was just 14s 6d (72.5p). It was advertised in *Trains Illustrated* which then cost 2s (10p). With magazines now costing just over £4 few tour operators offer such excursions at the equivalent price of around £14.50 for a junior fare. Motive power was not skimped on either as this was the then almost brand-new No 92220 *Evening Star* throughout from Paddington to Swindon. A good day out!

A great attraction of visiting the railway workshops was that they always produced a huge number of loco 'cops' as there were many locos brought together in the one place from all over the region, that would otherwise have taken a lot of tracking down. This applied especially to the northern works like Crewe, Derby and Doncaster, being in parts of the country I didn't visit so often at that time.

The freedom to wander around in the workshops and yards was quite unlike anything that would be permitted today in far less busy and cluttered facilities. Had today's restrictive health & safety regime been in force during the steam era, a book of memories, observations and photos such as this simply would not have been possible. On all these visits, often with some hundreds of participants, I was never aware of even the smallest of accidents.

Weather conditions on some of the works trips were not really conducive to photography, certainly not colour, so most of my works photos were black and white and some visits appear to have produced no photos at all. With so much to see in the limited time available, there was often not sufficient opportunity to take many snaps while jotting everything down.

THE HOME COUNTIES' RAILWAY CLUB ARE
RUNNING A SPECIAL TRAIN ON

SUNDAY, 9th OCTOBER

VISITING

SWINDON LOCOMOTIVE WORKS

AND SHED

FARES ARE: 14/6 ADULT   7/6 JUVENILE (UNDER 16)

The train will leave Paddington at approx. 11.15 a.m. and is due back at 5.0 p.m. We regret that we are unable to accept enthusiasts under the age of 12.

If you wish to take part in this event kindly fill in the attached form or write by letter to Mr. R. Walker, 17, Keswick Gardens, Wembley, Middlesex. Tickets will be sent by return.

To Mr. R. Walker. 17, Keswick Gardens, Wembley, Middlesex.

Please send me ......Adult and/or ......Juvenile ticket(s) for the Home Counties' Railway Club special on 9th October.

I enclose Cheque/Postal Order value............ (All cheques and postal orders to be made payable to "Home Counties' Railway Club" and crossed) also a S.A.E. in which the ticket(s) will be sent.

Name (block letters) ....

Address ....

The advertisement from *Trains Illustrated*, August 1960, that was so tempting. I was slightly under 12½ years of age, so only just 'qualified'. We did not know then that we were going be hauled by *Evening Star* – the last steam loco built for BR – completed at Swindon that March.

Swindon Works

The first visit to a works was Swindon, on
9 October 1960, when we travelled there and into
the works yard behind No 92220 *Evening Star*
(see Chapter 8). This was a very gloomy day and
I have read since that others found photography
difficult, so not so surprising then that results
were none too good.

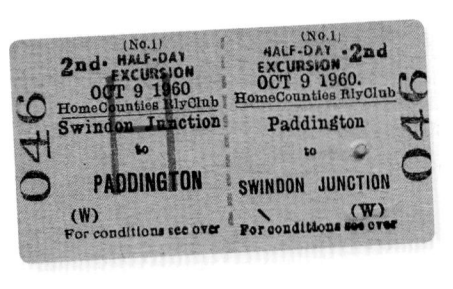

↑ Among the ex-works locos seen at Swindon on
9 October 1960, and not yet reunited with their tenders,
were Nos 7012 *Barry Castle* and 5988 *Bostock Hall*.

← Seen at its lowest ebb, No 6000 *King George V* in the
fog at Swindon on 8 December 1963. Although listed for
preservation it was uncared for and sent to Stratford
Works in 1964 for storage. It returned to Swindon two
years later and after another two years was pulled from
the Stock Shed and given a new lease of life.

➜ Something of a mystery now as
to why I should have taken just the
one photo on my second visit to
Swindon Works, especially as the
sun was shining. Recently
outshopped, the now-preserved
'Manor' 4-6-0 No 7802 *Bradley Manor*
is seen in steam on the occasion of
the visit by means of the Ian Allan
railtour of 27 April 1962, which
travelled from Waterloo to Swindon
via Southampton Docks.

GRAND EASTER HOLIDAY

LOCOSPOTTERS' EXCURSIONS
from LONDON
ON THURSDAY APRIL 26th 1962 TO
DONCASTER WORKS

Fare: 22 6 Under 16;   45 - Adult
KING'S CROSS   Depart: 10.10 a.m.   Return: 7.11 p.m.

from LONDON
ON FRIDAY APRIL 27th 1962 TO
SOUTHAMPTON DOCKS
Visits to BALCONY OCEAN TERMINAL
DOCK LOCOMOTIVE DEPOT · DOCK MODEL ROOM
and
SWINDON WORKS

Fare: 21 - Under 16;   42 - Adult
WATERLOO   Depart: 8.10 a.m.

The trains will include a buffet car from which light refreshments can be obtained.
A limited amount of accommodation will be reserved for adults, or adults accompanying not
more than one child. Please specify if you wish to use this accommodation.
Juveniles need not be accompanied by an adult. The train will be supervised by our own
staff and guides will be provided on the tours of the Works.
It is regretted that bookings for visitors to join the party at the Works cannot be
accepted as the trips are limited to those travelling on the special trains.

.... USE THIS BOOKING FORM ....

2nd Special Excursion 2nd
C.M. 8068   27th APRIL 1962
IAN ALLAN LOCOSPOTTERS
CLUB EXCURSION
Child under 16 years of age.
Waterloo to
SOUTHAMPTON D'KS.
THENCE TO SWINDON Via Westbury
RETURNING TO WATERLOO
Via Reading & Ascot
(S)   (S)
FOR CONDITIONS SEE OVER
CHILD 0368 9   CHILD 0368 9

The ticket and booking form flyer for Ian Allan's railtours to Doncaster and Swindon Works in April 1962. The precise arrival time from Doncaster at the end of the day was perhaps optimistic. Motive power for the Southampton Docks and Swindon Works trip on 27 April was 'West Country' No 34094 *Mortehoe*. On another trip behind this loco the train never arrived back in London at all when the Bulleid Pacific ran out of coal at Aylesbury (see Chapter 8).

Long after the official end of steam on BR, workshop facilities were retained for the overhaul of such engines. As late as 1975, it was possible to put 'Princess Coronation' No 46229 *Duchess of Hamilton*, obtained on loan for the National Collection from Butlin's Minehead holiday camp, through Swindon for restoration to working order for use on main line specials.

← The leaflet issued to Ashford Works visitors.

Ashford Works

Visited Wednesday, 5 April 1961 on the 'Ian Allan Railfan Excursion to Ashford/Eastleigh'. We arrived at Ashford at 10.22, and departed at 12.25 including the walk to and from the station, so it was quite a quick visit to so busy a place.

→ Schools class No 30933 *King's-Canterbury* in the yard at Ashford looking neglected, but it was not withdrawn for another seven months.

⬇ A murky view of the 'scrap line' at Ashford with spotters getting their last viewing of stored and recently withdrawn locos. Left to right are three 4-4-0s: D1 class 4-4-0 No 31487, 'Schools' No 30932 *Blundells*, L class No 31776 and H class 0-4-4T No 31276.

Brighton Works

I never had the opportunity to visit the former LBSCR works at Brighton, although it was the birthplace of many of my favourite locos. However, I was lucky enough on 11 May 1961 to see the A1X 0-6-0T which was the former Brighton Works shunter, when it worked into the station and back out again while I was on the platform end. This was No 32635, originally No 35 *Morden* and later numbered 377S and then DS377 when in departmental stock. It had replaced the similarly

liveried No 380s (No 82 *Boxhill*) when withdrawn for preservation in 1946.

No 32635 had been repainted in full LBSCR Stroudley 'improved engine green' yellow ochre livery when taking up work shunter duties, which it retained when reinstated in capital stock in 1959. Regrettably, although ten other 'Terriers' have been preserved, this celebrity member of the class was broken up in September 1963.

Eastleigh Works

The first of several visits to this important works was on the same day as to Ashford, on the Ian Allan railtour on 5 April 1961. The train ran right into the works yard behind Ivatt 2-6-2T No 41293 which took over from 'Schools' class No 30913 *Christ's Hospital* at Eastleigh station. We only had 70 minutes to visit the works and yards. Perhaps because of this, I have only one picture.

Unlike Ashford, several further visits were made to the slightly more local Eastleigh Works in the steam era, including public open days. At the time I was rather put out by the kids clambering all over

⬇ T9 class 4-4-0 No 30729 awaiting scrap at Eastleigh on 6 April 1961. It had been withdrawn ten months before and was broken up before the end of April.

the locos and spoiling the photo opportunity. Now, I look at these in disbelief and delight in the fact that such scenes of freedom were captured. The second visit to Eastleigh was on 1 August 1962 when the public were allowed to roam freely.

➡ The last T9 class 4-4-0 in traffic was No 30120. In 1962, it was repainted in LSWR green livery and returned to operation for use on enthusiasts' specials. It remained in capital stock until July 1963 when withdrawn and classified as preserved.

⬅ Among the locos on display in the yard at Eastleigh for the 1 August open day was B4 class 0-4-0T, dock tank No 30096. It is better known today as the Bluebell Railway's *Normandy*.

↑ A scene unlikely to be recreated with any 'Battle of Britain' in preservation today: No 34075 *264 Squadron* attracts attention from the more adventurous enthusiasts at Eastleigh Works on 1 August 1962. Meanwhile, a member of staff touches up the paintwork of the nameplate plaque.

→ Perhaps because of its more rounded boiler top, 'Merchant Navy' No 35022 *Holland-America Line* – another Bulleid which is still extant but unrestored – was treated with more respect. A pair of smoke deflectors is propped up in the foreground.

← BR Standard Class 4 2-6-4T No 80137 was on display in ex-works condition at Eastleigh on 1 August 1962.

The next Eastleigh open day I attended was on 7 August 1963, and what a surprise was in store! I thought that ex-LBSCR, A1 class 0-6-0T No DS680 was a loco I was going to miss. For some while it had been used exclusively in Lancing Carriage Works, which I had never visited, thinking it was 'only a carriage works'. Withdrawn in June 1962, I had heard it had been presented to the

Canadian Railroad Museum at Delson, Quebec, despite being the only 'Terrier' surviving in its original form with short smokebox, apart from the officially preserved No 82 *Boxhill*. It was not until I arrived at the works that I discovered it had been cosmetically restored but not yet despatched from the UK and was on display – fantastic! One shot at most was only ever allowed for any loco, and the majority seen did not even have that, but this was special. Restored to its original guise as No 54 *Waddon*, in Stroudley's fully lined 'improved engine green' it was the subject of no fewer than five different views being taken from all angles, including this one. It was later despatched to Canada with 21ft of LBSCR rail from a siding at Lancing.

At the time of writing, late 2012, the 'Terrier' was the only ex-BR loco resident in North America following the repatriation of all the others that had been sent there in the 1960s (see Chapter 6).

→ Claimed for the National Collection, 'Battle of Britain' 4-6-2 No 34051 *Winston Churchill* seems destined never to run again. Withdrawn in September 1965, it languished in the yard at Eastleigh Works on 29 September 1967, having been stored at Hellifield shed in the meantime.

An appeal fund for cosmetic restoration was launched by the Friends of the NRM in April 2011 with the aim of having it restored for static display in time for the 47th anniversary of Sir Winston Churchill's funeral train on 30 January 2012. During that year the loco appeared at the Great Dorset Steam Fair and at the Mid-Hants Railway, on static display, to encourage fund-raising. By October, with about £20,000 of the required £35,000 raised, the target for completion had been revised to 2015 – more appropriately the 50th anniversary of the funeral train.

← With everybody firmly on the ground at this year's open day, 7 August 1963, 'Battle of Britain' No 34084 *253 Squadron* makes for a better photograph than the example at the previous year's event.

Crewe Works

I have been to the former LNWR/LMS works many times, witnessing much change, and of course decline. The first time was on 3 April 1966 when it was the second works visit of the day, after Derby. The special train was run by the Epsom Railway Society (see Chapter 8). The train ran right into the works yard and this proved to be my best ever visit photographically to Crewe in steam days. The number of locos seen and the vastness of the works was almost overwhelming.

↑ Even as the train drew in to the works yard at Crewe I was able to get a shot from the window of Class 4F 0-6-0 No 44405, less its tender, and 'Jinty' 0-6-0T No 47649 behind.

↓ As we walked to the main works we passed another 'Jinty', No 47615 with a row of fireboxes as a backdrop.

↑ Once in the erecting shop, which was full of locos receiving attention, it was light and airy. I had no light meter or automatic camera then, so exposure's were always guesswork, but I did not do too badly here. First up was Ivatt Class 2 No 46443. Now preserved on the Severn Valley Railway, this 2-6-0 was bought by R C J Willcox from BR following withdrawal in March 1967, and so was never a Barry scrapyard resident like other survivors of its type.

← Row upon row of locos under repair. From left to right: 9F 2-10-0 No 92016, 8F 2-8-0 No 48392, 9F 2-10-0s Nos 92077 and 92227, with another, No 92002, on the second track, right.

↑ One of several 9Fs in works that day, No 92227 with another, No 92002, right.

↓ 'Black Five' 4-6-0 No 45447 is duly noted down.

↑ 'Britannia' 4-6-2 No 70041 *Sir John Moore*, with wheels out.

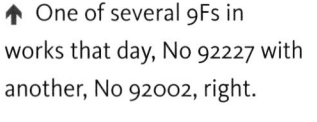

↓ Avoiding the obvious was not always possible, as wherever one stood there would have been a lamp post protruding from one or other of the locos. Besides, there would have been a whole bevy of people all jockeying for position, trying to get the best shot and there was no time to linger until others had finished and moved on. To get the view of all three locos, it was simply this, or nothing, and I still recall the altercation with the man who stepped in front just as I was taking it as he accused *me* of being ill-mannered! Left to right: 'Britannia' No 70038 *Robin Hood*, Class 4MT 4-6-0 No 75009, and Black Five No 44659.

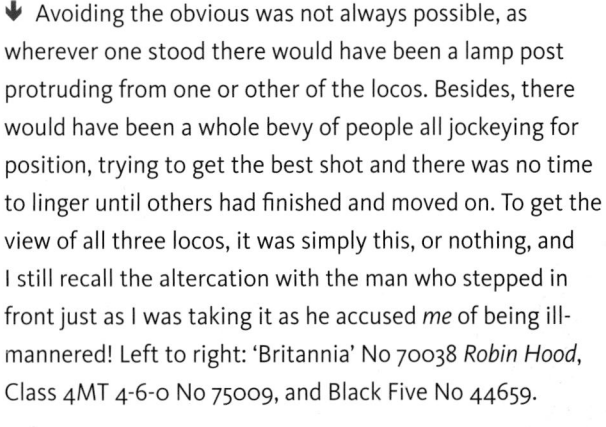

↑ Stripped of cylinders, motion and chimney, 8F class 2-8-0 No 48037 awaits attention. Following this it returned to traffic until withdrawal in December 1965.

→ A feature of many loco works and sheds was old loco boilers put to use as static steam generators.

↑ I was really pleased to see the unique Class 8P 4-6-2 No 71000 *Duke of Gloucester* was still intact, complete with its Caprotti valve gear, although it had been withdrawn in November 1962. Originally scheduled for official preservation there was now considerable doubt about this and as is now well known, all that was retained for the Science Museum was the valve gear from one side, the loco then being disposed of for scrap to South Wales. (With hindsight, such valve gear could perhaps have been retrieved from an LMS or BR Standard Class 5 4-6-0.)

The subsequent rescue of this unique loco by

enthusiasts and its restoration to main line running order is one of the most remarkable and commendable achievements of the railway preservation movement. Let us hope its present problems can be overcome and it sees main line operation again in the not too distant future.

I had seen No 71000 before, but only in the depths of Camden shed so was pleased to have what was probably going to be this last opportunity for a photo. It stands outside the Crewe Works paint shop. This 16-road building had housed many interesting locos in storage over the years, some of which survive today in preservation.

Derby Works

← The railtour on 3 April 1966 had also taken in Derby Works earlier in the day, but was not so productive for photos as was Crewe that afternoon. One of those was diesel too, but it was such an interesting loco even I could not resist it at the time. This was the pioneer main line diesel-electric LMS No 10000, awaiting its sad demise in the Derby scrap line. (Beyond are Southern diesel-electrics Nos 10202 and 10203.) Even then, I thought that such a historic loco should be saved for future generations. It is good to see the next best thing is now being pursued in the form of a new-build replica, a project I am pleased to support.

Doncaster Works

⬇ Just the one photo from the works part of the Home Counties Railway Society trip to Doncaster on 9 June 1963 (see also Chapters 2 and 8). It is nevertheless a particularly interesting and notable loco that caught my eye, as we hurried around the works yard. It was Gresley A4 Pacific No 60014 complete with its *Silver Link* nameplates. At the time, we were informed it was being retained for possible preservation. It was the first of the class to be withdrawn by BR, together with four others, in December 1962. Unfortunately, it was broken up in August, and what a shame this famous member of the class was not saved. (No doubt much to the relief of the correspondent who wrote a letter to *The Railway Magazine* bemoaning the preservation of No 60007 *Sir Nigel Gresley*, which he considered was one A4 too many as *Mallard* had already been preserved and two others, Nos 60008 and 60010, were also preserved, albeit in North America!)

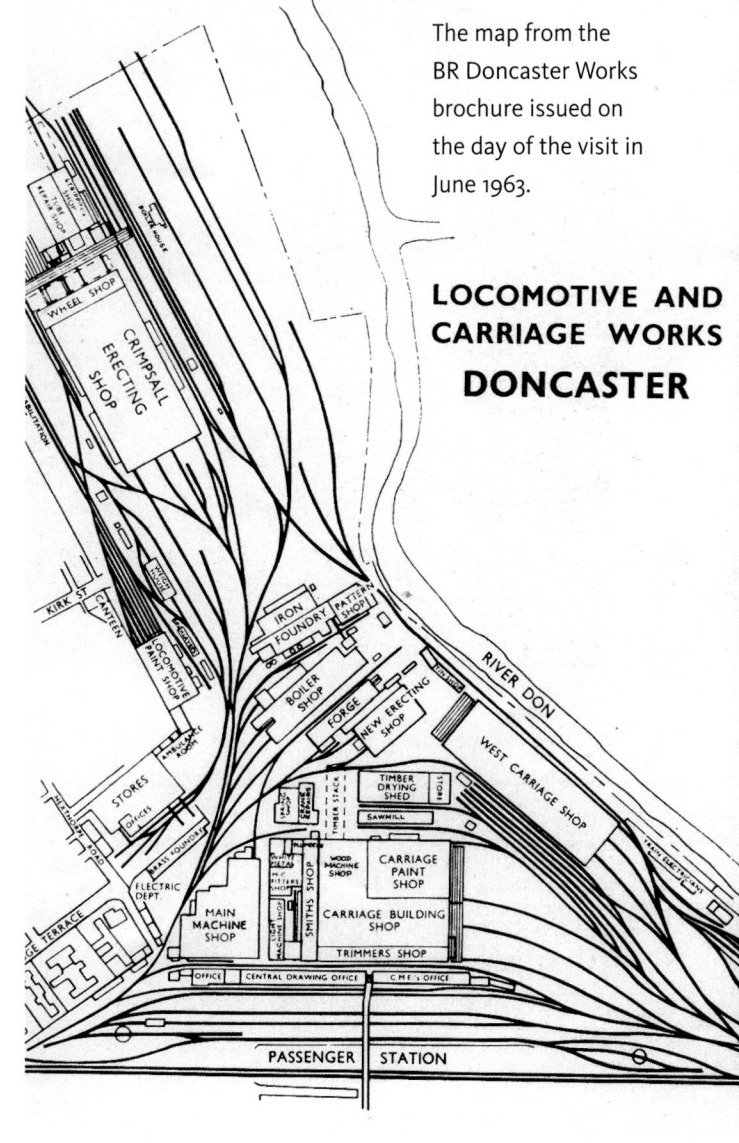

The map from the BR Doncaster Works brochure issued on the day of the visit in June 1963.

LOCOMOTIVE AND CARRIAGE WORKS DONCASTER

CHAPTER 4

ISOLATED STEAM

*The Isle of Wight:
summer holidays and the last day*

MY FATHER WAS not one for holidays. One week each year was just about tolerated, and he never wanted to go too far from our Surrey home. This was mainly because he did not like leaving his beautifully kept decorative garden and greenhouses, which he tended and watered daily – no vegetables allowed, other than a row of runner beans each year for their traditional appearance! It suited me that overseas holidays were never considered (father having 'done' more than enough 'going abroad' in the 1940s when serving with the RAF in North Africa).

Even from an early age though, I wished to go further than West Wittering – beyond the Southern electric network; anywhere where we could see some steam! A compromise was found – the Isle of Wight. Not too far to travel, and a bit like Thomas's Island of Sodor, it had lots of railways.

Admittedly the Isle of Wight was never a great place for loco 'cops' after the first visit, but the whole atmosphere of the 'railway that time forgot' was so fascinating that it helped me to develop my interest in railways as a whole, rather than simply marking off loco numbers in a book. Nevertheless, these locos really were isolated from the national network with even major repairs undertaken in the works at Ryde, so the only way to track them down was to visit the island.

Having already seen most of the locos on my first day-visit with school friend John Hattom, I started to look at the rolling stock, stations and signalboxes. The rakes of pre-Grouping carriages were particularly fascinating, especially when I discovered some were of the railway that we modelled, the LBSCR, as were some of the goods wagons. These were among the first occasions I made a point of photographing rolling stock, detail close-ups, and a few general railway scenes. As these were all part of the steam age, I have included a few of them here as a slight diversion from the general theme of steam locos in their different environments.

The island system

By the time of my island visits and holidays the island's railways had already been cut back considerably and I can only imagine what it would have been like in their heyday. I probably would have wanted to live there!

The line ran as it does today, from Ryde Pier Head down through Brading and Sandown to Shanklin, but then went on through Wroxall to terminate high up on the hill at Ventnor. The only other surviving line was that which branched off at Smallbrook Junction to Cowes via Newport. Surprisingly, I only ever ventured round on the Cowes line once, choosing to spend my time between Ryde Pier Head, St John's Road and Ventnor. Perhaps it was because as the locos and stock could all be seen on this section, the trains were no different passing through Newport or arriving at Cowes. That I virtually ignored that line, never stepping foot on Newport station other than to buy a platform ticket for the collection, for instance, is now something I very much regret.

The final visit in BR steam days was for the last day, on 31 December 1966. Being mid-winter the sun was low and many of the photos taken on that occasion were spoilt because of the sun, rather than the usual lack of it. There was little restriction on where we could wander and I was also able to enjoy a footplate ride during the run-round at Shanklin, the section to Ventnor already having closed on 18 April.

I have been delighted to see the reopening and development of the Isle of Wight Steam Railway, which is one of my favourite heritage railways. Interestingly, this is on the section I only travelled that one time in 1964, so I have been able to make up a bit of what I almost missed completely. What a shame though that it has not been possible to return all the way to Newport, or even Cowes.

Confirming their isolation from the rest of the BR national system, the Isle of Wight locomotives were never renumbered into the main series, so did not take up Southern Region 30000 numbers. When the Southern Railway was formed at the 1923 Grouping, the first attempt at renumbering the locomotives absorbed from the various companies, which inevitably suffered from extensive number duplication, introduced a letter prefix series.

The initials used did not follow the name of the former company or the three area divisions, Eastern, Central and Western as might have been expected, but that of the works responsible for a particular locomotive's maintenance. So, former SECR (Eastern section) locos took up an 'A' prefix for Ashford Works, LBSCR (Central section) locos were given 'B' for Brighton Works, and LSWR (Western section) had 'E' for Eastleigh Works. As I understand it, the Isle of Wight engines were given the 'W' prefix at that time, which they retained through to the BR era until their withdrawal. Therefore, their numbers were a throwback to the earliest days of the Southern Railway. The only place the 'W' was carried in BR days was on a metal plate affixed to the rear of the coal bunker. The front bufferbeam and cabside numbers did not show the letter after 1931, and the number moved from the tank to the bunker side when the locos received their tank-side nameplates.

The ex-LSWR, William Adams-designed, O2 0-4-4Ts were transferred to the island soon after the SR takeover of the independent lines, to replace the motley collection of motive power inherited at the 1923 Grouping. The first two ex-LSWR 0-4-4Ts, which became Nos W19 and W20, arrived from the mainland in April that year. The last, Nos W35 and W36, were delivered in March 1949, after the 1948 Nationalisation.

My first visit to the Isle of Wight was a day trip on 2 August 1961. By then, all four of the ex-LBSCR E1s had been withdrawn, but No W4 was still intact at Ryde St John's shed. The others had been Nos W1 *Medina*, W2 *Yarmouth* and W3 *Ryde*, disposed of in the late 1950s. Four of the ex-LSWR O2s had been withdrawn and scrapped in the 1950s: Nos W15 *Cowes*, W19 *Osborne*, W23 *Totland*, and W34 *Newport*.

BR LOCOMOTIVE STOCK ON THE ISLE OF WIGHT IN THE 1960s

Number	IoW name	Previous number/name	Withdrawn
Ex-LBSCR E1 class 0-6-0T			
W4	*Wroxall*	131 *Gournay*	10/1960
Ex-LSWR O2 class 0-4-4T			
W14	*Fishbourne*	178	12/1966
W16	*Ventnor*	217	12/1966
W17	*Seaview*	208	12/1966
W18	*Ningwood*	220	12/1965
W20	*Shanklin*	211	12/1966
W21	*Sandown*	205	5/1966
W22	*Brading*	215	12/1966
W24	*Calbourne*	209	3/1967*
W25	*Godshill*	190	12/1962
W26	*Whitwell*	210	5/1966
W27	*Merstone*	184	12/1966
W28	*Ashey*	186	12/1966
W29	*Alverstone*	202	5/1966
W30	*Shorwell*	219	9/1965
W31	*Chale*	180	3/1967
W32	*Bonchurch*	226	10/1964
W33	*Bembridge*	218	12/1966
W35	*Freshwater*	30181	10/1966
W36	*Carisbrooke*	198	6/1964

*Preserved by the Isle of Wight Steam Railway

Note: BR, the Southern Railway and its predecessors including the LSWR, used a letter plus number designation for most classes. Therefore, the ex-LSWR 0-4-4Ts were classified O2 and not 'zero 2' as is so often incorrectly printed in many otherwise authoritative publications. Other examples, which back this up, were classes T1 and M7 0-4-4Ts, G6 0-6-0T and H15, N15 and S15 4-6-0s. It was the same with the LNER 'O' class 2-8-0s.

↑ Visits to the Isle of Wight in the early 1960s always included travel on one of the BR paddle steamers, *Ryde, Sandown* or *Whippingham,* from Portsmouth Harbour to Ryde Pier Head, one of which is seen in 1964. What a tragedy, that having survived for so long in static use after withdrawal in 1970, it was not possible to save PS *Ryde.* As it is a popular holiday destination, I thought naively, as a boy, that the paddle steamers would for ever be maintained as part of the experience and enjoyment of visiting the island.

↓ The BR ticket for the Solent crossing, Portsmouth Harbour to Ryde Pier – 'Including Pier Tolls', but 'Exclusive of Tramway or Train' – dated 2 August 1961; my first Isle of Wight adventure.

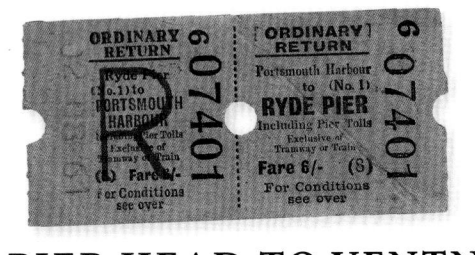

A RIDE DOWN THE LINE – RYDE PIER HEAD TO VENTNOR

Ryde Pier Head

↓ Platform ticket dated 2 August 1961.

→ My first journey on the Isle of Wight railway system, 2 August 1961, from Ryde Pier Head to Sandown and return.

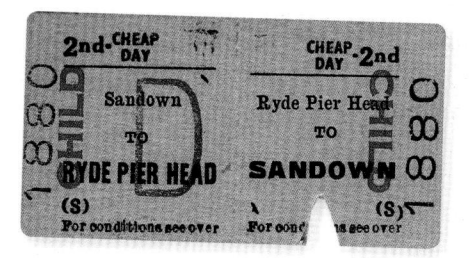

→ My first sighting of an Isle of Wight loco was upon arrival at Ryde Pier Head station on 2 August 1961 when aged 13, on a very brief day trip, accompanied by my slightly older school friend, John Hattom. This was O2 class 0-4-4T No W36 *Carisbrooke.* The coalbunker extension, unique to the island's tanks, is clearly seen.

The name of this station also appears to be something that is often misquoted in many of the numerous books on the Isle of Wight railways. The signalbox and tickets, for instance, clearly showed the title as Ryde Pier Head, rather than Pierhead.

trailer trundle towards Esplanade station, passing an engineer's train and the inner home signal on the approach to Pier Head. Beneath the arm is a route indicator which was set electrically when the points were set, showing the platform number as the signal cleared.

The tramway operated as two separate single tracks and remained in operation until 1969. Railcar No 1 was scrapped, but the power car of set No 2 survived into preservation, just. Its body was scrapped but the remains were used as a works vehicle, first at Newport and then Havenstreet when the preservation project moved there in 1971. However, for 40 years it had been left untouched until 2012 when a major project to restore the vehicle to its original form was launched. This will see a diesel engine fitted in place of the original petrol unit, new bodywork made, and the construction of a replica trailer, for operation on the IWSR.

↑ Although the pier section had been closed for reconstruction work before the last day of steam on 31 December 1966, the little pier tramway running parallel to it was in operation. However, it was unable to cope with the large influx of enthusiasts arriving to travel on the last trains so I walked the length of the pier, which enabled me to get a shot of one of the two petrol railcars as it passed. Baguley-Drewry railcar No 1 and

Ryde Esplanade

→ No W31 *Chale* waits at Esplanade station on a Ventor train, on 2 October 1966. The curved canopy was an unusual feature here.

↓ Platform ticket dated 2 October 1966 – now costing 3d.

Ryde St John's Road

← With the end of steam on the island looming, a day trip was made on 2 October 1966, just in case a last-day visit was not possible. No W17 *Seaview* was seen passing through the station en route to the shed.

↓ No W22 *Brading* departs from Ryde St John's Road on 21 July 1964 with a down train, passing the lovely signalbox, which survives today

↓ Within a few minutes of the departure of No W22, No W14 *Fishbourne* brought in a train of coal from Medina Wharf, the last commercial freight service on the island's railway.

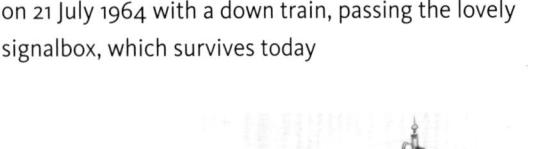

70H Ryde (IoW) Shed and Works

↓ Although only very few photographs were taken on this initial exploration of the island's railway on 2 August 1961, three of them were of a really rare and exciting 'cop':

E1 class 0-6-0T No W4 *Wroxall*. We were not sure until our arrival whether it would still be extant as it had been withdrawn nearly a year before, in October 1960. We found the 'prize' nicely displayed on a siding at the rear of the shed looking almost like a preserved loco on plinth. We wondered if this rare engine had in fact been set aside for preservation as we thought it was the last member of the class to survive. Alas no, and it was broken up.

A few years later I learnt that another of Stroudley's E1s still existed, No 110 *Burgundy*, despite being withdrawn by the SR as long ago as February 1927. It had been sold into industry where it remained in relative obscurity until rescued for preservation. Marvellously and appropriately, it was shipped over to the island to join the IWSR collection in late 2012.

➜ A visit to 70H Ryde (IoW) shed alongside Ryde St John's Road station was always a very happy experience, rarely any trouble with access, and although only ever a handful of locos were present, what a delightful scene they provided. Here, on 21 July 1964, No W33 *Bembridge* is in steam outside the small shed building, with No W27 *Merstone*, between turns.

← A general view of the front of the 'new' Ryde shed on the west side of the line, which dated from 1930 and replaced the 1874–1930 building. Nos W26 *Whitwell* left, and W33 *Bembridge,* are seen on 21 July 1964. Unknown to me at the time, I was photographed while taking this photo (see Introduction).

➜ Inside the shed building on 2 October 1966 were Nos W20 *Shanklin*, left and W28 *Ashey*, right, with behind that, Nos W33 *Bembridge* and W24 *Calbourne*. For all but one, their days were numbered.

➜ A loco crew are seen deep in conversation as they walk through the shed yard at Ryde on 21 July 1964, with No W26 *Whitwell* beyond, and No W27 *Merstone* to the right.

↑ Having seen No W17 *Seaview* passing through the station earlier, on 2 October 1966, we followed it round to the shed, for probably our last visit there.

← No W22 *Brading* at rest between the shed, right, and the coaling stage, on 2 October 1966.

➜ Also on shed on 2 October 1966 was No W35 *Freshwater*. The O2s sent to the island had certain modifications made, the most obvious being the fitting of Westinghouse air brakes as can be seen by the pump on the side of the smokebox, and the reservoir on the left-hand tank top. Also, the coal bunker was extended to increase capacity and steam hooters were fitted. This work was undertaken at Eastleigh Works prior to despatch. Thereafter, all repairs including reboilering were undertaken at Ryde Works.

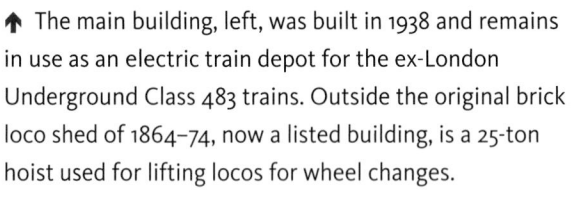

↑ On the opposite (east) side of the line to the engine shed at Ryde St John's was the compact and very busy works, much of which survives in use today. Here, wooden wagons receive attention in the open air, this being ten-ton five-plank wagon No S64392. No W16 *Ventnor* is also visible, on 21 July 1964. This was where many of the steam locos were later broken up.

Smallbrook Junction

→ It may have been a very small junction, but it became well known to railway photographers in BR steam days. Seen from a passing up train on 2 October 1966, the line to Newport and Cowes was no longer in use. The site is now much developed with a terminus station for the Isle of Wight Steam Railway and a platform for the Island Trains, but it is not currently an actual, rail-connected junction.

↑ The main building, left, was built in 1938 and remains in use as an electric train depot for the ex-London Underground Class 483 trains. Outside the original brick loco shed of 1864–74, now a listed building, is a 25-ton hoist used for lifting locos for wheel changes.

Brading

← With a fine rake of pre-Grouping coaches, No W18 *Ningwood* heads south from Brading station on 23 July 1964.

→ No W29 *Alverstone* approaches Brading station with a down train on 23 July 1967. It is most pleasing to see that this entire station, including the signalbox, has been beautifully restored and maintained as the Brading Station Visitor Centre. It continues to be served by the Island Line's electric trains, and is well worth a visit.

Lake

← It has to be admitted that as on the BR main line, I spent little time waiting for passing trains to photograph on the island. Here is one such occasion though, as No W27 *Merstone* passes Lake Crossing on 10 June 1962 with a down working.

↓ No W35 *Freshwater* passes Lake on 20 July 1964. The station here, seven miles from Ryde Pier Head, was not opened until 9 July 1987. No W35 was one of two Class O2s to be delivered to the island in BR days, and was the only IoW loco to have carried a BR number previously, 30181.

Shanklin

→ Just under eight miles from Ryde Pier Head is Shanklin station, which today is the terminus of the electrified line, the section to Ventnor having closed in April 1966. Here, No W21 *Sandown* arrives with a down train on 21 July 1964.

↓ This was followed by No W31 *Chale* on the next southbound train. The signal arm below the starting arm is a shunt-ahead signal used by locos running round when trains terminated at this station. This loco, together with the now-preserved No W24 *Calbourne*, was retained in service following closure of the line to steam on 31 December 1966 until withdrawal in March 1967, for use on electrification trains.

Ventnor

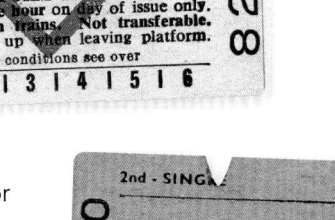

➜ The ticket for my journey on the section that subsequently closed in 1966, Ventnor to Shanklin, dated 23 July 1964.

⬆ William Adams-designed Class O2 No W20 *Shanklin* runs round at Ventnor on 23 July 1964, which required it to run into the tunnel.

➜ Ventnor had a couple of unusual features, one of which was the gangplank which provided the only passenger access to the island platform. The author, then aged 16, was caught making his way across by father's camera, on 23 July 1964. (How much smarter he then looked than a few years later, in the hippy era!)

⬅ The other distinctive feature of Ventnor station was the caves carved into the chalk cliffs alongside the goods yard, which were used by coal and builders' merchants (23 July 1964).

SMALLBROOK JUNCTION TO COWES

Newport

Medina Wharf

⬇ The sidings at Medina Wharf were situated alongside the River Medina, between Newport and Cowes. Originally opened in 1877, the sidings were upgraded by the Southern Railway in 1928 from when locos and rolling stock being transfered to and from the island passed through here.

Viewed from a passing train from Cowes on 21 July 1964, a well-filled coal train is in the foreground. Coal came in through the wharf for domestic and locomotive use. The yard remained open until 1967 with materials for the electrification, including conductor rails, being received from the mainland.

Haven Street

⬇ Little did I know when passing through this small station on 21 July 1964, how important and well-known it would become. It is now the HQ of the Isle of Wight Steam Railway.

Cowes

↑ No W14 *Fishbourne* following arrival at Cowes station on 21 July 1964. After passengers had alighted, the loco backed the train along the platform, stopping under the footbridge, as seen here. It then uncoupled, ran forward then back over a crossover and past the train to run round to the other end. While doing this the train was allowed to run back down to the buffer stops under the control of the guard in the brake coach. The engine then coupled up ready for the return to Ryde Pier Head.

No W14 was the lowest-numbered O2 and although not the first to arrive on the island (being shipped to the island in May 1936) it was the oldest IoW O2, built in 1889. It took up the number of 'Terrier' 0-6-0T *Bembridge,* which returned to the mainland the

same month. As No 2678 the A1X survived into BR days and is in preservation today on the Kent & East Sussex Railway.

The footbridge did not connect the platforms but served as public access across the station, linking Terminus Street with Cross Street. The line to Cowes closed to passengers on 21 February 1966 and the station was later demolished, the site now being occupied by a supermarket. The footbridge survives, and is today much used by passengers on the Mid-Hants Railway at Medstead & Four Marks station.

The station opened on 16 June 1862, the first on the Cowes & Newport Railway, which became the Isle of Wight Central Railway in 1887.

At one time it was important enough to have a WH Smith book stall.

FAREWELL TO IOW STEAM

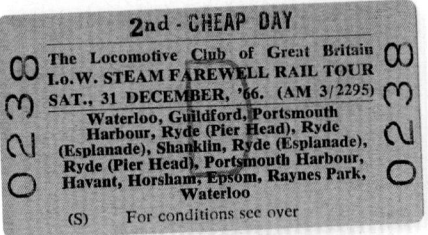

↑ The last day of passenger steam services on the Isle of Wight was 31 December 1966. By that date, operations were confined to the line which was to become electrified, Ryde Pier Head to Shanklin. This was another day trip, courtesy of the LCGB and the 'Isle of Wight Steam Farewell Rail Tour' from London Waterloo (see also Chapter 8).

Heading the LCGB special from Ryde Esplanade were Nos W24 *Calbourne* and W31 *Chale*, seen on arrival at Shanklin at 12.34. (The pier section was already closed for electrification work, and Shanklin to Ventnor had closed completely on 18 April.)

↑ This Ryde Pier Head to Shanklin ticket, dated for the last day of BR steam services, 31 December 1966, must have been bought as a souvenir, as my journey would have been covered by the LCGB railtour ticket, above.

← Following arrival of the special at Shanklin, No W27 *Merstone* departed on a service train, running bunker first to Ryde Pier Head as did all the 0-4-4Ts.

⬇ No W14 *Fishbourne*, suitably adorned with a wreath inscribed 'Farewell to IOW Steam' as well as its distinctive headboard bearing the crest of the LSWR and Isle of Wight Railway, prepares to pull forward from its train after arrival at the Shanklin terminus. On the footplate was Passed Fireman Ron Brett. An enthusiast was making a sound recording which will have the distinctive 'thump' of the Westinghouse brake pump, as the loco waits to move off from its train at the southern terminus for the last time.

⬇ There was very low cloud on this last day of 1966, but the sun did manage to break through and pick out the only member of the class destined for a brighter future – No W24 *Calbourne*.

⬇ The coaches on the Isle of Wight were formed into permanently coupled sets. No 500, with appropriate inscription, was used for the LCGB 'IoW Steam Farewell' tour and is waiting to depart from Shanklin at 13.37. Just arrived and carrying a more colourful headboard than that provided by the LCGB, was No W14 *Fishbourne*.

CHAPTER 5

RAIL ROVER

All Britain for less than £20

THIS WAS A LAST-MINUTE idea as far as I was concerned. Two pals of mine at the Epsom & Ewell Model Railway Club, John Bennett, aged 17 and Brian Small, 18, had been planning this epic trip for some while. The idea was to buy a seven-day All-Line All-Stations BR Railrover ticket and travel the national network to see as many locos and experience as much steam haulage as possible, excluding the 'home' Southern Region.

At that time, aged nearly 18, I had already started to see what other railway interests could be developed to take the place of the rapidly disappearing BR steam scene. I had gone with another friend of mine, Martin Limb, to the Isle of Man during the summer to see what this 'narrow gauge' was all about. It had not perhaps been the best year for such a venture: the seaman's strike meant there were no boats to the island, and it was the only year that the Isle of Man Railway was not to run at all.

It was not easy or cheap, but we had managed to book a flight to the island from Blackpool, the cost of which left little available for a rail rover trip. However, the more I heard, the more I wanted to join Brian and John on what sounded like the holiday of a lifetime. It was the ticket itself that was the stumbling block as this was no less than £18! On the other hand, this included night-time accommodation as John had come up with the idea of sleeping on overnight trains. For instance, if

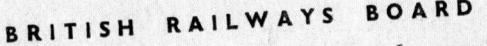

BRITISH RAILWAYS BOARD

SECOND CLASS   N⁰ 2044
                RATE £18 : 0 : 0

FROM 30 AUG 1966

TO 5 SEP 1966

AVAILABLE BY TIMETABLE AND ADVERTISED EXCURSION TRAINS
BETWEEN
ALL STATIONS
ON
BRITISH RAILWAYS
ALSO
BY STEAMER SERVICES OPERATED BY
THE CALEDONIAN STEAM PACKET CO. LTD.
BETWEEN CLYDE COAST PIERS AND LOCH LOMOND PIERS
NOT AVAILABLE
BY CONTINENTAL BOAT AND OCEAN LINER TRAINS OR
BY SERVICES OPERATED BY LONDON TRANSPORT

Issued subject to the Conditions and Regulations in the Board's
Publications and Notices applicable to British Railways.
The usual supplements are payable on Pullman and Observation Cars.

Name of Holder MR. P. NICHOLSON.
NOT TRANSFERABLE

BRITISH RAILWAYS
WISH YOU
PLEASANT JOURNEYS
and
INTERESTING VISITS

BR 3501/11

ALL-LINE
RAILROVER TICKET
SECOND CLASS
SEVEN DAYS
UNLIMITED TRAVEL
BETWEEN
ALL STATIONS
ON
BRITISH RAILWAYS

Date of Expiry

5 SEP 1966

we were having a couple of days in Scotland, we would travel back to London in an ordinary carriage overnight, returning during the early hours on another train similarly, so as to be back in Scotland first thing the next morning.

This swayed it, and so I too applied for one of these fabulous tickets. Yes, it did turn out to be the holiday of a lifetime – a completely unrepeatable experience.

Planning the itinerary

The journey was organised mainly by John who enjoyed working out multi-day rail trips with tight connections, if only as an exercise, but this was going to be for real. We took it for granted then that trains would run on time, or not far from it. Although it was agreed that we would be flexible enough to take up any unforeseen opportunities for steam haulage, John hoped we would not stray too far from his mapped-out course as this would throw out his plans for later in the week. This would jeopardise visiting all the places and travelling on the routes intended.

It was certainly not going to be an attempt to travel the most miles or travel on the maximum number of trains in a week just for the sake of it, as that seemed totally pointless to us. The idea was to use the ticket to travel to various steam 'hot spots' where some rewarding and enjoyable haulage, spotting and photographic time would be spent. The fact that nearly 50 years later I can look back on the week with such happy memories, and feel it is worth writing up and illustrating, proves we got it right.

The only minor disagreement as I recall, was early on as Brian and myself wanted to include a visit to Barry scrapyard. In hindsight, this was an unnecessary deviation from our basic aim. However, it must be remembered that at the time it was generally thought the situation there would not persist for much longer. We argued that if we did not go then we would never have another opportunity to see all the locos gathered together there, as most if not all would almost certainly be scrapped over the coming winter. Therefore, it would be too late if we were to leave it until the

following year. John was not keen on spending time on this trip viewing dead locos as it was seeing the locos in action and on shed that he considered it was all about.

John did a fantastic job in keeping us on the go, to be in the right places at the right time throughout the seven days. We passed through Edinburgh Waverley on our way south from Dundee on Thursday afternoon, our through coaches being attached to the 'Heart of Midlothian', departing the Scottish capital at 14.00. We went home that night via London, and passed through Cardiff General en route to Barry, between 14.30 and 15.10 on the Friday so nearly passing through the three capitals within 24 hours.

Taking a certain amount of provisions was one thing, plus the essentials including cameras, film, binoculars, notebooks and pens, as well as (very) few changes of clothes and basic toiletries, plus in John's case, his tape recorder. But there was just one more thing, or rather four more – the all-important railway timetables. This was 1966, before the single-volume, all-systems BR timetable was introduced, and long before the days of smartphones.

At this time, each region had its own comprehensive timetable, and they were huge, and heavy! Each was as big as the eventual all-Britain timetable. It was agreed we would have to have a separate bag for these weighty tomes, which we would take in turns to carry. Essential timetables were the London Midland, North Eastern, Scottish – and now because of this Barry business – the Western Region. Our only Southern Region travel would be to Waterloo, on trains we all knew well, so that was not needed. It was not thought the Eastern Region one would be required, so we were able to leave that one behind too. Nevertheless, it was a lot to lug about all day and night, but was absolutely vital for constant reference as the journey progressed and changed as the week went by.

It was also decided we would have a midweek return home for various reasons – a proper night's sleep, change of clothes, a good wash, and a good home-made meal by our respective mothers.

Telling the story

The following is based on my notes and memories of those seven days of continuous rail travel. I had contact with the other two about ten years ago for the first time since going our separate ways, and we discussed then that we should get together and produce a book on the trip. This came to nothing and I have not been able to consult with them regarding this adventure appearing as a chapter here with its two appendices. If they do now see this, I trust they do not disagree too much with how it is reported as no doubt we each have different memories.

I did have sight of some notes drafted by John and he either jotted down more details at the time, or has a much better memory for details than I do, and I hope he does not mind that just a few things I had forgotten have been quoted.

Recorded here are the basic train details (Appendix I), written in a dedicated notebook as we went, a small selection of the photos I took, and the loco shed lists (Appendix II). It is actually quite a brief summary of what we saw and where we went.

I would like to take this opportunity to thank both Brian and John, somewhat belatedly perhaps, for allowing me to join them on such a fantastic seven days. When we arrived at Woodham Bros in Barry, John could see why we two had been so insistent on going there, and agreed it was worthwhile to see so many locos awaiting their fate. He even got some interesting sound recordings of the wind howling through the locos and rattling loose parts.

Steam tour highlight

The key moments of the seven-day rail journey are told within the captions and tables, but in a week packed full with the excitement of tracking down steam at work and at rest, it may be asked what the real highlight was. Well, it in fact involved a diesel, or rather two diesels!

The story started with one of those events we could not possibly have planned in our itinerary. We were on the platform at Crewe on the Friday, Day 4, en route from our visit to Barry to Glasgow to catch the 09.55 from Buchanan Street for the last A4-hauled BR passenger service. This was something we simply could not afford to miss through any diversions. Over the years I had begun to wonder if the following actually did happen, or had I got so tired I had fallen asleep, dreamt it, and then, looking back, woven it into the story, it was that amazing.

About 35 years later, when I briefly re-established contact with Brian and John, who kindly supplied me with his notes, the first thing I did was look up Days 4 and 6. Almost to my astonishment, he described our journeys exactly as I believed I had remembered them.

The story started on the Friday, just after we arrived at Crewe, at about 23.15 and before we caught the 00.17 to Wigan to make our way to Glasgow, so we did not have a great deal of time to kill. However, at the end of the platform was 'Flying Pig' 2-6-0 No 43112 in typical scruffy condition, on a short train of parcels vans.

John set up his tape recorder in the hope of catching some good sound effects as it pulled out. I stood back, quietly, but Brian had wandered off somewhere else along the platform. Just as the loco was about to pull out, the driver shouted across to John saying something like: 'Wouldn't you get a better recording from up here in the cab?' I then saw John climbing aboard, and of course rushed over to join him. Never mind Brian, sorry…

For the next half hour or so we shunted up and down, rearranging parcels vans in the sidings just outside the station. The driver was very interested to hear about our exploits and what we were planning for the rest of the week with our rover tickets. Then he said that he was working an overnight train to Holyhead and back and we would be welcome to join him in the cab for that, but it was only a diesel, so we might not be interested. However, such an offer is something not to be refused, even if it was 'only' an English Electric Type 4 – or Class 40 as they became under TOPS (BR's Total Operations Processing System) – which later became one of my favourite loco classes.

We were a little sceptical of course as to how

genuine the offer was, but he seemed sincere and convincing enough, so arrangements were made for us to be waiting on the platform at Crewe in the early hours of Sunday morning, after we had had that last A4 trip. The £18 ticket was now beginning to look like quite good value.

We then realised that while we were talking the 2-6-0 had come to a stop, some way out from the north end of the station. The passage of time suddenly hit us and we asked when we would be going back into the platform, to which he replied: 'Oh, not for some time yet, about 2 o'clock. Is that OK?'

No it was not, we had to get the train up to Glasgow for the following morning for the 'Streak' farewell, and then we also remembered we were missing one person from our party who would be wondering what had happened to us! 'In that case,' he said, 'you'll have to walk back to the station. Just follow the concrete covers between the tracks, but do be careful and keep an eye out for any trains. These electrics can move pretty smartly!' We climbed down in the darkness and carefully followed the concrete covers, which could just be seen in the occasional light with the bright lights of the station looking a long way off in the distance. We picked our way along until coming to a mass of pointwork. I'm sure our heads were spinning round and round looking for the light of any oncoming trains as we scrambled across several tracks, hurrying as fast as we could to the safety of the platform.

We became aware of an electric loco approaching, which sped us up and had either of us tripped I dread to think what would have happened. We just got across the points when the train went thundering by, just a very few yards away and towering above us. It was too dark for anyone to have seen us and as we reached the platform there was nobody about to question or reprimand us, or get the steam loco driver into trouble, which was our concern of course.

Then we looked for Brian, who we found frantically checking all the platforms and waiting rooms, becoming extremely concerned as to what had happened to us. We did not fully explain, but would tell him later what he had missed, and no doubt get a telling off from him for being stupid – as he had not been able to join us! There was just time to have some quick refreshments in the all-night café on platform 4 before continuing our journey north.

The second part of this story is the diesel cab ride from Crewe to Holyhead and back. As this is really outside the scope of a book about steam, I will keep it as brief as possible. We took up our place on the end of platform 1 at Crewe, to await the 21.21 'Emerald Isle Express' to Holyhead. Each in turn said this was a waste of time and we'd been had, only for the other two to reassure that we just had to be patient. The train did roll in, on time and there was our driver. He explained he was taking over at Chester and so we rode with him and his secondman 'on the cushions' in the front compartment, reserved for the crew.

On arrival at Chester we made a quiet transfer into the rear loco cab of No D294 and worked our way through the engine compartment as it revved up and accelerated away from the station. Being in the front cab of the powerful diesel speeding through the night was an experience that would never be forgotten. Something we soon noticed was the difference between the bright electric colour light signals and the very dim oil lamps of semaphores.

We arrived at Holyhead about quarter past eleven and then had to hang around until returning to Crewe on the 00.40 departure, which was delayed until 01.00 due to loco failures. Again, while waiting for the driver to arrive we began to have doubts as to whether this really was going to happen. When he did turn up and let us into the rear cab he told us to sit on the floor so as not to be seen and only make our way to the front once we had left the station.

As exciting as this all was, keeping awake to take it all in was becoming a real problem as we had not had any proper sleep since the early hours of Saturday morning, and that was only for an hour or so. We took it in turns to sit in the secondman's seat and John describes how I promptly dropped off. No surprise perhaps, when looking back years later, I wondered if the whole thing had been a dream – or a nightmare, in the case of crossing the tracks in the dark at Crewe.

On arrival at Crewe, which was not a scheduled passenger stop, but fortunately for us, a signal check as predicted by the driver, we were bundled out of the rear cab and our bags virtually thrown out after us by the co-driver. As we picked ourselves up we saw the train accelerating away towards London. Had that all really happened? Well John says it did, and that's how I remember it. Also, I do have some brief notes written at the time to back

it up, but no name quoted for that driver, which is probably just as well. I hope he realised what a fantastic, unrepeatable experience he had given us three lads, something we would remember for the rest of our lives.

We still had a couple more days with our tickets, which were to be very different, but nevertheless memorable occasions as we fitted in a number of shed visits. This included Crewe South where we were able to catch up with Ivatt Mogul No 43112, this time in broad daylight, and what a scruffy-looking loco it was.

That rover ticket was £18 well spent, I have always thought.

Day 1 30 AUGUST

↓ Our first loco destination was one that had been recommended by a fellow member of our model railway club, and that was Mirfield. We were told there was plenty of heavy freight loco action to be seen there. Having travelled from Marylebone along the doomed Great Central line to Sheffield, we caught a train to Wakefield Kirkgate to get another from there to Mirfield. But, before we could even get off the train, a grubby WD 2-8-0 went thundering through one way then,

while we got our cameras ready, another running light went clanking its way in the other direction.

We had a good clear view and decided to spend some time here. There was no need to travel further as the 'Dub Dees' were forming a procession right here in front of us. Here, No 90664 heads through the station on what was just a typical day at Kirkgate, but was so unlike anything experienced by us on the Southern Region, and we thought the constant passage of such locos quite remarkable.

← A few minutes later, WD No 90074 was caught running light through Wakefield Kirkgate and we were rapidly compiling a list of these locos that were normally so elusive for us lads from south of the River Thames. BR had 733 of these former War Department, Riddles-designed class of 8F 'Austerity' 2-8-0s. The total built was 935, with many being sold after the Second World War for use by overseas railways. Amazingly, and inexcusably, not one BR example survived into preservation in Great Britain, as they were obviously not even deemed significant enough to be nominated for inclusion in the National Collection. Fortunately, it has been possible to fill the gap with a loco repatriated from Sweden and now numbered 90733, which is based on the Keighley & Worth Valley Railway. There are also three of the 2-10-0 variants preserved in the UK, but none of these is an ex-BR example.

→ Wakefield Kirkgate, a former Lancashire & Yorkshire and Great Northern Joint station, had such a constant cavalcade of these powerful locos in atmospheric conditions, with the smoke from one not really clearing before the next arrived, I soon became concerned I was getting through too much of my colour film – and this was only the first port of call on a seven-day marathon. So it was out with the black and white camera for the rest of our stay here. The subject was basically monotone anyway, and here, No 90074, its smokebox number barely visible, is seen again heading another heavy freight through Kirkgate. The 2-8-0s would have been based at 56A Wakefield or 56D Mirfield shed.

↓ Two at a time at Kirkgate, as No 90684 heads a train of mineral wagons through the station, as No 90361 awaits the signal, while running light. We did not really know what all these trains were, where they were coming or going but I have since learnt that eastbound trains, such as this empty one, would have been returning to the Yorkshire coal pits, while the westbound workings would

have been loaded, heading to Lancashire. Some were probably local trip workings going to or from Healey Mills yard for making up fully loaded trains and these often involved tender-first running.

Apparently, this was not a hot spot for photographers at the time as it was just grubby old WDs passing through a very unscenic location, day in day out.

WD 2-8-0S SEEN AT WAKEFIELD

Class WD 'Austerity' 2-8-0s seen working through Wakefield Kirkgate station on Tuesday, 30 August, between 14.20 and about 16.00, and for an hour or so again later in the evening*. Some locos passed through more than once, on full or empty trains, or running light.

90056*	90361	90610
90061*	90382	90631
90074	90407	90639
90099*	90415	90664
90135	90417	90684
90348	90427*	

Day 2 31 AUGUST

↑ Our first steam haulage of the day was the 09.12 from Kirkgate to Scarborough behind 'Black Five' No 44896. Arriving a minute early was a help, enabling this shot to be taken as we had but four minutes to get round to the other platform to catch the DMU to York, where we visited York Railway Museum (see Chapter 6).

→ Our two-hour stop in York on Day 2 allowed us to have a quick view of the old railway museum, which as it turned out was my only ever visit there. We then headed to Manchester on a DMU and after walking the length of the longest platform in Europe, at 2,238ft, linking Manchester Victoria with Exchange, we caught the 16.30 to Llandudno Junction. This was a steam service with BR Standard Class 5 No 73157 in charge. The 9H Patricroft-allocated 4-6-0 is seen about to depart from Exchange, which was the former LNWR station opened in June 1884. Previously, the LNWR had shared the adjoining Victoria station with the Lancashire & Yorkshire Railway. Exchange closed on 5 May 1969 but trains continued to run through its train shed.

Day 3 1 SEPTEMBER

↓ The station clock at Buchanan Street shows 6.30, which was am, not pm. We had travelled continually from leaving Manchester the day before, via Llandudno Junction to Holyhead – where we had just 11 minutes, so we did not exactly get to know the town well – and then Crewe to Glasgow Central. The train from Holyhead turned out to be our worst night as it was so crowded

we could not get any much-needed sleep. On arrival in Glasgow we walked across the city to catch the 08.25 'Grampian' from Buchanan Street to Aberdeen, which we had learnt was still A4 hauled.

Imagine our disappointment to find instead that a North British Type 2, No D6123, was at the head. Years later of course I was really pleased to be able to look back and find I had had such rare and interesting haulage, and am now disappointed I had not taken a photo, but at least I photographed the station approach. Buchanan Street was opened by the Caledonian Railway in 1849 and demolished in 1967.

← This called for a quick change of plan as there was now no need to travel all the way to Aberdeen. We detrained at Perth, as John had checked the timetables and said we were now going to go back to London for our midweek return home for a night, travelling via Dundee.

To make up for our steam haulage loss earlier we decided to visit the former NBR, 62B Dundee Tay Bridge shed, which must have been a bit of a rush as we only had 45 minutes between trains, so the three-minute early arrival would have been appreciated. Not a huge number of engines present, but very interesting ones nevertheless, including all four ex-North British Railway, LNER Class J37 0-6-0s still in traffic, including a nicely positioned No 64547.

Day 4 2 SEPTEMBER

Having returned home for Thursday night we made our way back to London the next morning, travelling from Leatherhead and Ewell West by 4-SUB EMU. This provided a much more familiar and totally different scene to that experienced in the days previously, but we were pleased to have a brief glimpse of Southern steam and normality after our hectic time in the North.

We then travelled west and spent the afternoon wandering around the scrapyard at Barry (see Chapter 9).

Day 5 3 SEPTEMBER

→ Following the disappointment on Thursday when a nondescript North British Type 2 worked the 'Grampian' from Glasgow Buchanan Street, we returned for another attempt at 'Streak' haulage on the Saturday, Day 5 of our trip. This time, we had been assured it would be a Gresley A4 on the 09.55 departure, an eight-coach 'Grampian' relief of special note, being the last scheduled run on BR of a member of this prestigious class.

We were not let down this time, and shortly after arrival at Buchanan Street we were greeted with the arrival of a gleaming No 60019 *Bittern* backing down on to train, complete with white-painted buffers.

↑ It was a very memorable journey with the lineside full of enthusiasts and other people waving the train on as it literally streaked through the countryside, with frequent whistling. We got talking to a chap in the buffet car before we realised who he was. He mentioned that he had a Gresley Pacific himself, it being none other than Alan Pegler, who I got to know better many years later. Whether he was being entirely honest or not I don't

know, but he did mention on one occasion many years later that he recalled talking to three rather unkempt but enthusiastic young lads that day.

The stop at Stirling was sufficient for us to nip across to the opposite platform for a couple of quick shots of No 60019. What a magnificent scene, I assumed this would be the last occasion I would ever see this marvellous locomotive in operation on BR.

It is therefore ironic, that just a couple of days before writing these captions, No 60019 in LNER garter blue as No 4464, headed the 'Torbay Express' from Bristol to Paignton and Kingswear, passing within a couple of miles of my home here in Somerset, almost 46 years to the day we travelled behind this loco on its 'last' run.

However, this is not quite the same.

↑ Unfortunately, we had to leave the 'Grampian' at Perth as we had done previously, not this time in disgust at the motive power, but so as to get back in time to Crewe for an unusual appointment. We had been given the offer of a footplate ride to Holyhead and back, even though it was to be in a diesel, but who could refuse such an invitation? We took this one last look at *Bittern* as it was about to depart for Aberdeen, and journey's end, or so we thought, for Gresley's streamlined Pacifics.

↑ We decided to catch the 14.12 back to Glasgow Buchanan Street, which gave us time to visit 63A Perth shed, and have some lunch. After a bit of persuasion, the shedmaster permitted us to have a look round. On shed were mainly 'Black Fives', including No 45475, and a number of BR Standard 2-6-4Ts.

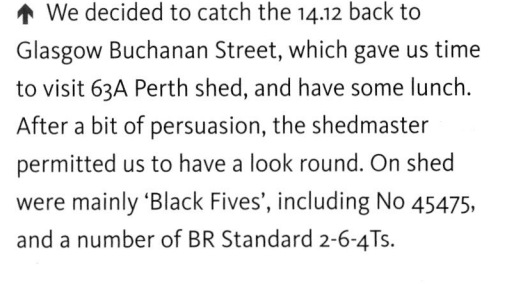

→ However, there were two A4s present; No 60034 *Lord Faringdon*, in a row of diesels outside the shed, minus its tender, and in the works was No 60026 *Miles Beevor*, as seen here. Both were to be scrapped, No 60034 in January 1967, and No 60026 in January 1968.

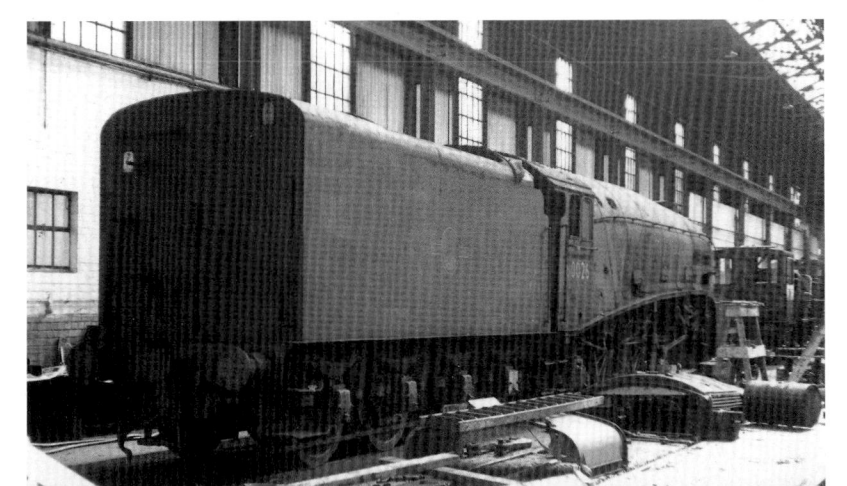

Day 6 4 SEPTEMBER

After our night-time adventures from Crewe, travelling first to Holyhead and back, much of it in the driving cab of an EE Type 4, and then a return trip to Euston in an attempt to catch up with some sleep, we had the best shed visit of the trip, to 5B Crewe South. There was no problem with access and with so many other enthusiasts wandering around it was like an unofficial open day.

↘ With nearly 40 'Black Five' 4-6-0s on shed, I can see now why I never felt too excited at seeing the type in those days. It is perhaps only in the preservation era that I have come to fully appreciate Stanier's masterpiece. The sight and sound on a 2012 visit to the North Yorkshire Moors Railway when two 'Black Fives' departed from Grosmont station within a couple of minutes of each other is one of the most memorable steam moments of recent times. It made me understand even less those who have criticised 'duplication' of types in preservation. Perhaps such people should confine their interests to collecting postage stamps? Here, No 45421 is seen at rest at Crewe South on Day 6.

↓ On entering the shed yard we were greeted by this sight of Class 5s, LMS and BR Standard types, Nos 45107 and 73160, running back from the coaling stage, and bathed in lovely sunshine.

↑ Freshly painted black with its cabside number still to be applied was BR Standard Class 2MT 2-6-0 No 78036, with its Type BR3, 3,000-gallon tender to the fore.

↓ Now visible in daylight and at rest, Ivatt Class 4MT 2-6-0 No 43112. This was the loco on which John and I had our footplate ride, shunting parcels vans out from Crewe station in the dark, and from which we had to return, walking along the main line tracks to the platform.

↑ Smartly turned out and looking magnificent,
BR Standard Class 7MT 4-6-2 'Britannia' No 70051,
formerly *Firth of Forth*.

↓ Ivatt 2-6-0s Nos 43113 and 43151, with 'Britannia'
No 70025 (*Western Star*), have just been topped up at
the coaling stage.

↑ The next in line for coaling at Crewe
South was 8F class 2-8-0 No 48758.

→ Just after we had left the shed , two 9F class 2-10-0s
passed by, running light under the wires: No 92114 and the
penultimate example, numerically, No 92249.

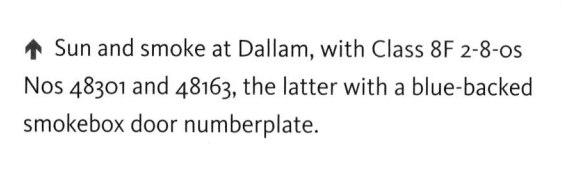

↑ Sun and smoke at Dallam, with Class 8F 2-8-0s Nos 48301 and 48163, the latter with a blue-backed smokebox door numberplate.

↑ Later that Sunday afternoon, after our wonderful experience of visiting Crewe South shed, we made our way to 8B Warrington Dallam shed, which involved a lengthy walk across town. As we made our way down the approach road we were welcomed by a vista of locos in steam, which looked like a 'mini Crewe'. In view is No 45232 with behind and to the right, Nos 92224, 92156, 45129, 48301, 48163, 92086 centre front, and 44935, right.

Day 7 5 SEPTEMBER

↓ The visit to 12A Carlisle (Kingmoor) shed was another early start, on this, the last day of our rail roving, and the light was again noteworthy. Unusually clean for the period, 'Black Five' No 45254 was a pleasing sight as we approached the large shed complex.

↑ Although I had previously seen all the BR Standard 'Britannias' in service except one, the large number of the class now concentrated in the North West, including previously Western and Eastern Regions engines, was always a rewarding sight. The one I missed was the first to be withdrawn and scrapped, in 1965, No 70007 Coeur-de-Lion. Here, on Kingmoor, is the only one of the class of 55 Pacifics never to have received a name, No 70047.

↑ Wheezing and snorting, 'Jinty' No 47471 slowly pulls along three other engines; 9F 2-10-0 No 92008 sandwiched between 'Black Fives' Nos 45236 and 45018 in the early morning light at Kingmoor shed.

←↑ That morning there were 31 Stanier 'Black Fives' on Kingmoor, including these two, Nos 45185 and 45212. Together with the 39 at Crewe South, 11 at Warrington Dallam and another four at Carlisle Upperby, we had seen 85 members of this class in only a few hours, as well as several others on the journeys in between the shed visits.

➜ LMS 3F 0-6-0T, No 47531 awaits its next call to duty at Kingmoor. Of the 422 Fowler-designed 'Jinties' built for the LMS in 1924–31, mainly by private loco building companies, ten have survived into preservation.

← Passing Kingmoor shed running light engine, shortly after sunrise, was 'Black Five' No 45432.

↑ No 46458 crossed the yard and picked up a short rake of 16-ton mineral wagons while we made our way back to the footbridge that crossed the main line and sidings, to get a grandstand view. Here, it approaches, viewed while looking around the top of the coaling stage. In the background is 2-6-2T No 41217.

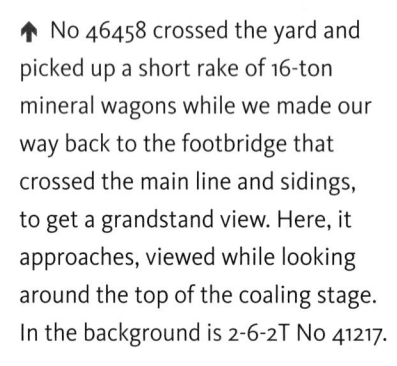

↓ The Ivatt Class 2MT passed under the footbridge, covering us with glorious smelling smoke and steam, passing at walking pace into the sunshine again. The shunter walks alongside the Mogul.

↑ Although 12B Carlisle (Upperby) shed was about the smallest visited during our week's travels, with only 19 locos present, it was particularly enjoyable. On arrival we had a friendly reception and were given the OK to wander around and take photos as we pleased. A far cry from many of today's heritage railways, which purport to exist to preserve the scenes of the past for 'educational' purposes but then largely restrict this from view; fare-paying passengers only please!

On entering the modern-looking roundhouse we found Ivatt 'Mickey Mouse' 2-6-0 No 46458 on one of the roads around the turntable. We did not have to wait long before it rolled out into the sun and on to the turntable in order to exit the shed.

↑ Ivatt Class 2MT 2-6-2T No 41217, with a mixed rake of a parcels van and wagons, posed under the footbridge at Upperby.

→ We then went back for a look round the shed to see what else was lurking in there. Another 'Britannia', but one that is perhaps rather forgotten today, No 70022. The original plates had been removed but the name had been re-applied: *Tornado*. A name that today is more associated with new-build A1 4-6-2 No 60163.

↓ When we returned to Carlisle Citadel station to make our final journey home we found another Ivatt 2-6-2T, No 41264, shunting various items of stock.

↓ As we made our way south on a DMU, travelling via Whitehaven and Barrow-in-Furness to Preston, it started to rain, the worst weather of the week. We were interested to see 'Britannia' No 70031 *Byron* on a goods train as it had not been long before that we had seen it being coaled up at Upperby. We noticed that its neatly applied name, which we had seen earlier, had been applied to the left-hand side only.

The weather got worse the further south we travelled and although we passed various other steam locos in action, on goods, running light and on a passenger train at Barrow-in-Furness, photography was impossible. But, we had had a fantastic week of tracking down steam.

CHAPTER 6

PRESERVATION PIONEERS

Museums and the first preserved
steam railways

THE IDEA OF RETAINING redundant locomotives for their historical and technical interest dates back to 1862 when *Puffing Billy* and Stephenson's *Rocket* were put on display at South Kensington, London. They formed part of the Patent Office Museum collection housed within the South Kensington Museum, which had opened in 1857. This was a collection of items representing industrial and decorative arts from the 1851 Great Exhibition, and it became the Science Museum in 1909.

Further locomotives were added to this display, and various railway companies held on to a few old locos, mainly kept in their works. These were only ever considered as static exhibits with no thought given to making them operational again. The retention of historical railway items was not seen as being any different from the museum display of other items from human history, such as Roman pottery, suits of armour and old coins.

Apart from a few exceptions this remained the policy in the UK for many years. The LNER was the most go-ahead in railway preservation, not only with the opening of its own museum at York, but also with the restoration of Stirling Single No 1 to working order in 1938. This was used to promote new rolling stock for the non-stop London to Edinburgh 'Flying Scotsman' service, and to commemorate the 50th anniversary of the 1888 'Races to the North'.

When British Railways was formed there were a few locos on static display at various stations as well as the Science Museum and York collections. There was certainly no formal policy of keeping representatives of the later types of locomotives and this did not occur officially until a list was drawn up by the British Transport Commission (BTC) in 1960 (see Appendix III).

Preserved locomotives accounted for a very small proportion of those I needed to see, and as far as I was aware, the following was a complete list of those of main line company origin I had to track down when I started pursuing them in the early 1960s. This is as per Ian Allan's *abc British Railways Locomotives Combined Volume*, summer 1961, which included 'Historic Locomotives Preserved in Store'.

Western Region – three: Nos 2516, 4003 and 4073
Southern Region – three: Nos 82, 563 and 737
London Midland Region – eleven: Nos 3, 80, 118, 158A, 790, 1008, 1439, 3020, 54398, *Lion* and *Pet*
Eastern Region – seven: Nos 1, 66, 251, 910, 990, 1463 and 1621 (note: No 1275 was omitted)

Of these locos the following were of particular interest, because as well as being main line company locos they had also carried BR numbers until withdrawal:

Ex-GWR/BR Nos 2516, 4003 and 4073
Ex-SR No 737/1737 (BR No 31737)
Ex-LMS No 80/2148 (BR No 41966) and No 1008/10621 (BR No 50621).
BR No 54398 – later broken up.

The others had been withdrawn prior to Nationalisation, but had passed into the ownership of the BTC.

PRESERVED LOCOS IN WORKING ORDER LISTED IN THE 1961 IAN ALLAN'S *ABC* AS CAPITAL STOCK:

Western Region

4-4-0   GWR   3440   *City of Truro*
(Withdrawn as GWR No 3717 March 1931 and displayed at York Railway Museum. Returned to operational condition in 1957 and taken into BR capital stock until May 1961 when withdrawn again and placed on display in the GWR Museum, Swindon, renumbered again as 3717.)

Southern Region

None, but ex-LSWR T9 4-4-0 No 30120 was restored to its pre-Grouping livery as No 120 and operated on the main line in 1962–63.

London Midland Region

4-6-0   HR   103   Jones Goods
(LMS No 17916, withdrawn and preserved in 1934)

4-2-2 CR 123 Caledonian single
(LMS No 14010, withdrawn and preserved in 1935)
4-4-0 MR 1000 Three-cylinder compound
(LMS No 1000; BRs Nos M1000 and 41000,
withdrawn in 1951 and stored at Crewe. Restored
to working order 1959–62, but transferred to
Clapham Museum December 1962.)

Eastern Region

4-4-0 GNSR 49 *Gordon Highlander*
(LNER Nos 6849 and 2277; BR No 62277,
withdrawn and preserved in 1958.)
4-4-0 NBR 256 *Glen Douglas*
(LNER Nos 9256 and 2469; BR No 62469,
withdrawn and preserved in 1959.)

One reason why works visits were so important was
that many of the above could only be seen there,
often stored in the paint shop. I was unaware at
that time that other ex-main line steam locos were
still at work in industry (see Chapter 11). So the
only other ex-BR locos I was really aware of that
were not in Ian Allan's *abc* were the two Corris
narrow gauge saddle tanks, the two Stockton &
Darlington survivors on Bank Top station, and
those ancient machines at South Kensington. Also,
no doubt, *Shannon* on Wantage Road station as this
would have been seen from passing trains.

Other, non-BR steam locos were known to be
owned by London Transport, but were a bit of a
mystery and those in industry were so anonymous
and unreported or unrecorded anywhere that
they were of lesser interest in my pursuit of 'cops'.
However, there were the 'Red Panniers', 11 Class
5700 0-6-0PTs operated by London Transport from
1956 to 1971, but we rarely saw any of these on our
numerous trips to London. Of the 16 survivors of
this class, no fewer than six finished their working
life with London Transport.

The 1961 edition of Ian Allan's *abc* made no
reference to the BTC official list of locomotives
preserved or to be preserved, which was announced
early that year. This included 27 locos scheduled to
be preserved in addition to 44 already so designated
officially.

The full list as produced by the BTC in 1960
forms Appendix III, which was the foundation for
what became known as the National Collection.
Being under the auspices of the BTC meant that
British Railways, subsequently as the British
Railways Board, was responsible for the majority
of locos preserved. In the mid-1960s, it was made
very clear that the BRB wanted to divest itself
of this responsibility and the dispersal of the
collection including stock at Clapham, Swindon
and York museums was being suggested. It was
not until 1975 and the formation of the National
Railway Museum that responsibility was taken
on by a newly established branch of the Science
Museum. This was to include the locomotives at
South Kensington and the museum in Swindon,
as well as Clapham and York, but not Glasgow.
Other locomotives, including former main line
company examples, have since been added to the
National Collection, such as an LNER A3 Pacific
and a rebuilt Bulleid 'Merchant Navy' Pacific, albeit
sectionalised.

What we know today as the National Collection
came out of the 1968 British Transport Act, which
set up the National Railway Museum at York and
defined the remit for the collection. At that time
the collection inherited from the BTC had trams
and buses removed from it and it was agreed that
the Scottish engines would be vested in what was
then the Glasgow Transport Museum. Similarly,
no locos or stock from Northern Ireland were to
be included, and the only item from Wales turned
out to be Taff Vale Railway 0-6-2T No 28, but no
Welsh rolling stock. Therefore, the oft referred to
'National Collection' is very much an English affair.

When it became known that the BTC was to
announce which locomotives were going to be
scheduled for retention, I well remember the great
anticipation of publication of this very important
list. It was carefully studied and discussed at great
length in the playground at school, certainly far
more so than any exam results would have been.
We were surprised and relieved to see such a good
Southern representation and had not expected a
'King Arthur', 'Lord Nelson' and a 'Schools' all to

be included, but no Maunsell Mogul? The obvious omissions, which we could not understand, especially in view of the number of Southern locos chosen, was the absence of important LNER types such as Classes A1, A2, A3 and B1, as surely these were needed to continue the East Coast collection instigated by the LNER at York?

Likewise, from the LMS, no 'Royal Scot', 'Patriot', 'Jubilee', 8F 2-8-0, or even a 'Jinty' – surely some mistake? And for the GWR, no 0-4-2T and no pannier tank other than the atypical 9400, which we looked upon as more a BR development of the classic GWR design. Surely a 5700 was worthy of preservation, as was a Prairie tank (large or small), 'County', 'Hall'/'Modified Hall' or 'Grange' and perhaps a 'Manor' or a 4300 Mogul? The omission of an 'Austerity' 2-8-0 also appeared to be a major oversight, especially as the type, along with the 2-10-0s, had served the country during the war so well, as had the LMS 8Fs. Who decided on this list, we wondered?

Older and therefore obviously wiser people said, as they always seem to do, 'you can't save everything'. We were not expecting 'everything', just the most important, key types of locos that had survived until then. We did not think it unreasonable to see a wider and more representative collection saved by and for the nation, and for future generations.

It was becoming obvious that there was not going to be anything like a sufficient number of steam locos left in Britain, even if there were to be as many as half a dozen preserved railways throughout the country, to maintain a full-time interest in steam railways, for me or enthusiasts in general.

A miracle was needed and incredibly, that is what happened. The survival of no fewer than another 200 steam locos could not have been anticipated, but that is exactly what occurred.

This book is not an attempt to depict every preserved locomotive of this period, but a selection showing them in their different situations, such as in museums, on plinths, on the earliest preserved railways, and stored in sheds or works. They were well scattered about!

RAILWAY MUSEUMS AND THE FIRST PRESERVED RAILWAYS

In my quest to see every main line loco there were a number in museums and on static display or in store that needed to be tracked down. A comprehensive and accurate list of all these locos was not easy to come by in the early 1960s. However, it appeared that the future of steam was going to be pretty static as that was the way they had always been put on show when their revenue-earning days were over. Traditionally, retired locomotives were displayed to the public either in museums or exposed to the elements on plinths. Although some historic locos had been restored to working order and run on the main line, this was only for a very limited time for special occasions and they soon returned to the safe haven of an old-style museum.

It seemed to be a case of seeing these last few locos once and for all, and that would probably be it. There would be little point going round the country looking at the same locos again and again in exactly the same situation, year after year.

There were a few operational preserved railways being established, the first to run passenger trains being the Middleton and Bluebell railways in 1960. When these railways were being set up locos were acquired from BR and from industry, very much as a museum-type collection, saved for their historic and/or local interest.

Fortunately, locos were not bought just for their potential commercial use in hauling trains of fare-paying passengers, which is often the case today, but with an eye to the future as historic artefacts. The term 'heritage railway' has since been coined, perhaps as a polite phrase to cover those railways which now use steam primarily to attract the general public – the 'family market' as it is termed – to part with their cash for a nostalgic train ride, rather than the preservation and exhibition of historic railway items in their own right and interest.

The official opening dates for the early preserved railways, only three of which were before the end of BR main line steam in August 1968, were as below. These started with acquiring locos of historic interest, and the railway was generally regarded as somewhere where restored examples could be demonstrated in action, with the others set aside for static display.

1960, June	Middleton Railway (for one week only; regular services from July 1969)
1960, August 7	Bluebell Railway
1968, June 29	Keighley & Worth Valley Railway

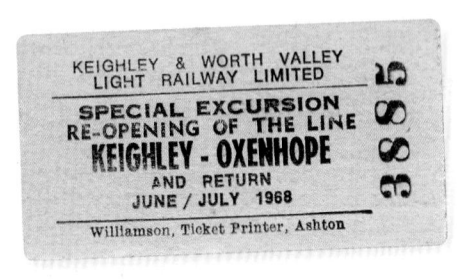

Other projects were under way, some with stock being acquired, included the following which opened later, along with many other now well-known heritage railways. These opened as follows:

1969, May 17	Dart Valley Railway
1970, May 23	Severn Valley Railway
1973, Apr 22	North Yorkshire Moors Railway
1973, Sep 30	Great Central Railway
1974, Feb 3	Kent & East Sussex Railway
1976, Apr	North Norfolk Railway
1977, Jun 1	Nene Valley Railway
1979, May 19	Yorkshire Dales Railway (Embsay & Bolton Abbey Steam Railway)

Some of these lines had run passenger trains prior to official opening, notably the North Norfolk and Severn Valley railways, which ran numerous 'members' specials'. The SVR offered 'day membership' at 2s (10p).

Railways such as at the Scottish Railway Preservation Society's Bo'ness & Kinneil, Bluebell, Severn Valley and Keighley & Worth Valley, maintain collections of locos on display in purpose-built buildings as an added attraction to the ride on the line. They clearly appreciate and understand the value of railway heritage and what it was that kick-started the movement more than 50 years ago. Other lines, of which perhaps the West Somerset Railway, although providing a marvellous travel experience, is perhaps the prime example, are only interested in accommodating locomotives that have revenue-earning potential, with no space available for anything else.

NATIONAL MUSEUMS

The establishment of a large building displaying a big collection of static locomotives, a few items of rolling stock and small artefacts, was for many years considered the ultimate in railway preservation. No thoughts of running these engines and stock were even considered.

Science Museum, South Kensington, London SW7

I visited this museum from a very early age and so its original loco collection was familiar to me. They were looked upon very much like the dinosaur skeletons in the nearby Natural History Museum as they were all from before the pre-Grouping railway companies had become established, let alone the 'Big Four'. It was only later I realised there was a distinction between some of these antiques, in that some had been employed at one stage of their careers by a main line railway company, such as the Liverpool & Manchester Railway, while others had only ever been in industrial use on the early colliery lines.

→ The Land Transport Gallery closed for redevelopment and for additional exhibits to be displayed and the time taken to complete this work seemed interminable. We heard this was to include GWR 4-6-o No 4073 *Caerphilly Castle*, and also the prototype 'Deltic' diesel. I had seen *Deltic* in operation at King's Cross, but the 'Castle' was a loco still to be marked off in Ian Allan's *abc*.

The 'Castle' had been formally handed over to the museum at Paddington station on 2 June 1961 and two days later it was moved by road, amidst much publicity, into the new building, which was still under construction. This gallery was not opened to the public until 17 October 1967, and requests to see it in the meantime were always declined. This photograph was taken on 6 April 1968.

← The most famous and historic locomotive in the Science Museum collection is Robert Stephenson 19 of 1829, better known as *Rocket*. The original locomotive has been at South Kensington since 1862, other than for occasional visits elsewhere, including overseas. This is one of the oldest surviving main line company locomotives, having been purchased by the Liverpool & Manchester Railway following its success in the 1829 Ranhill trials. It was used by the LMR until 1834 when it was returned to Stephenson's.

It was resold into colliery service in 1836, working in Cumberland until 1840 and was then kept in store until being presented to the South Kensington Museum, but without its distinctive beer barrel tender. It is today one of just three locos kept in the London museum, along with *Puffing Billy* and Grand Junction Railway 2-2-2 No 49 *Columbine* of 1845. It is seen here in the then recently re-opened Land Transport Gallery, on 6 April 1968.

→ Hackworth's *Sans Pareil* was a long-time Science Museum resident. It was another of the Rainhill contestants and was also acquired for use on the Liverpool & Manchester Railway, so gained a main line pedigree. Sold to the Bolton & Leigh Railway in 1832 and following withdrawal in 1844, it passed to Coppull Colliery, Chorley, where used as a stationary engine until 1863. It was presented to the Patent Collection in 1864 but today is on display, in pride of place, in the Welcome building at the Soho end of the Locomotion museum site at Shildon.

⬆ Although never a main line railway company engine, *Puffing Billy*, as it has always been known, is one of the world's most famous and historic locomotives so is included here, despite its industrial railway origin. It was built by William Hedley, Jonathan Foster and Timothy Hackworth in 1814 for Wylam Colliery, Northumberland. It is 5ft gauge, but the working replica built for Beamish in 2006 is standard gauge.

The original *Puffing Billy* joined the South Kensington collection in 1862, and together with the similar *Wylam Dilly* displayed in the National Museum of Scotland, Edinburgh, is claimed to have been the world's first successful steam loco to have run with flanged wheels on edge rails, without use of an adhesion-assisting cogged rail.

The Museum of British Transport, Clapham High Street, London SW4

The large exhibits section of the museum at Clapham opened on 29 May 1963 and was a very welcome destination for enthusiasts. At last, it made available for viewing a large number of the locomotives and other vehicles that had been officially preserved and cosmetically restored but

which had been kept in secure storage at various locations throughout the country. Many had not been accessible to the public for a long time and my first visit, on the opening day, produced some very interesting and long-awaited 'cops'.

Although the building itself, a former tram and bus depot, was light and airy, and the exhibits were well spaced, most of my visits were made when photography was difficult. The opening day brought forth a huge crowd of people. It was an ideal venue for special events attended by large numbers of railway society and trade stands, but these also limited the view of the exhibits. It finally shut its doors in 1974 with the National Collection exhibits mainly transferred to the new National Railway Museum at York. The London items were retained for display in the Capital, most in a former greenhouse at Syon Park before transfer to the new museum at Covent Garden Piazza.

A summary of the locos on display at Clapham:

Furness Railway No 3 'Coppernob 0-4-0 1846
GCR No 506 *Butler-Henderson* (BR No 62660) 1920
GER No 87 (BR No 68633) 0-6-0T 1904
GER No 490 (BR No 62785) 2-4-0 1894
LBSCR No 82 *Boxhill* 0-6-0T 1880
LNER No 4468 *Mallard* (BR No 60022) 4-6-2 1938
LNWR 790 *Hardwicke* 2-4-0 1873
LNWR No 3020 *Cornwall* 2-2-2 1858
LNWR *Pet* 0-4-0ST 1865 1ft 6in gauge
LSWR No 563 4-4-0 1893
LYR *Wren* 0-4-0ST+Tender 1887 1ft 6in gauge
Metropolitan Railway No 23 4-4-0T 1866
MR No 1000 (BR No 41000) 4-4-0 1902
SECR No 737 (BR No 31737) 4-4-0 1901
Wotton Tramway Aveling & Porter 807, 4wWT 1872

Notes
No 4468 was delivered to the museum on 29 February 1964.
No 23 was extracted from the museum prior to opening, for display at the Metropolitan Railway Centenary Exhibition, Neasden depot in May 1963, returning to Clapham on 11 January 1964.

The Museum of British Transport

Clapham High Street, London SW4

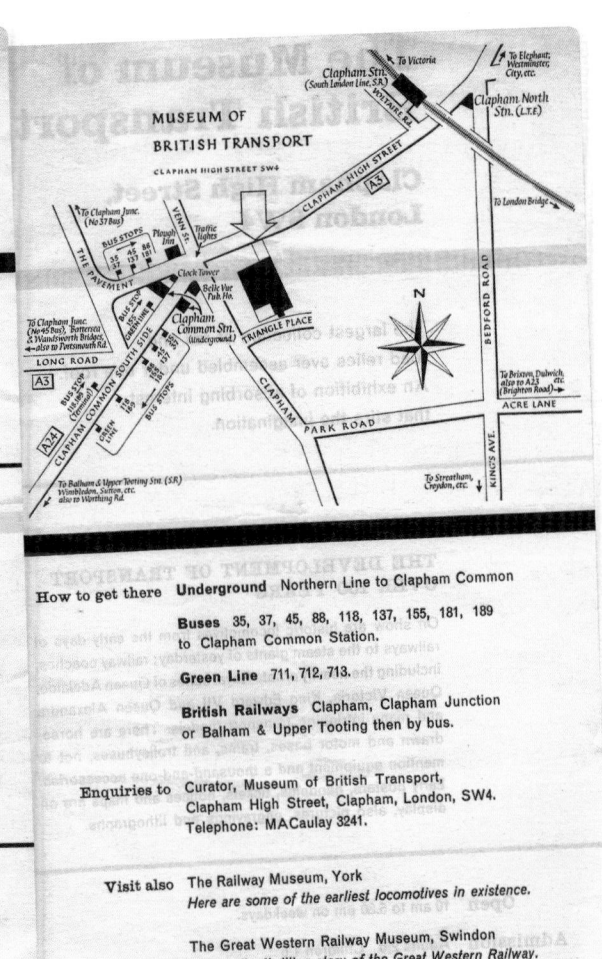

The largest collection of rail and road relics ever assembled under one roof. An exhibition of absorbing interest that stirs the imagination.

HERE IS HISTORY ON WHEELS

THE DEVELOPMENT OF TRANSPORT OVER 150 YEARS

On show are historic locomotives from the early days of railways to the steam giants of yesterday; railway coaches, including the heavily ornate Royal suites of Queen Adelaide, Queen Victoria, King Edward VII and Queen Alexandra and many intriguing transport models. There are horse-drawn and motor buses, trams, and trolleybuses, not to mention equipment and a thousand-and-one accessories. Early posters, handbills, tickets, notices and maps are on display, also pictures, engravings and lithographs.

Open 10 am to 5.30 pm on weekdays.

Admission Adults 2/6 Children 1/6
Special rates for school parties.

How to get there **Underground** Northern Line to Clapham Common

Buses 35, 37, 45, 88, 118, 137, 155, 181, 189 to Clapham Common Station.

Green Line 711, 712, 713.

British Railways Clapham, Clapham Junction or Balham & Upper Tooting then by bus.

Enquiries to Curator, Museum of British Transport, Clapham High Street, Clapham, London, SW4. Telephone: MACaulay 3241.

Visit also The Railway Museum, York
Here are some of the earliest locomotives in existence.

The Great Western Railway Museum, Swindon
Here is the thrilling story of the Great Western Railway.

➡ Ten of the 50 LBSCR 'Terrier' 0-6-0Ts survive in preservation. The first to be saved was No 82 *Boxhill*, which remained in original form as Class A1, ending its working days as Brighton Works shunter, No 380S. Withdrawn in 1946 and restored to Stroudley 'improved engine green' livery, it is seen at Clapham in August 1963.

⬅ Another Clapham resident was LNWR 2-2-2 No 3020 *Cornwall*, built at Crewe in 1847, which underwent several rebuildings during its operational life. Withdrawn but retained for preservation in 1902, it was photographed on 11 June 1966.

➜ A personal favourite at Clapham was SECR D class 4-4-0 No 737. This loco was not withdrawn until 1956 and so had been numbered in BR stock as No 31737. Before being restored in 1960 and displayed at Clapham it had been stored in Tweedmouth, Northumberland so was a 'cop' on my first visit to the museum, but this view dates from early 1965.

➜ One of the most famous locos in the Clapham collection was LNWR 2-4-0 No 790 *Hardwicke*. Built at Crewe in 1873 it was a participant in the 1895 'Races to the North'. Preserved by the LMS when withdrawn as No 5031 in 1932, it was restored to pre-Grouping condition and kept in the paint shop at Crewe Works. Following extraction from Clapham it returned to the main line in 1976, but is now in the NRM, York. Seen at Clapham on 11 June 1966.

← I was never quite sure if the London Transport system and its predecessors counted as 'main line', especially as they did not appear in the Ian Allan BR loco *abc*s, but they were not industrial, so an early loco from this system is included here.

This is the only surviving example of a Beyer Peacock 4-4-0T. Metropolitan Railway No 23 was built in 1866 becoming London Passenger Transport Board No L45. Withdrawn in 1948, it was restored to 1903 condition, as seen at Clapham on 11 June 1966.

→ 'Coppernob' copped. Furness Railway No 3 is well known as 'Coppernob' because of its prominent, dome-shaped copper firebox. This is only a nickname and it has never been carried by the loco. This remarkable survivor was built in 1846 by Bury Curtis & Kennedy of Liverpool. Withdrawn in December 1898, it was thought to be the oldest working loco in the country at the time and was placed on display at Barrow station in a large glass case. It remained there until 1941 apart from a visit to the Wembley exhibition in 1924/25. It received some damage during an air raid and so was removed to Horwich Works. From there, it was later moved to Clapham Museum, there photographed on 11 June 1966.

National Trust Industrial Railway Museum, Penrhyn Castle, Bangor, Caernarvonshire

The National Trust loco collection of standard gauge and narrow gauge locos and rolling stock included one main line loco for a while.

This was LNWR Webb 'Coal Tank' 0-6-2T No 1054, built at Crewe in 1888. Withdrawn in October 1958 as No 58926 it was purchased by a group of enthusiasts and was presented to the NT in 1963 and placed on display at the castle, adjacent to the stable yard. It arrived on 11 March 1964, coming from storage at the Railway Preservation Society's Hednesford depot, Staffordshire.

This was one of a few ex-BR locos that remained to be tracked down following the end of main line steam and was first seen, as depicted, on 11 July 1969. After nine years on display here it was taken into the care of the Bahamas Locomotive Society for restoration to working order at the since-closed Dinting Railway Centre. Today, it is fully restored again, as LMS No 7799, based on the KWVR.

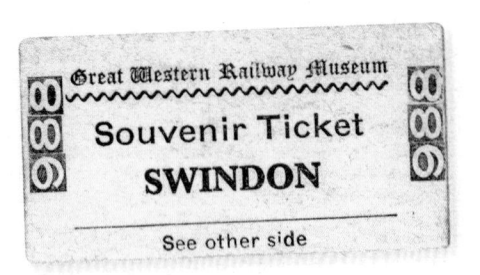

Great Western Railway Museum, Emlyn Square, Swindon, Wiltshire

Swindon Corporation opened this museum jointly with the British Transport Commission, so the locomotives displayed here were from what became the National Collection. The building was designed as a lodging house for GWR craftsmen but it was never used as such, becoming a Wesleyan chapel. The last service was held in September 1959 and it passed to the corporation for conversion into the GWR museum. This was somewhat belated perhaps, as the GWR had many years previously, broken up its two most famous locomotives, which it had preserved, *North Star* and *Lord of the Isles*. A full size, non-working replica of *North Star* had been built as a replacement in 1925, and is claimed to incorporate some original parts, but apart from *Tiny* at Newton Abbot no other GWR broad gauge locos were allowed to survive. The driving wheels from *Lord of the Isles* were saved, and displayed in Swindon.

This museum has since been superseded by the much larger STEAM museum, which opened in 2000.

Steam locos displayed in Swindon museum were:
North Star 2-2-2 replica 1925
No 2516 0-6-0 1897
No 3717 *City of Truro* 1903 (later replaced by No 6000 *King George V*)
No 4003 *Lode Star* 4-6-0 1907
No 9400 0-6-0PT 1947

York Railway Museum, Queen Street, York

The first dedicated railway museum in the world, this was opened by the LNER at York. Primarily it was intended to conserve the history of the East Coast Main Line and artefacts of the LNER and its constituents, but as the only such permanent indoor display of locos in the UK, a representative of each of the other 'Big Four' railways was also included. From the Southern was the ex-LBSCR No 214 *Gladstone* – the first loco to be bought for preservation by enthusiasts, the Stephenson Locomotive Society in 1927; ex-Grand Junction Railway *Columbine* from the LMS, and from the GWR there was the speed record-breaking No 3717 *City of Truro*.

The museum closed in 1974 and the building was later demolished, superseded by today's National Railway Museum in York, which opened in 1975. The original museum never included any locos that were numbered in BR stock.

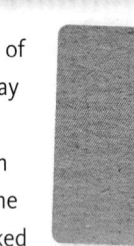

➜ The other side of the national railway museum tickets, Clapham, Swindon and York, which the purchaser was asked to see.

Locos exhibited at York Railway Museum were:
GNR No 1 4-2-2 1870
GNR No 251 4-4-2 1902
GNR No 990 *Henry Oakley* 4-4-2 1898
GWR No 3717 *City of Truro* 4-4-0 1903 (Removed in 1957 for restoration to working order.)
LBSCR No 214 *Gladstone* 2-4-0 1882
LNWR No 49 *Columbine* 2-2-2 1845
NER No 66 *Aerolite* 2-2-4T 1851
NER No 910 2-4-0 1875
NER No 1275 0-6-0 1874
NER No 1463 2-4-0 1885
NER No 1621 4-4-0 1893

Also, two former industrial railway locomotives
Hetton Coal Co. 0-4-0 1822
Shutt End Colliery Railway *Agenoria* 0-4-0 1829

All photographs in this museum were taken on 31 August 1966, this being visited during the Rail Rover tour, as described in Chapter 5.

→ Great Northern Railway A2 class No 1, the Stirling Single. This loco was preserved by the GNR when withdrawn in 1908 and displayed that year at the Franco-British Exhibition, White City, London. It was restored to working order and headed a number of specials in 1938, including one for the Railway Correspondence & Travel Society, the first enthusiast-organised railtour.

← Retaining an example of each East Coast Main Line express passenger locomotive was a prime purpose of the LNER's museum, so two GNR Atlantics, Nos 251 and 990, were saved. Class C2 No 990 *Henry Oakley*, the first 4-4-2 in Britain, was withdrawn in November 1937 and placed on display following restoration, in January 1938. It was restored for main line use in 1953 to commemorate the centenary of Doncaster Works, but soon returned to the museum. Apart from 4-6-2 No 1470 *Great Northern* in 1922, it was the only GNR loco to be officially named. It is currently on display at Bressingham.

→ Former LBSCR B1 class 0-4-2 No 214 *Gladstone* was the first engine purchased by enthusiasts for preservation in 1927, paid for by members of the Stephenson Locomotive Society. Finding a suitable home for it was a problem, until the LNER agreed to take it for the museum at York. It remained there until transferred to the new museum in 1974.

➜ One of the non-LNER group locos to find a place at York was Grand Junction Railway 2-2-2 No 49 *Columbine*. Dating back to 1845, it was withdrawn from the LNWR's Engineer's Department, as *Engineer Bangor*, in 1902 and placed in store at Crewe Works. It was accepted at York in 1934. Together with *Gladstone*, it was one of two locos transferred from York to the new museum at Clapham.

← Ivatt Large Atlantic Class C1 No 251 was withdrawn in 1947 and joined its older, smaller sister in the museum. It too was restored to working order in 1953 and subsequently returned to the museum but today is housed in Barrow Hill Roundhouse.

⬇ Wilson Worsdell-designed NER M class 4-4-0 No 1621, built at Gateshead Works in 1893, was withdrawn in 1945 and took up its place in the museum at York in 1947. It is now at Locomotion, Shildon.

Glasgow Corporation, Coplawhill Transport Museum, 25 Albert Drive, Pollokshields, Glasgow

The officially preserved Scottish locomotives, which were never part of the National Collection, were put on display in this museum, which was located in the former paint shop of Coplawhill tram depot, in 1966. This included the four locos retired from main line operation on enthusiasts' specials in 1965, following their restoration to working order in 1958/59. This museum later closed and the collection put on display at the Glasgow Museum of Transport in Kelvin Hall in 1987. This closed in May 2010, replaced by the new Riverside Museum at Glasgow Harbour, which opened in June 2011.

Main line locos displayed in the Coplawhill museum:
Caledonian Railway No 123 4-2-2 1886
Caledonian Railway No 828 (BR No 57566) 0-6-0
    1899 (Privately owned, on loan to the museum.)
Glasgow & South Western Railway No 9 0-6-0T
    1917
Great North of Scotland Railway
    No 49 (BR No 62277) 4-4-0 1920
Highland Railway No 103 4-6-0 1894
North British Railway No 256 (BR
    No 62469) *Glen Douglas* 1913

➡ The truly historic 'Jones Goods', the first 4-6-0 in Britain. Withdrawn by the LMS as No 17916 in October 1934, it was restored in HR green livery in 1935 and stored at St Rollox Works. It obtained its distinctive yellow livery when restored to working order for main line operation in 1959. Taken out of traffic in October 1965, it was moved into the museum at Coplawhill in June 1966 and is seen there on 24 December 1967.

➡ Using the Ian Allan *abc* books as a reference I was led to believe no locos of the Glasgow & South West Railway had survived. It therefore came as a very pleasant surprise to learn that 0-6-0T No 9, a 5 class loco, was still in existence. Built by North British (21521 of 1917) it became Class 322 No 324 in 1919, and was withdrawn by the LMS as No 16379 in April 1934. It was then sold for colliery use in North Wales.

Several previously published references to its industrial life were rather confused as to where this was, but this has been established as being Hafod Colliery near Johnstown, Ruabon, where it was moved in April 1934. On withdrawal in March 1962, it was presented to the BTC by NCB North Western Division, No 5 Area and placed in store at Oswestry Works in November. When I saw it there on an unofficial visit, not expecting to find very much there, it was one of the most unexpected 'cops' ever! This unique survivor returned to Scotland, going to the Coplawhill museum in June 1966, where I saw it again, but looking a lot smarter, on 24 December 1967.

Lytham Motive Power Museum, Lytham, Lancashire

Although a private museum, this is featured here as it was presented as a mini national museum for industrial locos, but included one main line loco on display. The locos, which were nearly all 0-4-0STs, were beautifully restored and nicely displayed in a specially constructed building which formed a roundhouse, the tracks radiating from a small, boarded turntable.

Public opening was limited by staff availability, but a polite request to look round usually gained access. It was established by J M Morris of the Helical Spring Co, now part of the international Helical Technology Group, which celebrated its 50th anniversary in 2012. Most of the locos would otherwise have been lost to the scrapman and many have since passed to other sites, but three industrial standard gauge locos remain here.

In 1994, ex-GWR 4-6-0 No 4979 *Wootton Hall* was given storage space on land outside the building, when it had to be removed from its first home at Fleetwood after leaving Barry scrapyard. Owned by the Furness Railway Trust, it was moved to its present site at the Appleby Heritage Centre in 2007, with transport sponsored by the Lytham museum.

OPEN AIR DISPLAY

For many years the only way to preserve locomotives, other than in museums, was on display in public places such as stations, parks and the like. They were often totally exposed to the elements regardless of how historic the loco was, and many of today's survivors from the earliest days of railways were at one time kept in such a way for long periods.

Most of these have been moved to more appropriate accommodation and some have even been returned to working order. There was a time when redundant locos from local industries were installed in children's play areas as climbing objects. It was later realised that this was not good for the loco, or the children who clambered over them precariously, and these too have been moved to better homes or fenced off.

Canterbury, Kent

One of the most well-known and historic locomotives to have been displayed in a public park in Britain was *Invicta* (Robert Stephenson 24 of 1830). This 0-4-0 was withdrawn as long ago as 1839, having worked on the Canterbury & Whitstable Railway, including the inaugural

← The only main line loco in the original Lytham Motive Power Museum collection was ex-North British Railway No 42 of 1887, BR Y9 class No 68095, and like most of the others at Lytham, it was an 0-4-0ST. It was bought for the museum in 1966 from J McWilliams & Sons Ltd, scrap merchants at Shettleston, who acquired it for scrap following withdrawal by BR in 1962. Photographed at Lytham on 19 June 1971, it is now in the Scottish RPS collection at the Bo'ness & Kinneil Railway.

train on 3 May 1830, then replaced by stationary engines. It passed into the ownership of the SER which exhibited it, minus its tender, at the Stockton & Darlington Railway Golden Jubilee in 1875, and at the Stephenson Centenary in Newcastle in 1881. It was presented to the City of Canterbury for public display in 1906. Following restoration in 1977 by the NRM, it returned to Canterbury for the 150th anniversary of the Canterbury & Whitstable Railway on 3 May 1980, and has been housed since then in Canterbury Museum.

Furness Railway 0-4-0STs

Two remarkable survivors with Furness Railway origins were put on display in 1960. They were built by Sharp Stewart as 0-4-0 tender locos with six others between 1863 and 1866. The first six were sold in 1870 to the Barrow Haematite Steel Co, which at the time was claimed to be the biggest iron and steel works in the world. It is believed that Sharp Stewart rebuilt the locos then as 0-4-0STs prior to delivery. On withdrawal in 1960, the last two were presented for display at local schools.

↑ Ex-Canterbury & Whitstable Railway *Invicta* is seen here in the last year of BR steam, on 21 April 1968, while still exposed to the elements in Dane John Gardens, Canterbury.

➜ A former Furness Railway loco as displayed in rebuilt form as an 0-4-0ST at the George Hastwell School, Abbey Road, Barrow-in-Furness on 10 July 1968.

This loco is better known today as 0-4-0 FR No 20 having been rebuilt back into original form in 1996–98 at Steamtown Carnforth. It was during this work that its identity was confirmed as Sharp Stewart 1448 of 1970, it previously having been believed to be Sharp Stewart 1435, FR No 18. Now owned by the Furness Railway Trust this loco was on display at Locomotion, Shildon, at the time of writing in late 2012.

The other surviving Furness Railway Sharp Stewart (1585 of 1865) remains in its rebuilt form as an 0-4-0ST. It was displayed at Stone Cross Special School, Ulverston, but is now at the West Coast Railway's Carnforth depot, so is not readily accessible for public viewing. Investigation has confirmed its identity as FR No 25.

Newton Abbot station, Devon

Not fully exposed to the elements, but very much out in the open, was the only surviving 7ft 0in gauge (broad gauge) loco, *Tiny*, which was displayed on the station at Newton Abbot from 1927, where I saw it on 2 June 1973. This vertical boiler loco was built by Sara & Co of Plymouth in 1868 for the South Devon Railway where, as No 151, it was used on the Sutton Harbour branch. It became GWR No 2180 when the railway was absorbed and it was then used for shunting at Newton Abbot. Following withdrawal in 1883 it was retained as a stationary engine in Newton Abbot Works until it was retired in 1927. It is now in the present-day South Devon Railway's museum at Buckfastleigh.

Butlin's Holiday Camps

Sir Billy Butlin made a very valuable contribution to railway preservation when he decided to display a selection of locomotives at his holiday camps. He bought no fewer than eight locos from BR, four large LMS types and four small Southern tank engines, in 1963. Today, all are preserved elsewhere and several have been restored to working order including two, and hopefully soon three, to main line operational condition.

The locos were cosmetically restored by BR prior to sale, the LMS locos at Crewe Works. When GWR 'King' class No 6018 *King Henry VI* was requested, the quote from the Western Region apparently insisted on full restoration to working order by Swindon, resulting in too high a purchase price for a loco intended for static display. The offer was therefore declined and the loco broken up.

Dispersal from the holiday camps took place during 1970–73 when it was found that the attraction of static locos for holidaymakers was waning, and maintenance commitments were escalating. Butlins attempted to find new homes for them through the Transport Trust but this resulted in controversy including a court injunction placed on one loco, so they were eventually sold.

Locomotive	Camp where displayed	Current home
LMS 4-6-0 'Royal Scot' class 6100 (BR No 46100) *Royal Scot*	Skegness	Crewe Heritage Centre
LMS 4-6-2s 'Princess Royal' class 6203 (BR No 46203) *Princess Margaret Rose*	Pwllheli	Midland Railway-Butterley
6229 'Princess Coronation' class (BR No 46229) *Duchess of Hamilton*	Minehead	Locomotion, Shildon
6233 (BR No 46233) *Duchess of Sutherland*	Heads of Ayr	Midland Railway-Butterley
LBSCR 0-6-0T A1X class 40 (BR No 32640) *Brighton*	Pwllheli	Isle of Wight Steam Railway
62 (BR 32662) *Martello*	Heads of Ayr	Bressingham
78 (BR 32678) *Knowle*	Minehead	Kent & East Sussex Railway
LSWR 0-4-0T B4 class 102 (BR No 30120) *Granville*	Skegness	Bressingham

Note: No 6229 is now part of the National Collection and was at one time restored for use on the main line. Currently a static exhibit, it has been re-streamlined in its original style. A return to the main line in this guise is being considered.

← LMS No 6203 *Princess Margaret Rose* when on display at Butlin's Pwllheli holiday camp, July 1969.

⬇ No 6229 *Duchess of Hamilton* at Minehead holiday camp, 1973.

⬇ Brighton 'Terrier' BR No 32640 at Butlin's Pwllheli holiday camp in July 1969, devoid of name and number.

➜ LBSCR A1X class BR No 32678 at Minehead holiday camp in 1973.

Beaulieu Motor Museum, Hampshire

Lord Montagu acquired Southern Railway 'Schools' class 4-4-0 No 928 *Stowe* for open air display at his motor museum, arriving in February 1964. An inauguration ceremony was performed by Lord Robertson of Oakridge on 24 March. Like all the Butlin's locos, I had seen it previously when in operation on BR, but made a visit to view the loco in its new environment in August 1969. It was displayed with Pullman cars *Agatha*, *Fingall* and Car No 35.

This loco is now owned by the Maunsell Locomotive Society and is undergoing long-term restoration on the Bluebell Railway.

THE FIRST HERITAGE RAILWAYS

Only two standard gauge railways officially operated a regular passenger service prior to BR's last day of steam in August 1968, but several were preparing for re-opening soon afterwards, with new lines being added to this ever since.

⬆ On arrival at the Middleton Railway on 17 September 1967 I was delighted to see the beautifully restored ex-North Eastern Railway H class 0-4-0T No 1310 on display. It was withdrawn by the LNER in 1931 as a member of the Y7 class and sold into colliery use. It had been acquired for preservation by the Steam Power Trust in June 1965 from NCB Watergate Colliery, Gateshead, for the price of £300.

Middleton Railway

This is often claimed to have been the first standard gauge preserved railway to have operated a passenger train, even before the Bluebell Railway opened. This is correct, but it was diesel-hauled, the passenger vehicle was an old electric tram car, it was only for a few days during the university rag week in June 1960, and it was on an industrial railway. The Middleton Railway Preservation Society ran numerous goods trains subsequently, but it was not until July 1969 that a regular, advertised passenger service was run.

The tram, which was the only surviving car from the historic Swansea & Mumbles Railway, No 2, was later scrapped following a fire.

The Middleton always was an industrial railway and most of its locomotives have been of industrial origin. However, two ex-main line locos have been in the collection from the earliest days and were seen on my first visit to this historic railway in September 1967. This was by means of a railtour, as described in Chapter 10. Passenger trains were run on the MR especially for the visiting party, with a brake van train hauled by 0-6-0D *John Alcock* (Hunslet 1697 of 1932), which had been LMS No 7401, later 7051.

← What was of particular interest to me at the Middleton Railway was ex-BR No 68153, later BR Departmental No 54, and former LNER Y1 class No 59. This is a Sentinel (8837 of 1933) vertical-boiler four-wheel, geared steam loco, of a type I had never managed to see in BR service. It had been withdrawn by BR in September 1961. The Middleton locos were kept in Clayton's yard at the end of the Dartmouth branch, where it was found on 17 September 1967.

Bluebell Railway

Running a regular steam-hauled passenger service, with passenger coaches, from 7 August 1960, the Bluebell Railway can rightly lay claim to being the first standard gauge preserved railway to open fully to the public, using steam on a former BR line. My first visit was in March 1961 and I went back again many times later, becoming a regular volunteer with the Maunsell Locomotive Society in the 1980s. Since moving to Somerset I have been unable to visit the line as often as I would like, but it remains my favourite heritage railway, with the finest collection of locos. (Being such a good, representative collection of Southern engines and rolling stock, that almost goes without saying.)

The railway today is now completely different from when I first went there and needs little introduction. A small selection of photographs is included here, confined to the period when steam could still be seen on BR.

That first visit to the Bluebell Railway, which was of course also

THE MIDDLETON RAILWAY

INSTRUCTIONS FOR OPERATING SPECIAL TRAINS BETWEEN HEADSHUNT AND OVERBRIDGE ONLY

SUNDAY 17th. SEPTEMBER 1967 BETWEEN THE HOURS OF 14.50 AND 17.00 Hrs.

OPERATING SUPERINTENDENT To detail crew (2) of Diesel 0-6-0 and to arrange crew (2) of Bagnall 0-4-0. To detail train Guard and one relief guard. To detail 3 flagmen for Moor Road Crossing (to be superintended by P.W.Inspector)

All rolling stock to be previously completely checked and lubricated.

P.W.INSPECTOR. To clamp personally all switches concerned (certain switches bolted up the previous day).

DETAILS SUNDAY SEPT 17th 1967.

1. The only locomotives allowed to move between 14.00 hrs and 1700 hrs are (1) Diesel 0-6-0, (2) Bagnall 0-4-OT (steam).
2. The train will comprise One steam locomotive, one brake van, one diesel locomotive. The locomotive facing direction of travel will be in charge. Normal "brake whistles" and "banking whistles" codes will be used if required.
3. Bagnall 0-4-OT will carry single line token in charge of driver (to be inspected before starting operations)
4. Visitors 12 plus guard travel in brake van under insurance arrangements and will on no account attempt to join or alight from moving train. Guard will ensure that safety bars are correctly positioned on brake van and that all couplings are correct.
5. SPEED WILL NOT EXCEED 5 M P H at any place.
6. 3 members equipped with red flags will be on duty to protect Moor Road Crossing in charge of the Permanent Way Advisor/Inspector who ALONE is authorised to give the signal for trains to cross Moor Road. He will appoint a deputy if necessary. All trains will stop at Moor Road Crossing and await instructions.
7. The train will carry one white light at the front and one red at the rear on each journey. The loco. crews and guards will be in possession of all equipment as required by British Railways Rules 127 to 129 (No Detonators).
8. Permanent Way Advisor/Inspector will issue any necessary instructions regarding permanent way matters in writing. Switches to be clamped/bolted/blocked are Headshunt, Parkside Incline, Whitakers Siding switches, Moor End Siding, Upper Loop Switches. P.W.A. to see to this personally. All facing points will be fixed clamped or bolted.
9. If the steam loco. requires to take water intermediately it will be detached from the van and diesel locomotive which will remain on the headshunt. The guard is authorised to unclamp the switches. The steam loco. will be preceded by a flagman to and from water column. On return of locomotive, the guard will reclamp headshunt switches in the straight direction.
10. Train will have steam locomotive at the Balm Road end, and the Diesel loco. at the opposite end.
11. Rolling stock in Dartmouth Yard will be positioned so as to allow steam locomotive free access to water column.
12. On no account will passenger carrying train traverse Clayton's curve or enter Dartmouth Yard.
13. ALL PERSONELL employed on Sunday September 17th 1967 will be in possession of a copy of this notice and any subsequent amendments, and of a copy of the operating Regulations.

TAKE NO RISKS WHATEVER !

Signed R.F.Youell, Chairman.
R.C.Lawrence, Permanent Way Advisor and Safety Precautions Officer.
J.Lodge Operating Superintendent.

14th September 1967.

my first to any preserved railway, was a very exciting occasion. Although out of season for passenger trains, a couple of locos were in steam and there was much activity at Sheffield Park. This was partly due to the presence of a German TV crew who asked my uncle to drive back out of the car park and come in again following our arrival. They were rather taken with his brand-new, white Triumph TR3 and wanted to get a shot of it coming into the yard. I wonder if that film survived?

↓ The functional display board at the entrance to Sheffield Park station on 14 August 1963, my first visit in colour.

TIME TABLE 1963

Every SATURDAY and SUNDAY from 30th March to 27th October.
EASTER MONDAY 15th April.
Every WEDNESDAY from 15th May to 25th September inclusive.
DAILY from 1st June to 9th June (inclusive) and 20th July to 8th September (inclusive).
BOXING DAY 26th December CHRISTMAS SPECIAL (see footnote).

UP		a.m.	a.m.	p.m.	p.m.	p.m.	p.m.	p.m.	p.m.	p.m. A
SHEFFIELD PARK	dep.	10.50	11.50	1.50	2.50	3.50	4.42	5.50	6.50	
FRESHFIELD	dep.	10.58	11.58	1.58	2.58	3.58	4.50	5.58	6.58	
HOLYWELL (Waterworks)	dep.	11.03	12.03	2.03	3.03	4.03	4.55	6.03	7.03	
BLUEBELL HALT	dep.	11.08	12.08	2.08	3.08	4.08	5.00	6.08	7.08	
HORSTED KEYNES	arr.	11.10	12.10	2.10	3.10	4.10	5.02	6.10	7.10	
HORSTED KEYNES (S.R.) to HAYWARDS HEATH and beyond	dep.	11.16d	12.16d	2.16d	3.16ns	4.16d	5.08ns	6.16d	7.16 nsa A	

DOWN		a.m.	p.m.	p.m.	p.m.	p.m.	p.m.	p.m.	p.m. A
HORSTED KEYNES (S.R.) from HAYWARDS HEATH and beyond	arr.	11.14d	12.14d	2.14d	3.13ns	4.14d	5.03ns	6.14d	7.12nsb A
HORSTED KEYNES	dep.	11.20	12.20	2.20	3.20	4.18	5.10	6.20	7.15
BLUEBELL HALT	dep.	11.22	12.22	2.22	3.22	4.20	5.12	6.22	7.17
HOLYWELL (Waterworks)	dep.	11.26	12.26	2.26	3.26	4.24	5.16	6.26	7.21
FRESHFIELD	dep.	11.31	12.31	2.31	3.31	4.29	5.21	6.31	7.26
SHEFFIELD PARK	arr.	11.37	12.37	2.37	3.37	4.35	5.27	6.37	7.32

NOTES: A — not after 30th September.
Applicable to Southern Region train times at HORSTED KEYNES only —
d—Daily   ns—Not Sundays
nsa — Not Sundays. Departs 7.23 p.m. Mondays to Fridays.
nsb — Not Sundays. Arrives 7.05 p.m. Mondays to Fridays.
On Boxing Day (26th December) a special train with Father Christmas will leave Sheffield Park for Horsted Keynes, and back at 3.15 p.m. calling at all stations—due back at Sheffield Park at 4.10 p.m.
The famous National Trust Gardens at Sheffield Park (a few minutes walk from Sheffield Park Station) will be open at all times whilst Bluebell Railway trains are running.

→ I had never seen an ex-SECR P class 0-6-0T before and to see two of them in steam at such close quarters was wonderful. I was clearly going to find railway preservation fascinating, but how different and restricted access is to such places these days – a lot of the appeal has been thrown away. Nos 323 *Bluebell* (BR No 31323) and 27 (BR No 31027) pose by the water tank at Sheffield Park on 19 March 1961.

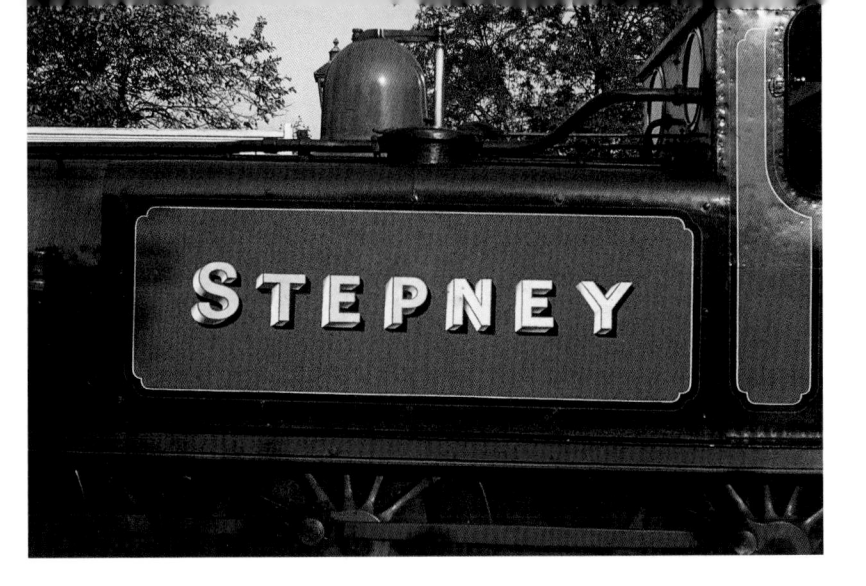

↑ In March 1961 there was a complete lack of covered accommodation, and certainly no such thing as a paint shop. I was fascinated to see Brighton 'Terrier' No 55 receiving its name again, which it had lost even before the 1923 Grouping.

↑ The finished article, as seen on 13 August 1964.

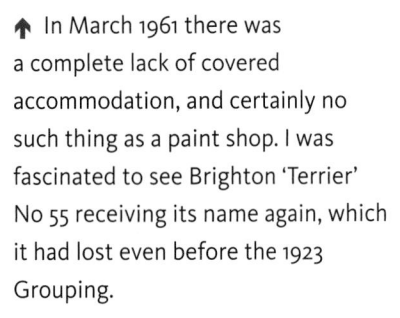

↓ The classic Bluebell loco from the earliest days, Brighton A1X 'Terrier' No 55 *Stepney* (BR No 32655) at Sheffield Park on 14 August 1963. Behind it is the platform signal frame, which was entirely open in LBSCR and BR days, but was enclosed to form a signalbox when the preservation society took over the station.

↑ A visit to Sheffield Park in August 1962 found another of my favourite locos in steam: LSWR Adams Radial 0415 class 4-4-2T No 488 (BR No 30583). The land beyond the station fence has since been developed by the railway with extensive sheds and workshop facilities.

← Ex-SECR P class 0-6-0T No 323 *Bluebell* (BR No 31323) at Sheffield Park on 14 August 1963.

→ Like all the early preserved railways, the Bluebell soon built up a collection of historic locos, not necessarily appropriate to the line historically, and included a few industrials. This ex-North London Railway 0-6-0T (LNWR No 2650, LMSR No 27505 and BR No 58850) was a very welcome arrival as far as I was concerned being a type I had never seen before. The locos were spread out in the yard in August 1963, making viewing and photography so much easier than we are used to on any of today's heritage railways.

↓ The Bluebell's second P class 0-6-0T, No 27 (BR No 31027), was turned out in full South Eastern & Chatham Railway livery, and no fictitious name, like sister No 323 *Bluebell*. This is seen on 15 September 1963 and the 'Blue Belle' headboard is being fitted to the bunker before leaving Horsted Keynes for Sheffield Park. This was the extent of the line at that time, but the electrified main line connection at Haywards Heath via Ardingly was still in use by BR. ('Horsted Keynes. Alight here for the Bluebell line.') This route enabled the 'Scottish Belle' railtour to run through that day, with Caledonian Single No 123 and LSWR T9 class 4-4-0 No 120, as shown in Chapter 10. In the white jacket is the autocratic manager of the line, Horace May.

↑ A welcome and perhaps more appropriate addition to Bluebell stock in late 1962 was No 473 *Birch Grove*, seen here arriving at Sheffield Park on 31 May 1964 with the Chesham set of coaches. I was very familiar with the ex-LBSCR Billinton E4 class 0-6-2Ts and had seen this loco many times as BR No 32473. However, it looked so different named and in LBSCR marsh umber, to when I had seen it in BR black.

→ This view of the ex-GWR 'Dukedog' at Sheffield Park on 5 July 1964 later proved to be more interesting than I was aware at the time. Although it carries *Earl of Berkeley* nameplates it was numbered 9017. By the time of its official naming on 13 June 1965, it had reverted to its original number, 3217. The nameplates were never carried in GWR days as originally intended, but some earlier members of the 3200 class did receive their names. A policy change saw these plates applied to the prestigious and larger 'Castle' class 4-6-0s, in this case, No 5060.

The 4-4-0 had been renumbered 9017 when the 32xx number was required for a new Collett 0-6-0 in 1946. The name and number plates were purchased from BR when the respective locos were withdrawn, so that the 'Dukedog' could take up its originally intended identity. No 3217 had been constructed at Swindon in 1938, using the frame and running gear of 'Bulldog' class No 3425 (built as No 3715 in 1906), and the boiler from 'Duke' class No 3282.

Keighley & Worth Valley Railway

The only other standard gauge line to officially open prior to August 1968 was the KWVR, on 29 June that year. This was the first true branch line to be re-opened, from its connection to the main line at Keighley, through to the original terminus at Oxenhope. (The Middleton was part of an industrial complex and the Bluebell was a section in the middle of a cross-country through route.)

My first visit to the KWVR was more than two years prior to opening, on 16 April 1967, again by means of a very cheap excursion with interesting, preserved motive power for much of the journey from London (see Chapters 8 and 10). A rapidly expanding collection of locos was being built up and these were well spaced out for photography in the yard at Haworth, where a special passenger train was run for the benefit of the visitors. There was something of an LNER bias with the locos being acquired for this former Midland Railway branch at the time. I was then of the belief, and was probably not alone in this, that each railway acquired locos as long-term additions to their collection, just as locos were kept in a museum like Clapham or York, for the foreseeable future. Today, locos are constantly on the move, either as longer-term transfers, for short-period hires or gala appearances. The locos seen today at those early railways are often very different from when they opened.

← An old design, but a new loco, No 69023 had only ever carried a BR number, as incredibly it was only 16 years old when seen on display at the KWVR on 16 April 1967. The Worsdell NER design dated back to 1898, but examples were built by the NER as Class E1, and the LNER as J72 from 1898 to 1925. The final batch was built after Nationalisation at Darlington Works in 1949–51, BR Nos 69001 to 69028. These were all withdrawn between 1963 and 1965, and despite their young age and suitability for use on preserved railways, this was to be the only survivor. It was bought privately and named *Joem*. This and No 69005 had seen further BR use until 1966/67 as service locos Nos 59 and 58 respectively.

➜ This LNER loco, BR No 69523 (just one digit different from the J72), is today a familiar sight on Britain's heritage railways as it makes frequent gala appearances. Currently, it carries its original livery and identity of GNR No 1744. It is the sole surviving example of Gresley's N2 class 0-6-2T, withdrawn in 1962 and acquired for preservation by the Gresley Society. Its first public preservation site was the KWVR, where it was turned out in LNER black as No 4744, as seen on 16 April 1967.

← A real pioneer of preservation: GNR J52 class 0-6-0ST No 1247. This was the first standard gauge steam locomotive to be bought by a private individual for preservation. Withdrawn as BR No 68846 in May 1959, the former King's Cross 'Top Shed' pilot loco was acquired by Captain W G 'Bill' Smith and put through Doncaster Works for overhaul. It was then used on main line specials.

Following a period of operating railtours on the main line the loco was moved to the KWVR in March 1965, where I saw it on 16 April 1967. However, the lack of covered accommodation and the fact that it was seeing little use there, as official reopening of the line did not occur until 1968, resulted in it being moved on to Tyseley. This historic loco, the only example of its type in preservation, was handed over to the National Collection in December 1980.

➜ When steam locos were being acquired for preservation directly from BR, they were more selectively chosen for their historic interest so there was little duplication, except perhaps for those like Brighton 'Terriers' and LMS 'Black Fives'. This was a time when locos were looked upon as museum pieces, even on future operational lines like the KWVR.

The LMS companies were represented at the KWVR prior to re-opening by ex-Lancashire & Yorkshire Railway No 957, a Barton Wright 25 class 0-6-0 of 1887, the sole survivor of its type purchased privately direct from BR.

➔ Also acquired from BR, by two individuals, H Foster and R Ainsworth, but more specifically for operation and use on the KWVR, was Ivatt Class 2 2-6-2T No 41241. Built by BR at Crewe in 1949 it was in operation on 16 April 1967 running for a few hundred yards from Haworth giving rides for the railtour visitors. This loco has remained a useful member of the railway's stock to the present day, although its boiler certificate has now expired and it has been withdrawn for overhaul.

Kent & East Sussex Railway

The first section of this line did not reopen until 1974. This should have been a lot sooner, and the fact that it did open then was down to the sheer determination and dedication of those involved. Authorities appeared to throw every obstacle possible in their path to prevent this happening and the KESR pioneers must always be remembered for their persistence in reopening one of Britain's most important heritage railways.

A visit to Rolvenden on 1 October 1967 found locos and stock being accumulated in the faith that 'right' would prevail and 'good would conquer evil'. Many of the locos were of industrial origin, as befitting this former Colonel Stephens line, and therefore eminently suitable for this country byway. The railway was fortunate to be able to also secure two very appropriate Brighton 'Terriers' as used on the line previously, one being an actual, original KESR locomotive, No 3 *Bodiam*.

⬅ The largest loco on site at Haworth at this time, April 1967, was LMS rebuilt 'Royal Scot' No 46115 *Scots Guardsman*. It was stored at Haworth on behalf of owner R A Bill, from August 1966 until April 1969. Today, it is a main line performer based at Carnforth.

⬇ A1X class 0-6-0T BR No 32670 was originally LBSCR No 70 *Poplar*, built in 1872, but was sold to the Rother Valley Railway in 1901, which became the KESR in 1904. The 'Terrier' became No 3 *Bodiam* and was absorbed into BR stock at Nationalisation. It was withdrawn in November 1963 and is seen at Rolvenden on 1 October 1967 when awaiting its return to traffic on the revived KESR.

The KESR's other 'Terrier' in the early days was ex-BR No 32650 (LBSCR No 50 *Whitechapel*). Following withdrawal by BR in 1963 it was purchased by the Borough of Sutton & Cheam in 1964 with a view to placing it on display at a new civic centre in Sutton, masquerading as No 61 *Sutton*, which had been scrapped the previous year.

Meanwhile, No 32650 was loaned temporarily to the KESR until the site was ready, but the scheme never materialised and it was restored to working order and given the name *Sutton*, and headed the inaugural passenger trains on the KESR in 1974. It was withdrawn from service in 1994 and kept on static display at Tenterden until 2004 when it was transferred to the Spa Valley Railway where it is slowly being restored to working order again within the old LBSCR Tunbridge Wells West shed. The KESR still has two 'Terriers', as ex-Butlin's No 32678, owned by the Terrier Trust, joined the collection later and was restored for operation on the line in 2001.

Robertsbridge, East Sussex

In anticipation that the KESR would be reopened from Tenterden through to its main line connection at Robertsbridge, some locos were kept there in the 1960s (see also Chapter 11). Although it is an on-going project with great strides made recently, this is yet to be achieved. It looked completely hopeless at one time and the stock was then moved to other locations.

↑ I made my first visit to the DVR on 31 October 1970 when stock could still be seen under the all-over roof at Ashburton station, including GWR 1400 class 0-4-2T No 1450.

Dart Valley Railway

Known today as the enthusiast-run South Devon Railway, this was the first steam railway to be reopened after the cessation of steam on BR. It was officially opened on 17 May 1969, but public trains had started running on 5 April. This was operated as a commercial enterprise by the Dart Valley Light Railway Co Ltd, which was not a preservation society. It stated at the time that it did not need to be as the Great Western Society was 'so well equipped to collect and preserve Great Western history and stock'.

For the first couple of seasons trains ran from Totnes, through Buckfastleigh to the original branch terminus at Ashburton, but the last two miles, and therefore access to the station and yard there, were lost when the A38 road was developed. The final train to Ashburton was a BR railtour on 2 October 1971.

← The sole surviving SECR H class 0-4-4T, No 31263, was kept at Robertsbridge initially, following purchase by the H Class Trust in 1964. Seen there on 1 October 1967, it was moved to its present home on the Bluebell Railway in February 1969.

RAILWAY CENTRES CLOSED, AND TEMPORARY STORAGE LOCATIONS

As the final day of BR steam neared, many groups and individuals were doing what they could to secure locos for the future. There was every reason to believe that this was the last opportunity and that everything withdrawn would soon be broken up if not purchased. No-one could predict what was going to happen at Woodham Bros, Barry.

For a while, some locos were being kept at various sites while their longer-term future was determined. It was not always realised then that the chosen base was only going to be temporary, but that was the way some turned out to be.

Other sites that opened in the 1960s, on the other hand, have been developed and have since grown considerably to become well-established railways or centres.

Caerphilly, Glamorgan

One early preservation centre was set up at the premises of South Wales Switchgear Ltd, Harold Wilson Industrial Estate, Caerphilly. This was the site of the former Rhymney Railway's Caerphilly Works which had been closed by BR in 1963.

When the Great Western Society South Wales Group was in need of a home for ex-GWR 2-6-0 No 5322, acquired from Woodham Bros, Barry, SWS Ltd agreed to them taking it to their Caerphilly site, and it arrived there in 1969. Following completion of restoration it was operated at a number of steam days until being moved to the Didcot Railway Centre in 1973. The Caerphilly Railway Society was then formed and a collection of industrial locos was built up, some of which were steamed occasionally, but limited public access to the site and persistent vandalism led to it being vacated as a railway centre in 1996–97, with the CRS moving to the Gwili Railway.

The 63rd Barry departure was Ivatt 2-6-2T

⬇ Former Taff Vale Railway O1 class 0-6-2T No 28, built at TVR's Cardiff Works in 1897, was withdrawn by the GWR as No 450 in 1926 and sold to the Longmoor Military Railway, and out of main line service. It later passed to the NCB and following withdrawal in 1960, was presented to BR for preservation in 1962. It later passed to the National Museum of Wales and is officially part of the National Collection.

It was first moved to Caerphilly Works but this was closed by BR on 24 June 1963 and the loco was transferred to Swindon Works for storage. It then went to Stratford, London but returned to Caerphilly in July 1967 when South Wales Switchgear, which had taken over the works premises, wanted to display the loco there for a few years, and it is seen there on 30 June 1969.

Railway enthusiast employees of SWS Ltd undertook its restoration, returning No 28 to steam in 1983, and it later moved to the Dean Forest Railway. A subsequent restoration proved abortive and today it is in a very sorry state. It lies dismantled, and forgotten, at the Llangollen Railway despite being the only Welsh loco in the National Collection. (Cosmetic restoration is a possibility.)

10A Carnforth MPD, Lancashire

Carnforth was one of the last BR steam sheds and even while still in use as a running depot, locos destined for preservation were stored there. It was initially intended that this would be the engineering base for the proposed Lakeside & Haverthwaite Railway, but it eventually became a separate organisation after closure by BR, being known as Steamtown Carnforth. As such it became an important operating base for main line steam locos as well as being a popular visitor attraction, complete with a 15in gauge steam railway. Today, it is the operational base of West Coast Railways and is strictly off-limits to the public. The only time in recent years when access has been allowed to enthusiasts was *The Railway Magazine*-sponsored open weekend in July 2008.

⬇ Ivatt Class 2 2-6-0 No 46441 (built BR Crewe in 1950) in pseudo LMS maroon as No 6441 for Dr Peter Beet. Photographed on 4 August 1968 during BR's last weekend of scheduled steam. It is now part of the large collection of mainly industrial locos at the Ribble Steam Railway, Preston.

⬇ Fairburn 4MT 2-6-4T No 42073 (built BR Brighton 1950), purchased for use on the Lakeside & Haverthwaite Railway, is seen in store at Carnforth on 10 July 1968. My previous encounter with this loco was during our Rail Rover holiday when it hauled us from Bradford Exchange to Leeds Central on 30 August 1966. It was withdrawn in October 1967 and was acquired for the LHR with sister loco No 42085, also stored for a while at 10A.

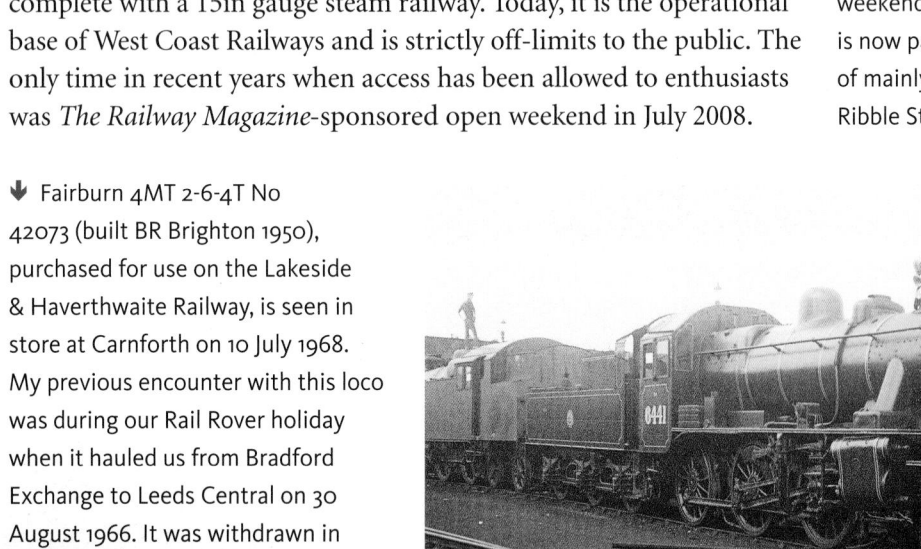

Longmoor Military Railway, Hampshire

Had this been allowed to develop it would now be one of Britain's leading heritage railways. This was a long-established training facility for the British Army and as well as extensive workshop facilities it had a lengthy track, which encircled the site, as well as having two main line connections.

As the military requirement wound down the possibility of it becoming a railway centre was beginning to look hopeful, as several major loco owners and groups moved their stock on site, including artist David Shepherd.

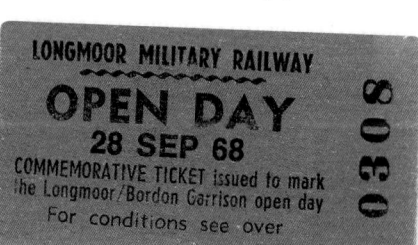

However, it was not to be. A handful of vociferous residents living not so nearby raised objections and the proposal was thrown out. Had it progressed this would no doubt have adversely affected several other railways we have today, and the East Somerset Railway would never have come into being.

The LMR held a series of well-attended open days, as well as accommodating incoming railtours.

The following views are from an open day on 28 September 1968, the month following steam's end on BR, when the preservationists appeared to be taking over Longmoor.

→ Looking ready for action is Ivatt Class 2 2-6-2T No 41298, owned by the Ivatt Locomotive Trust. Withdrawn in July 1967 and bought direct from BR in serviceable condition, it was moved to Longmoor in August 1967. When the LMR had to be vacated it moved to Quainton Railway Centre and a major overhaul commenced. This was never completed and the loco was transferred to the Isle of Wight Steam Railway in 2008. It is due to enter service following completion of restoration in October 2013, 46 years after acquisition for preservation in virtual working order. Next to the Ivatt is Bulleid Pacific No 34023 *Blackmore Vale*.

↑ One of David Shepherd's two BR Standards, Class 4MT 4-6-0 No 75029 *The Green Knight*. Withdrawn in August 1967, purchased April 1968 and named on 5 July, although the plates were not carried on this occasion. Resident for many years on the East Somerset Railway, which was opened specially for this loco and David's 9F, the 4-6-0 was later sold. It is now based on the North Yorkshire Moors Railway and is fitted with TPWS (Train Protection and Warning System) equipment for working trains on the Network Rail line to Whitby.

↑ David Shepherd's other BR Standard, Class 9F 2-10-0 No 92203, which he named *Black Prince*, on 8 June 1968. Withdrawn in November 1967 and purchased direct from BR, it was moved south to the LMR, by rail, in steam on 6–7 April (see Chapter 10).

➜ Unlike No 41298, but like Nos 34023, 75029 and 92203, this is a locomotive that has seen considerable use since it was on static display at Longmoor: rebuilt 'Merchant Navy' No 35028 *Clan Line*. Bought direct from BR in August 1967 by the Merchant Navy Preservation Society, it has been a consistent main line performer through to the present day.

← It is usually quite clear whether a locomotive can claim to have a 'main line' pedigree, either being built for a main line railway company, or acquired from industry subsequently, as in the case of some GWR absorbed locos. One loco whose status I have never felt quite sure about is the unique *Gazelle*. However, as it is such a delightful loco it is included here anyway, and it ran at least once on the national network. It was built by Alfred Dodman & Co of King's Lynn in 1893 for William Burkitt, who had running powers over the GER and M&GNJR, the 2-2-2WT having its own passenger accommodation despite its small size.

It was sold to the Shropshire & Montgomeryshire Light Railway in 1911, which had it rebuilt by Bagnall as an 0-4-2WT. It was requisitioned by the War Department in 1941 and transferred to the Longmoor Military Railway in 1950, where it was later put on display, as seen on 28 September 1968. Now part of the National Collection, it graces the Colonel Stephens Museum at Tenterden on the KESR, but it put in an appearance at the NRM's Railfest event at York in 2012.

RAILWAY WORKS

It was fairly common practice for locos that were deemed to be 'preserved' to be secreted away in railway workshops, usually in the paint shop. Not all such locos have survived to the present time, but it was a safe haven for many.

↙ *Lion* is one of Britain's most famous and historic locos, perhaps best known as the *Titfield Thunderbolt*, having played the starring role in that film in 1952. Built for the Liverpool & Manchester Railway by Todd Kitson & Laird in 1838, it was their No 57, later Grand Junction Railway and LNWR No 116. Withdrawn in 1859 it became a stationary pumping engine at Princes Dock, Liverpool until 1928, when it was acquired by the LMS. It has since been restored to working order on several occasions as well as having had a period on static display in Liverpool. At other times it was kept in Crewe Works paint shop, where I saw it on 3 April 1966. It is now on display in the new Museum of Liverpool.

➔ Also seen in the Crewe Works paint shop on 3 April 1966, following cosmetic restoration the previous year, was LMS 'Princess Coronation' Pacific No 46235 *City of Birmingham*. It had been claimed for official preservation, but never joined the National Collection as such, its place later taken by ex-Butlin's No 46229 *Duchess of Hamilton*. No 46235 has been kept in static isolation in Birmingham's science museum, today referred to as the 'Thinktank'.

BR LOCOMOTIVES PRESERVED IN NORTH AMERICA

There was just one other situation where ex-BR locos could be found following their retirement. Shortly after their withdrawal, several engines were purchased for preservation in North America or were sent to museums there.

Amazingly, at the time of writing in late 2012, all but one of these are back in the UK. Three have been repatriated permanently, while the two A4s have been brought over at considerable expense by the National Railway Museum for an exhibition marking the 75th anniversary of *Mallard*'s speed record-breaking run in July 1938. They will be returning to their respective homes in 2014.

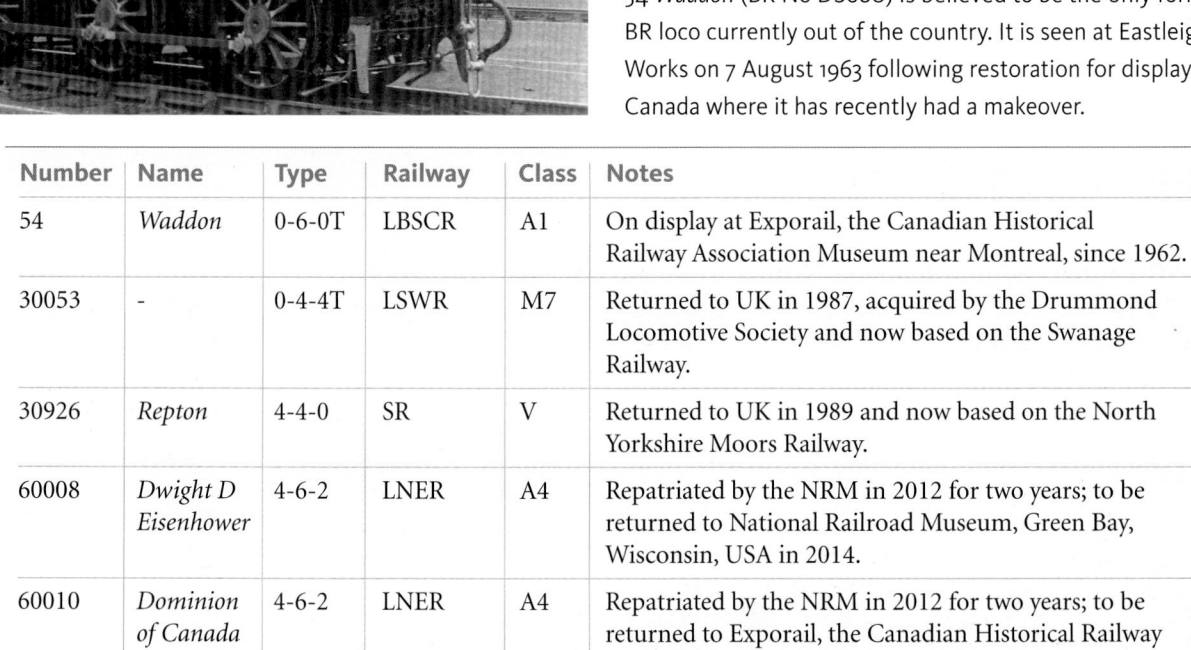

← At the time of writing, early 2013, ex-LBSCR 'Terrier' No. 54 *Waddon* (BR No DS680) is believed to be the only former BR loco currently out of the country. It is seen at Eastleigh Works on 7 August 1963 following restoration for display in Canada where it has recently had a makeover.

Number	Name	Type	Railway	Class	Notes
54	*Waddon*	0-6-0T	LBSCR	A1	On display at Exporail, the Canadian Historical Railway Association Museum near Montreal, since 1962.
30053	-	0-4-4T	LSWR	M7	Returned to UK in 1987, acquired by the Drummond Locomotive Society and now based on the Swanage Railway.
30926	*Repton*	4-4-0	SR	V	Returned to UK in 1989 and now based on the North Yorkshire Moors Railway.
60008	*Dwight D Eisenhower*	4-6-2	LNER	A4	Repatriated by the NRM in 2012 for two years; to be returned to National Railroad Museum, Green Bay, Wisconsin, USA in 2014.
60010	*Dominion of Canada*	4-6-2	LNER	A4	Repatriated by the NRM in 2012 for two years; to be returned to Exporail, the Canadian Historical Railway Association Museum near Montreal in 2014.
	Dunrobin	0-4-4T	Duke of Sutherland		Repatriated from Canada in 2011 for preservation at Beamish, following restoration at the Severn Valley Railway.

CHAPTER 7

MAIN LINE
NARROW GAUGE

The railway company-owned

steam locomotives

THIS CHAPTER TITLE MIGHT appear to be something of a contradiction in terms. However, several main line railway companies owned and operated narrow gauge lines, both as passenger railways and as workshop tramways. Some of these remained in operation, passing into BR ownership at Nationalisation in 1948. One notable example, the Vale of Rheidol Railway, actually outlived the national network as a steam-worked line, becoming BR's last steam service.

It was through the Great Western Railway that BR obtained its best-known narrow gauge lines and locomotives, namely the 2ft 3in gauge Corris Railway, the 1ft 11½in gauge Vale of Rheidol, and the 2ft 6in gauge Welshpool & Llanfair, all having been absorbed by the GWR previously.

The locomotives of these lines were taken into BR capital stock, and being part of the Western Region, in common with other inherited GWR locos, retained their original numbers.

No doubt like many railway enthusiasts, these locomotives were my first encounter with narrow gauge, being listed as they were in the Ian Allan *abc* books. In fact, for a while, I probably believed these were more or less the only narrow gauge steam locos in existence in the UK, apart from perhaps those on the Ffestiniog, Snowdon Mountain and Isle of Man railways.

The fact that Talyllyn Railway Nos 3 and 4 were actually owned by and had been numbered in BR stock gave them a more important status in some eyes, over the TR's own two original locos, No 1 *Talyllyn* and 2 *Dolgoch*. Because of this, those two locos are not featured in this book, which is devoted solely to 'main line' engines.

Corris Railway (2ft 3in gauge)

The Corris Railway was a slate-carrying railway which operated a passenger service from 1883, but this ceased in 1930 when the railway was absorbed by the GWR. Steam had been introduced in 1878 with No 3, one of the original 0-4-0STs, converted to an 0-4-2ST, surviving right through to Nationalisation and into preservation. Nos 1 and 2 were condemned in 1921 when a new locomotive, 0-4-2ST No 4 was purchased, which is the other Corris survivor today.

The line closed on 20 August 1948 after

SURVIVING MAIN LINE NARROW GAUGE STEAM LOCOS FROM PASSENGER LINES

Number	Name	Builder	Type	Gauge	Railway
1		Kitson 2551 T56 of 1882	0-4-0Tram	3ft	MR-NCC Portstewart Tramway
2		Kitson T84 of 1883	0-4-0Tram	3ft	MR-NCC Portstewart Tramway
3		Hughes 323 1878	0-4-2ST	2ft 3in	Corris Railway
4		Kerr, Stuart 4047 1921	0-4-2ST	2ft 3in	Corris Railway
7	*Owain Glyndŵr*	GWR Swindon 1923	2-6-2T	1ft 11½in	Vale of Rheidol
8	*Llywelyn*	GWR Swindon 1923	2-6-2T	1ft 11½in	Vale of Rheidol
9	*Prince of Wales*	GWR Swindon 1924	2-6-2T	1ft 11½in	Vale of Rheidol
822	*The Earl*	Beyer Peacock 3496 1902	0-6-0T	2ft 6in	Welshpool & Llanfair
823	*The Countess*	Beyer Peacock 3497 1902	0-6-0T	2ft 6in	Welshpool & Llanfair

Notes: No 3 – built as an 0-4-0ST by Hughes Locomotive & Tramway Engine Works Ltd, Falcon Works, Loughborough. No 9 – the builder of this loco is often given as Davies & Metcalfe Ltd of Stockport, builder's No 2 of 1902, but the so-called rebuild of 1924 by the GWR was almost certainly a complete new locomotive constructed at Swindon.

becoming part of BR, as flooding of the River Dyfi endangered the bridge, with services suspended immediately. This left locomotives Nos 3 and 4 marooned at Machynlleth, where they were sheeted over, awaiting their fate.

Fortunately, their unusual gauge of 2ft 3in ensured their salvation as the similar-gauge Talyllyn Railway was being taken over by enthusiasts at that time. They were bought in spring 1951 at a price purported to be £25 each, becoming TR Nos 3 and 4. Therefore, they had carried these same running numbers in the ownership of the Corris Railway, GWR, BR and now Talyllyn Railway. In TR ownership they have been named *Sir Haydn* and *Edward Thomas* respectively.

The present-day Corris Railway has a new-build version of Kerr Stuart 'Tattoo' class No 4, completed in 2005 and running as No 7. The Falcon Project is a new-build of No 3, which is currently under construction with a hoped-for completion date of 2015. It will of course be an 0-4-2ST from the outset, with the cost expected to exceed £100,000, somewhat more than the price of a genuine CR/GWR/BR example in 1951!

↑ Corris/GWR/BR/TR No 3 in a view somewhat later than this book's usual end-of-BR-steam cut-off date of August 1968. However, trying to photograph some locos, particularly preserved ones can be akin to waiting for an eclipse. Although I visited the Talyllyn many times in the late 1960s, I never had the opportunity to see and photograph No 3 complete, out in the open, with nothing in the way, let alone with no clouds between it and the sun.

A visit on 21 April 1973 however, found everything in alignment – including all five steam locos, Nos, 1, 2, 3, 4 and 6 at Tywyn Wharf where they were awaiting an annual steam test. Patience was rewarded.

Vale of Rheidol Railway (1ft 11½in gauge)

This railway opened between Aberystwyth and Devil's Bridge in 1902 and was taken over by the Cambrian Railways in 1913. Passing to the GWR in 1922 when the Cambrian system was absorbed, it became part of British Railways at Nationalisation in 1948. Although a tourist railway, the locomotives were not preserved, but remained in BR capital stock to outlive main line standard gauge steam when this was eliminated in August 1968.

This became the only steam railway operation on the BR network, right up to 1989 when the line was sold in its entirety to the Brecon Mountain Railway Co. The three 2-6-2Ts then passed out of main line railway ownership.

↑ My first visit to the narrow gauge railways of North Wales was in July 1967 and I was delighted to find ex-BR No 4 in operation on the Talyllyn Railway. At that time equipped with a Giesl ejector, it is seen on arrival at Abergynolwyn station on 9 July. Unfortunately, No 3 was in the back of the works at Pendre, completely dismantled for overhaul and it was several years later before I was able to see it complete.

→ VofR No 7 *Owain Glyndŵr* is prepared for a day's work at BR Aberystwyth shed on 10 July 1967.

↓ VofR No 8 *Llywelyn* at Aberystwyth on 10 July 1967.

↘ The tank-side nameplate and BR crest on Brunswick green VofR 2-6-2T No 8 *Llywelyn*, 10 July 1967. There has been much recent discussion as to whether the green used by BR was called Brunswick or not. The correct term was in fact 'middle chrome green' although the term 'Brunswick green' is the description of a type of green, not the name of a particular shade. So, whether that name was used by BR or not does not alter the fact that the green used falls technically within that range. Conversely, just because William Stroudley of the LBSCR referred to his yellow ochre livery as 'improved engine green' did not make it a green colour!

↑ No 8 *Llywelyn* and its two stablemates ensured BR continued with steam long after the official 'end of steam' in 1968. It is seen inside the old standard gauge shed, which was taken over by the narrow gauge line in 1968 following abandonment of the old facilities. This was the first application of 'Corporate' Rail Blue to these locos, complete with the double-arrow motif, which was later dropped from the tank sides and the nameplates mounted lower, and lining applied. Cast BR emblems then appeared on the cab side with the number plate mounted higher. This view is dated 8 July 1969.

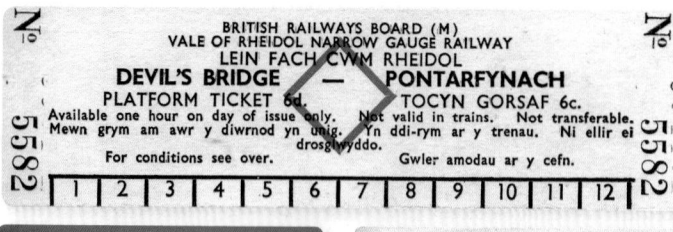

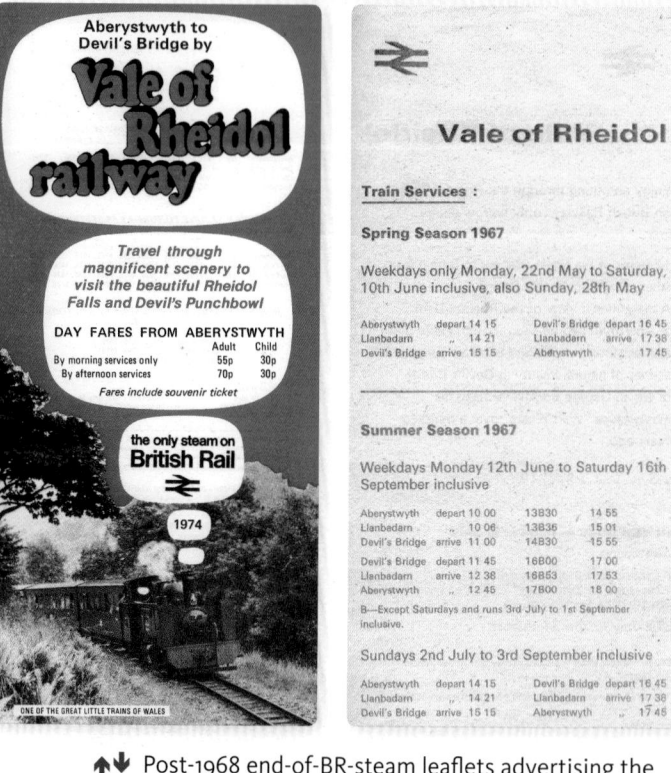

⬆⬇ Post-1968 end-of-BR-steam leaflets advertising the service provided by the Vale of Rheidol into the 1970s and '8os, showing this was still steam operated, and using it as a marketing feature.

⬆ No 9 *Prince of Wales* waits to depart from Aberystwyth station on 8 July 1969, nearly a year after the official end of steam on BR. The Rail Blue livery was applied as a result of the directive issued by BR on 9 June 1966 to repaint all locomotives in this livery, but this was never applied to other, standard gauge BR steam locomotives then in traffic. Such a move was highly controversial amongst enthusiasts of the day, but the VofR stock was not regarded as preserved at that time. It was retained to do the job for which it was intended, conveying passengers between Aberystwyth and Devil's Bridge.

At the same time the former standard gauge steam shed was taken over for VofR locos and carriage stock in 1968, the line was deviated into the main station to use the former Manchester & Milford Railway bay platforms 4 and 5. This eliminated the level crossing which was just outside the old GWR narrow gauge station.

Welshpool & Llanfair Light Railway (2ft 6in gauge)

This 2ft 6in gauge line opened in 1903 with just two locomotives, which remained the sole motive power throughout its life prior to preservation. The line was operated from the beginning by the Cambrian Railways, but the two locos were numbered 1 and 2 and named *The Earl* and *The Countess*.

When absorbed by the GWR in 1922, they were renumbered 822 and 823 respectively and lost their names. Passenger services ceased in 1931, but the line continued in use for goods well into the nationalisation period, closing in 1956. The two locos were placed in store at Oswestry Works until acquired by the preservation society, which reopened a section of the line in 1963. They reverted to Nos 1 and 2 and have since taken up Nos 822 and 823 again, with names shortened to *Earl* and *Countess*.

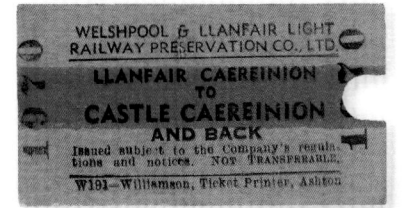

↓ No 1 *The Earl*, in lined-green livery, heads the ex-Chattenden & Upnor Railway 'combination' coach No 214 on 17 July 1967 as it waits to return from Castle Caereinion, which was as far as trains were running at that time from Llanfair Caereinion. Passenger numbers were clearly not as they are today. Even this accommodation was excessive that day as my friend Martin and I travelled back to Llanfair in the cab. Welsh narrow gauge generally was then a lot more relaxed and true to its humble origins than perhaps are some of today's 'mini main lines'.

↑ No 2 *The Countess*, in lined black, was in open storage at Llanfair Caereinion, awaiting restoration in July 1967. Other, non-BR locos, steam and diesel, were beginning to be acquired for the railway, and the fairly rare gauge of 2ft 6in resulted in some of the first preservation imports of steam locos and rolling stock from abroad.

Portstewart Tramway (3ft gauge)

The Portstewart Tramway opened in June 1982 connecting the town of that name with the main line station at Cromore, a distance of one mile. Within five years it was suffering financial problems and was acquired by the Belfast & Northern Counties Railway, which was taken over by the Midland Railway in 1903 and hence the LMS in 1923, and therefore became part of the Northern Counties Committee. Still losing money, the tramway closed on 31 January 1926.

Tram locos Nos 1 and 2 were placed in store at LMS-NCC York Road Works, Belfast. It is understood an attempt was made to offer No 1 to the London Science Museum, but this was rejected and the only regional museum interested and prepared to take it on was that at Kingston upon Hull, where it resides today. No 2 is perhaps more appropriately displayed at the Ulster Folk & Transport Museum, Cultra, although No 1 would not be out of place within the National Collection at York or Shildon.

← There are very few surviving steam tram locomotives in Britain of any gauge, and this is one of only two narrow gauge ones, Portstewart Tramway No 1. This is one of the least known, ex-main line company steam survivors, and certainly one that was not in the book (Ian Allan's *abc*). Lettered MR-NCC – Midland Railway - Northern Counties Committee – it was seen in the Hull Transport Museum on 21 July 1968, the first Irish 'main line' loco I tracked down.

NON-PASSENGER NARROW GAUGE LINES

Three other narrow gauge steam locos that saw service with BR and its predecessors on internal works systems survived into the 1960s and therefore the present day:

No 1	Bagnall 1889 1911	0-4-0ST	3ft	Beeston Creosote Works
Wren	Beyer Peacock 2825 1887	0-4-0ST+T	1ft 6in	Horwich Works tramway
Pet	LNWR Crewe 1865	0-4-0ST	1ft 6in	Crewe Works tramway

Crewe Works tramway (1ft 6in gauge)

The first part of the locomotive works at Crewe, Cheshire was opened in 1843 by the Grand Junction Railway. The GJR became part of the London & North Western Railway and the works developed and expanded to become one of Britain's largest and best known locomotive construction and repair facilities. The extent of the works called for a better system of internal transport than hand-carts and so an 18in gauge rail system was installed during 1861/62. This was extended over the years, and in 1878 track was laid on the lengthy footbridge which ran from the Old Works to Crewe station, this being known as the Spider Bridge.

From the beginning, steam power was used for hauling the wagons, with the first loco called *Tiny* built in 1862. Designed by John Ramsbottom, this was the first of seven steam locos built at Crewe for this railway. It was introduced more than a year before the Festiniog Railway's George England locos were delivered.

The second loco for the Crewe system was *Pet*, built at the works in June 1865. Along with the

→ *Pet* was withdrawn from use at Crewe Works in April 1929 and retained for preservation. It was put on display at the Museum of British Transport, Clapham in 1964, where I saw it on 11 June 1966. Following closure of this museum it was placed on loan to the Narrow Gauge Railway Museum at Towyn on the Talyllyn Railway in June 1967, but is now in the NRM at York. A remarkable survivor and a rare example of an 18in gauge steam loco which dates back to the earliest days of small, narrow gauge railways.

other locos, this was withdrawn in 1929. However, *Billy* was retained as standby to a Hudswell Clarke diesel loco, which were both later scrapped. The main part of the railway closed in 1932 with just a few sections remaining in use, worked by hand, until the early 1960s.

↑ The former Lancashire & Yorkshire Railway Horwich Works tramway loco, *Wren,* was restored to its original lined LYR black livery and put on public display at the Museum of British Transport, Clapham in May 1964. I saw it there the following year, amongst the trams and horse buses. Today, it is prominently displayed in the entrance hall to the National Railway Museum at York.

Horwich Works tramway (1ft 6in gauge)

The Lancashire & Yorkshire Railway opened its locomotive works at Horwich in 1887, and like the LNWR's Crewe Works, this was served by an 18in gauge rail system. This ran through the workshop buildings, where the rails were set in the ground tramway style, as well as connecting the various parts of the works externally. At its peak there was about seven miles of track and eight steam locos hauling metal 'tub' wagons.

As the importance of the works declined so did the use and extent of the tramway. Under BR, a new Ruston & Hornsby diesel loco, No ZM32, was introduced, and from then until closure of the system this was the sole motive power. However, one of the original steam locos, *Wren,* supplied new by Beyer Peacock in 1887, was retained as standby. This was officially withdrawn in 1961 and then classified as preserved, being placed on display in the old erecting shop in July 1961. No ZM32 also survives and is preserved on the Steeplegrange Railway, Derbyshire. Horwich Works was closed in 1983.

Beeston Creosote Works (3ft gauge)

Although built in 1911, this 0-4-0ST did not achieve 'main line' status until taken into BR departmental stock in July 1956. It was supplied by ME Engineering Ltd, dealers of light railway material and contractors' plant of Cricklewood, London NW3, for use at BR's creosote works at Beeston, Nottinghamshire. It had gone new to Judkins Ltd, Tuttle Hill Granite Quarries, Nuneaton, Warwickshire, where it was their No 1 and was used there until about 1950, when it was laid up.

It saw only occasional use at the BR depot and was replaced in 1958 by a Ruston & Hornsby diesel loco, No ED10. It was acquired for preservation in 1962 and spent some time in the yard of S A Burgess, Haddenham, Cambridgeshire for restoration. Passing through various private owners, it was acquired by the Amerton Railway, Staffordshire, arriving there on 18 March 2008. By then it was in a completely dismantled state and is now being restored as and when time and finances permit. It will be completed as a 2ft gauge loco and fitted with a cab or awning as it would have had when new.

↑ BR No 1, a 'Mercedes' class Bagnall 0-4-0ST of 3ft gauge with 6 x 9in cylinders and Bagnall-Price valve gear, was one of the last ex-BR steam locos I tracked down, not seeing it until 11 July 1971. It was in the yard of S A Burgess at Haddenham, waiting in vain for professional restoration.

CHAPTER 8

LAST TRAINS AND RAILTOURS

*The end of the line for steam classes
and destinations*

RAILTOURS FOR ENTHUSIASTS in the 1960s included many 'last trains'. These were the last trains to run over a line prior to it being closed, or the last train to be hauled by a particular loco class before they were withdrawn for scrap.

There were certainly plenty of such trains to choose from and I remember my mother querying how it was possible for me to go on so many trains purporting to be the 'last one'. These were run all over the country and produced some bizarre routes and motive power. Those I went on mainly worked north from London, or toured the Southern Region's lines.

Although I went on quite a number of last trains, this was nothing near as many as I would have liked as there were so many to choose from. Looking back now I wonder why I did not do more, but perhaps it was down to finances and simply time, as I was supposed to be studying for accountancy exams, not that it was ultimately a career I pursued.

Also, there was the explosion of rock music in the 1960s and gigs to attend whenever possible to see the huge number of great new bands coming on the scene. Some of these went on to become household names but others that I thought at least as good failed to survive, even if some of their members went on to become well known. My favourite band at the time was The Birds with a great guitarist – better known now as Ronnie Wood of the Rolling Stones. Other bands playing locally I went to see regularly were The Who, The Animals, Yardbirds, Fleetwood Mac, Pretty Things, John Mayall and the Bluesbreakers, the Groundhogs, and the only Liverpool band we rated, The Undertakers. Then from America came the greatest of them all, Captain Beefheart and The Magic Band, and they actually played in our local pub!

On top of this I was very interested in aircraft, attending air shows and visiting airports and airfields. I must have been to Heathrow a few times because my last spotting trip there, in the late 1960s, resulted in a long day without picking up a single 'cop' amongst the Boeing 707s, DC8s, Caravelles, BAC 111s, VC10s, Tu104s, Convair 990s

and Viscounts. I never went back there after that disappointing experience.

One of the attractions of going on railtours, which extended well into the 1970s, was that they provided a really cheap and easy way of getting to far-flung locations and back in a day. Trips to the embryonic KWVR, the Middleton Railway and the main BR workshops have already been mentioned in Chapters 3 and 6. Those using preserved motive power are covered in Chapter 10 while those using BR locos feature here.

Railtours were organised by many organisations. Some were long-established, such as the Locomotive Club of Great Britain (LCGB), Railway Correspondence & Travel Society (RCTS), Stephenson Locomotive Society (SLS), and of course, Ian Allan Travel. Many were run by newer set-ups, some of which ran just a very few trains, while others were fairly new to running such trains but had existed as spotters' clubs for many years previously.

One I used regularly, and which I thought always gave excellent value for money with a great day out, was the Home Counties Railway Club (Society from January 1963). It was formed in 1955 as the Middlesex Loco Spotters Club, becoming HCRC a few years later. However, I always felt let down that having supported so many of their trips that when it came to the Somerset & Dorset farewell trip I did not get a place, and I was not informed of the re-run in time to rebook and so missed that too! I never did get to travel this famous route and although disappointed at the time, did not know then that I was later to live so much within its shadow. I moved to Shepton Mallet in 1987, and more recently, to Burnham-on-Sea.

In addition to travelling on as many excursions as I could, others brought rare motive power into the local area and so these were an excellent way of seeing some rarities in action. A number of these are included here, from the Beattie well tanks from Cornwall, to A2 Pacific *Blue Peter* when still in BR stock and seen passing through Surbiton.

↑ We were overawed by the fact that our train boasted the almost brand-new 9F class 2-10-0 No 92220 *Evening Star* for haulage. It is seen at the head of the train in Swindon Works yard prior to the return to Paddington on this very dull day. It was not a 'cop' for me though, as I had been thrilled to catch a brief glimpse of it heading through Templecombe as we travelled west on holiday.

On that occasion I had only a few minutes earlier been admiring the colour plate of *Evening Star* in the latest issue of *The Railway Magazine*, which I had been treated to from WH Smith at Waterloo before we embarked on our journey to Sidmouth. At that time, *The RM* only splashed out on two colour pictures per year, as frontispieces in the January and July issues.

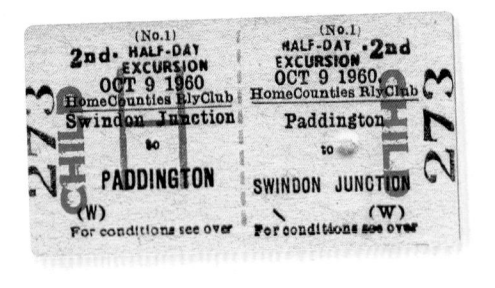

↑ My first ticket for a railtour, The Home Counties Railway Club's first excursion to Swindon Works on 9 October 1960. This trip was advertised in *Trains Illustrated*, August issue (see page 59) and the fare seemed remarkably cheap even then at 7s 6d (37.5p). I looked at it time and time again before the big day, wondering what it was going to be like on such a train. The day out more than lived up to expectations.

Taking them in chronological order, these are just some of the specials on which I travelled or went out to see locally. By 1967 my tactics had obviously changed. I had seen all the Southern locos so there was no longer a need for shed bashes to track down any 'cops'. In view of the impending demise of steam, which I was still finding difficult to take in, I went on a number of railtours for the last experience of travelling behind steam, probably for the last time on these lines.

Home Counties Railway Club 'Swindon Special' 9 OCTOBER 1960

This train was described in more detail in Chapter 3. It was my first experience of going on a railtour and the first time I had entered a railway workshop. It was a good example of interesting haulage to a very interesting destination at a most reasonable price. Even at the time we were pleased with how cheap the fares were for the accompanying adult (my dad) and half-fares for my friend Brian Davis and me.

RCTS/SLS the 'LSWR Suburban Tour' 2 DECEMBER 1962

One railtour brought rare motive power to the local area, using two of the three ex-LSWR Beattie well tanks from the Wenford Bridge branch, where they worked china clay trains. They headed this train from Waterloo via Point Pleasant Junction, East Putney, Wimbledon, Surbiton to Hampton Court Junction, then back to Wimbledon Yard. From there, more-familiar H16 class 4-6-2T No 30517 took the train to Chessington South and back to Wimbledon Yard. The well tanks headed the train from there to Shepperton and back to Waterloo via Richmond.

This was such a success it was repeated on 16 December. The three 0298 class 2-4-0WTs were withdrawn after these workings with the two depicted passing into preservation, and both are currently in working order. No 30587 (LSWR No 298) is in the National Collection, but based on the Bodmin & Wenford Railway, and No 30585 is kept at the Buckinghamshire Railway Centre, Quainton Road.

→ Class 0298 Beattie well tanks Nos 30585 and 30587 pass through Wimbledon station heading coach set No 278 on 2 December 1962, en route to Hampton Court Junction.

↓ One of the five magnificent ex-LSWR Urie Class H16 4-6-2Ts worked the 'LSWR Suburban Tour' from Wimbledon Yard to Chessington South and back on 2 December. It is seen running light through Wimbledon. Built in 1921/22 to work the transfer freights between Feltham Hump Yard and Willesden, all were withdrawn at the end of 1962 and broken up in 1963/64.

Home Counties Railway Society 'Crewe Special' 10 FEBRUARY 1963

This was one of those winter trips in poor weather. There was lots to see, but the only photo I seem to have taken, according to my negative register, was of 'Black Five' No 45031, never printed, and annotated 'underexposed'. Nevertheless, the tour, or at least the return journey, is worth relating.

Motive power from London Marylebone to Wolverhampton was Bulleid Pacific No 34094 *Mortehoe*. Other locos recorded for the day were 350hp shunter No D3095, which top-and-tailed the train with No 34094 back into Wolverhampton as it

had to set back more than once to get away. The 'West Country' then took the train on to Crewe, with 'Black Five' No 45340 taking the train into the works yard. *Mortehoe*, which for reasons now largely forgotten was always my least-favourite Bulleid Pacific, bringing a groan every time I found it at the head of a train on which I was travelling, was double-headed by B1 4-6-0 No 61409 from Crewe to Derby Friargate and Nottingham Victoria. From there the train was entrusted, and I would even have said at the time, unwisely, to No 34094 alone. We travelled via the Great Central main line, but only as far as Aylesbury. After having crawled along, with us constantly looking at our watches and thinking of the last train home from Waterloo, we eventually came to a dead stop at Aylesbury station, which was, as far as we were concerned, the 'middle of nowhere'...

We then became aware we were all being turned off the train as it was not going any further. On checking we found the tender devoid of coal apart from a few lumps being kept for the loco's return to shed. We were able to board a service DMU to Marylebone, arriving there at about 12.40am, the Bulleid having shot past us while en route, much to our surprise. We spent the night huddled in the compartment of a 4-SUB at Waterloo, awaiting the first train home in the morning.

I am indebted to the Six Bells Junction website's Railtour Files for filling in some of the details of this outing, which perhaps because of the lack of photos as an *aide-memoire*, is far more vague in my mind than any other such trip – apart from that arrival at Aylesbury which I recall vividly. Also, the fact that we had a 'Gronk', on the back at Wolverhampton, is something I only learnt while researching for this book, nearly 50 years after the event! The wonders of the Internet.

> A trainload of railway enthusiasts will visit Crewe engine works on Sunday in a train that will follow the former Great Central main line. 10·2·63

➔ Few railtours make the national press, but this one did, before and after the event. Apparently, there were more than 1,000 applications for the 600 seats, so were a lot of disappointed people that day.

2nd - HALF WAY EXCURSION
JUVENILE UNDER 16
10th FEBRUARY, 1963
Home Counties Railway Society
London (Marylebone) to
CREWE WORKS AND BACK
Outward via Northolt Junction, Banbury, Wolverhampton (High Level) & Stafford
Return via Stoke, Eggington Junction, Nottingham (Victoria) & Harrow-on-the-Hill
(M) For conditions see over   Fare £0

SIX-HUNDRED steamed-up train lovers returned dejected to Marylebone early to-day after a humiliating pilgrimage to the great Crewe engine works.
Their train — specially chartered from British Railways—arrived 85 minutes late and then ran out of coal at Aylesbury. The loco-lovers finally got back three hours late—and pulled by a diesel! Said one sad tripper: "It's the end for any self-respecting steam train lover." 11·2·63

Home Counties Railway Society 'Doncaster Special' 9 JUNE 1963

➔ This trip not only provided the opportunity to visit Doncaster Works, but the motive power all the way there and back from King's Cross was 'Princess Coronation' Tender Pacific No 46245 *City of London* in BR maroon livery. This magnificent engine is seen at Doncaster station prior to the return.

The change of motive power from that advertised in the April 1963 issue of *Modern Railway* was explained on the passenger information sheet with the following comment.

'The Motive Power will NOT be as advertised, due entirely to British Railways complete lack of co-operation inter regionally. After over four months of negotiations, the excuse given by Eastern Region was that Western Region Locomotives were "out of guage" [sic] (cylinder width clearances) despite the fact that they ran over the route we wanted in 1928 (Pendennis Castle) then again in 1948 (King Henry VI). After this disappointment we nearly cancelled this 'Special' but at the last minute British Railways Eastern Region agreed to let an Ex L.M.S. "Princess Coronation" Class Locomotive haul the train.'

No doubt among other passengers, I did not share the 'disappointment' of having a 'Castle' replaced by a 'Duchess', not that I have anything against one of the GWR's finest engines. On the return it was obvious a very high speed was reached when descending Stoke Bank and those with stopwatches were making some exciting claims. The actual speed does not appear to have been confirmed but I feel pretty certain that it would have been the highest speed I was ever hauled by a steam loco, and certainly in excess of 100mph.

2

SUNDAY 9th JUNE 1963

Schedule time.	OUTWARD Actual time.	Distance in miles.	Location	RETURN Schedule time.	Actual time.
9–20 am	9.21	0.00	KINGS CROSS	7.51 pm.	7.56
9–41 "	9.48	12.75	Potters Bar	7.26 "	7.32
9–47 "	9.54	17.25	Hatfield	7.21 "	7.24
10.01 "	10.10	32.00	Hitchin	7–07 "	7.12
10.50 "	10.30	43.00	Sandy	6.43 "	6.48
11.06 "	11.00	58.75	Huntingdon Nth	6.18 "	6.35
11.11 "	11.30	76.25	Peterborough "	6.00 "	6.10
11.20 "	11.45	80.00	Werrington Tghs.	5.56 "	6.06
11.33 "	11.58	98.50	Essendine	5.48 "	5.58
11.38 "	12.07	100.00	Stoke	5.38 "	5.40
11.42 "	12.11	105.25	Grantham	5.32 "	5.33
11.53 "	12.20	109.25	Barkston S.Jct.	5.28 "	5.27
12.13 pm	12.46	120.00	NEWARK Northgate	5.15 "	5.15
12.35 "	1.08	138.50	Retford	4.55 "	4.55
		156.00	DONCASTER	4.32 "	4.32

Home Counties Railway Society 'Third Swindon Special' 8 DECEMBER 1963

The destination and motive power made this trip irresistible: Swindon Works with haulage by a BR Class 6MT 'Clan' class 4-6-2. These ten former Scottish Region Pacifics were very rare birds for those of us living in deepest Surrey. Only a few years ago I had a telephone call from one of my friends on that trip. He asked: 'Have I been dreaming, or did we really have a 'Clan' haul us to Swindon Works one time?'

Overleaf is a photo to prove he was not dreaming. We had gone on the first Home Counties trip to Swindon on 9 October (not on the first of the month, as HCRS always subsequently published for some reason), when it was with BR's last steam loco, No 92220 *Evening Star*. Unfortunately we did not go on the second Swindon trip on 24 June 1962, which was behind No 30850 *Lord Nelson*, and I have no record of ever being hauled by a member of that class. That first railtour was on a very murky day, but the 1963 Swindon tour was run in even worse weather as most of the way there and back was in thick fog.

HOME COUNTIES RAILWAY SOCIETY

Paddington/Swindon 8th December 1963

The Motive Power is:—B.R. Standard "CLAN" Class No. 72006 "CLAN MACKENZIE"

The above train has been timed to run as follows:—

Mileage	Location		Booked time	Actual time	Remarks
			a.m.		
0.00	Paddington	Depart	10.40	10.40	
1.25	Westbourne Park	Pass	10.44	10.48	
5.25	Ealing Brdwy.	"	10.49	10.52	
9.00	Southall	"	10.53	10.57	
13.25	West Drayton	"	10.58	11.04½	
18.50	Slough	"	11.03	11.15	
21.00	Burnham	"	11.06	11.13	
22.50	Taplow	"	11.07	11.15	
24.50	Maidenhead	"	11.09	11.34	
31.00	Twyford	"	11.17	11.35	
36.00	Reading Gen.	"	11.22	11.41	
41.50	Pangbourne	"	11.28	11.46	
48.50	Cholsey & Moulsford	"	11.35	11.52	
53.25	Didcot	"	11.42	11.58	
56.50	Steventon	"	11.46	12.01	
60.50	Wantage Road***	"	11.50	12.05	
66.50	Uffington	"	11.56	12.11	
			p.m.		
71.50	Shrivenham	"	12.02	12.16	
77.50	Swindon Jct.	"	12.13	12.24	
78.50	Swindon Works Yard	Arrive	12.25	12.35	

Mileage	SWINDON WORKS — PADDINGTON		Booked time	Actual time	Remarks
0.00	Swindon Works Yard	Depart	3.40	3.40	
1.00	Swindon Jct.	Pass	3.52	3.48	
7.00	Shrivenham	"	4.00	4.00	
12.00	Uffington	"	4.07	4.06	
18.00	Wantage Road***	"	4.13	4.11½	
22.00	Steventon	"	4.18	4.15½	
25.25	Didcot	" ML.	4.22	4.19	
30.00	Cholsey & Moulsford	"	4.28	4.23½	
37.00	Pangbourne	"	4.34	4.30	
42.50	Reading Gen.	" RL	4.42	4.37	
47.50	Twyford	"	4.46	4.43	
53.00	Maidenhead	" ML.	5.01		
55.00	Taplow	"	5.03	4.50	
56.50	Burnham	"	5.05	4.52	
59.00	Slough	"	5.07	4.54	
64.25	West Drayton	"	5.11	5.06	
68.50	Southall	"	5.16	5.10½	
72.25	Ealing Brdwy.	"	5.20	5.14	
78.50	Paddington	Arrive	5.30	5.24	

ABBREVIATIONS:— ML. Main Line. RL. Relief Line.
*** SHANNON is preserved on the westbound platform. This tiny 0-4-0 Tank engine was built for the Bedfordshire Railway in 1857 and acquired by the Wantage tramway in 1878. This line opened in October 1875 but closed to passenger traffic in July 1925 and it remained open to Goods until December 1945. Then "Shannon" was removed to its place of honour on the platform.

An atmospheric view which proves it was not a dream, albeit dreamlike, of BR Standard 6MT class 4-6-2 No 72006 *Clan Mackenzie* at Swindon shed and works in the fog on 8 December 1963. The train was worked right into the works yard where the 'Clan', surely making the first visit of the type there, ran round, was turned and serviced ready for the return run. The misty conditions added to the mystique of the occasion.

Guildford to Horsham line closure 12 JUNE 1965

Most of the last trains I went on were in fact specials organised by railtour clubs, and not the actual service trains. The exception was the Southern steam-worked line between Guildford and Horsham (but see also Chapter 4 for the last day of Isle of Wight steam). The section being closed was from Guildford to Christ's Hospital, with an official date of 14 June 1965, but it was the 12th that was regarded by passengers as the final day, there being an almost carnival atmosphere along the line. Footplate rides on Ivatt 2-6-2T No 41287 were freely available, for at least parts of the journey, and we each took it in turn to join the footplate crew.

→ Christ's Hospital 'A' signalbox, viewed from the footplate of Ivatt 2-6-2T No 41287 on the last day of services between Guildford and Horsham, 12 June 1965.

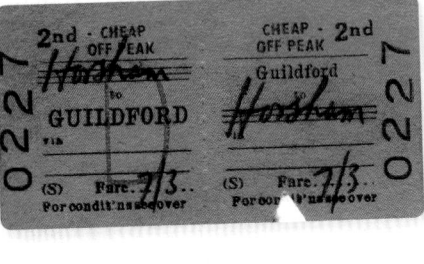

← Presumably stocks of tickets from one end of the line to the other had been exhausted as the closure date approached, and it was not prudent to have ordered more. So it was a hand-written ticket I was issued with at Guildford for Horsham on the last day of service, 12 June 1965. As the 7s 3d (36p) in effect included a 'footplate pass' for part of the journey, it was good value.

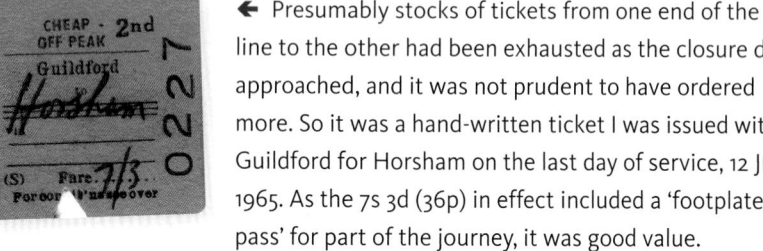

→ No 41287 on the last day of Horsham services is watered up at Guildford station. The gentleman on the right, holding up the water column, is someone I did not know at that time, but got to know well a year or so later when I became involved with the narrow gauge Brockham Museum near Dorking. He was the 'CME' and is the well-known Southern railwayman and author, A W 'Tony' Deller.

Epsom Railway Society 'Midland Enterprise' 3 APRIL 1966

This was one of several railtours organised by our locally based Epsom Railway Society. It was another occasion where the organiser states their disappointment with BR: 'British Rail have let us down! At the last moment, having been promised one, we were told that there were no Buffet Cars available for our use.' It then stated the ERS was running its own buffet service manned by society members and, 'We hope, also, to demonstrate that we are at least as efficient as British Rail in catering – and considerably cheaper as well!'

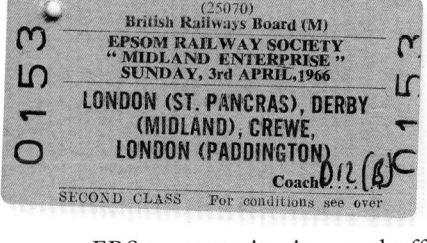

One of the three organisers of ERS railtours was young Adrian Shooter, who went on to carve himself

↓ The steam section of the ERS Crewe and Derby trip was worked by 'Britannia' No 70012 *John of Gaunt* of 5B Crewe South shed. It is seen ready to back on to our train at Crewe station for the return to London, running as far as Banbury where Brush Type 4 No D1701 took the train on to Paddington.

'something' of a career in the railways, notably as head of Chiltern Railways. This train was to take us to both Crewe and Derby Works. It was worked from St Pancras to Crewe by BR Sulzer Type 4 'Peak' No D100 *Sherwood Forester*. I could never have imagined then that this fairly new diesel loco would one day be acquired for preservation, as No 45060, by my good friend Michael Jacob of the Pioneer Diesel Locomotive Group. While I kept to owning things like 2ft gauge Lister petrol locos, Michael moved up in scale.

RCTS 'Longmoor Rail Tour' 16 APRIL 1966

This was a fairly short-distance railtour, just over 121 miles, but a very interesting and unusual one. The freight-only Bentley to Bordon branch had closed completely on 4 April 1966 and from that date traffic to and from the Longmoor Military Railway went via Liss. The military authorities kindly agreed to a last through railtour over the LMR, including the Hollywater Loop.

The train departed from Waterloo behind a pair of soon-to-be withdrawn Maunsell Moguls. From Woking, motive power was, uniquely, the LMR's 'Austerity' 2-10-0 No 600 *Gordon*, running via Guildford and Haslemere to Liss. It must have been a first for this loco to run with a passenger train on the national network.

To accommodate everyone from the main train, and to provide photo opportunities, a train was run twice from Longmoor Downs, around the Hollywater Loop with LMR stock. This comprised two ex-SECR 'birdcage' brake coaches, a GWR coach, and two brake vans hauled by Austerity 0-6-0ST No 196 (carrying fictitious BR number 68011 on the smokebox).

The main train then continued, top-and-tailed on the LMR with Austerity 0-6-0ST No

195, from Liss to Longmoor Downs and Bordon. It then ran on the recently closed line to Bentley, and worked via Aldershot, Frimley Junction, Camberley, Ascot, Virginia Water and Staines to Staines Loop behind the big blue engine. From there to Windsor & Eton Riverside we had No 77014, one of the 20 BR Standard Class 3 2-6-0s, which in itself was a rarity so far south. The two Maunsell Moguls took over again for the return to Waterloo.

This excursion proved so popular that it was run again on 30 April, but the first and last sections out and back into Waterloo were by Maunsell U

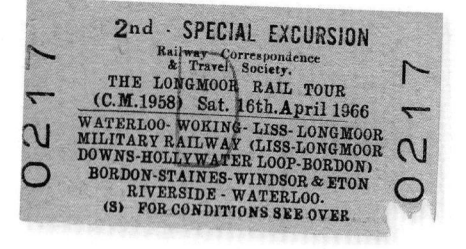

class Moguls Nos 31791 and 31639 instead of N class No 31411 and U class No 31639, as the N had been withdrawn during those two weeks, and no others of the class were fit to run. BR Standard Class 5 4-6-0 No 73114 *Etarre* ran in place of the Class 3, which was not passed for use that day either.

← Another dull wet day out as N class 2-6-0 No 31411, with U class No 31639 behind, wait to leave Waterloo on 16 April 1966 with the 'Longmoor Rail Tour'. The two Maunsell Moguls took the train to Woking where it was handed over to LMR 2-10-0 No 600 *Gordon*. Just a few weeks later, on 5 June, the last of the Maunsell Moguls, which had been such a mainstay of the Southern for so long, were all withdrawn, the last being U class Nos 31639 and 31791, and N class Nos 31405 and 31408.

Fortunately, thanks to Woodham Bros, Barry, we still have five examples of this classic design: U class Nos 31618 and 31638 in the care of the Maunsell Locomotive Society on the Bluebell Railway, and Nos 31625 and 31806, and N class No 31874 on the Mid-Hants Railway.

↘ The Riddles-designed 'Austerity' 2-10-0 was built by the North British Locomotive Co for British Army use overseas during the Second World War. After the war, 25 of the 150 built passed into BR stock as Class WD, but none of these survive in preservation, the Longmoor Military Railway's No 600 *Gordon* never being owned by a main line railway company. However, it made a very rare outing on BR metals with a passenger train when it worked the RCTS's railtour on 16 April 1966. It is seen in Woking station waiting to run round and couple up to the train destined for the LMR via Liss.

This loco is still owned by the

Ministry of Defence and is on long-term loan to the Severn Valley Railway where it is on static display. Two other 'Austerity' 2-10-0s and one 2-8-0 have been repatriated from overseas for preservation in England.

↑ As I was not travelling on the A2 railtour I was able to photograph No 60532 *Blue Peter* approaching Surbiton station on its way down to Exeter. This loco was withdrawn on 31 December 1966 and placed in store until purchased for preservation in 1968 by Geoff Drury. A return to the main line did not take place until 1992, and today it is in Barrow Hill roundhouse while finance is being raised for a further restoration.

LCGB A2 'Commemorative Railtour'

14 AUGUST 1966

Many rare and unusual loco workings could be seen during this time thanks to some imaginative rostering for railtours. A good example was the LCGB's 14 August 1966 train which saw a Peppercorn A2 class 4-6-2 running on the Southern and Western regions. Still in BR stock, No 60532 *Blue Peter* worked the train from Waterloo to Exeter Central via Yeovil Junction, returning to Westbury via Taunton and Castle Cary. The final leg, from Westbury to Waterloo via Salisbury and Basingstoke, was behind 'Britannia' No 70004 *William Shakespeare*, one of the two former SR 'Golden Arrow' members of the class.

On checking my notes, wondering why I had not seen or photographed the 'Brit' on the way back to London, I see that after stopping at Surbiton to see the A2 in the morning, I continued my journey by bike to Heathrow Airport for a day's aircraft spotting. (That's what I would now call a misspent youth.)

LCGB 'Isle of Wight Steam Farewell Rail Tour' 31 DECEMBER 1966

This was definitely a 'last train' rather than an excuse to engage exotic motive power over an unusual route. It was a very sad day for me to witness the last steam workings on the Isle of Wight. (See Chapter 4.)

The outward journey from Waterloo was behind BR Standard Class 5 4-6-0s Nos 73065 and 73043 which took the train down to Portsmouth Harbour. The Solent crossing, each way, was on board MV *Southsea* and haulage on the island was by Class O2 0-4-4Ts Nos W24 *Calbourne* and W31 *Chale*. The train travelled from Ryde Esplanade only as far as Shanklin, where the locos ran round for the return. Motive power from Portsmouth Harbour back to Waterloo was in the hands of rebuilt 'West Country' No 34013 *Okehampton*.

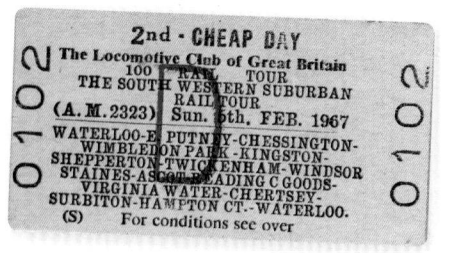

← BR Standard Class 5 4-6-0 No 73065, with No 73043 behind, are seen on arrival at Portsmouth Harbour on the last day of 1966 with the LCGB's 'Isle of Wight Steam Farewell Rail Tour'.

LCGB 'South Western Suburban Rail Tour' SPL 100 5 FEBRUARY 1967

This was only a 147-mile journey and the destinations were none too exotic, but no fewer than six locos with nine changes during the day made this an interesting tour of Southern lines.

This was the 100th railtour organised by the LCGB and a commemorative booklet was issued, detailing them all from No 1 on 6 September 1953 to the Wye Valley, through to and including the basic itinerary for the day of SPL 100.

The roster for the day was:

77014 Waterloo–Clapham Junction–Point Pleasant Junction–East Putney–Wimbledon–Raynes Park–Motspur Park–Chessington South (run-round)–Wimbledon–Wimbledon Park.

80145 Wimbledon Park–Wimbledon–Raynes Park–Kingston–Fulwell Junction–Shepperton.

34100 *Appledore* Shepperton–Fulwell Junction–Twickenham.

77014 Twickenham–Feltham–Staines–Windsor & Eton Riverside.

34100 *Appledore* Windsor & Eton Riverside–Staines–Staines Loop.

76033 Staines Loop–Staines–Ascot–Reading Spur–Reading General.

76058 Reading General–Southcote Junction–Reading Central Goods (run-round)–Southcote Junction–Reading General–Ascot–Virginia Water.

34077 *603 Squadron* (replacing No 34100 which had run a hot box on the tender) Virginia Water–Weybridge–Surbiton.

77014 Surbiton–Hampton Court.

34077 *603 Squadron* Hampton Court–Hampton Court Junction–Wimbledon–Clapham Junction–Waterloo.

The First Hundred

SPL 100

Rail Tours 1953 - 1967

THE LOCOMOTIVE CLUB OF GREAT BRITAIN

→ This was a rare loco that became a common sight on the Southern Region in latter days, it being No 77014, one of the 20 BR Standard Class 3 2-6-0s built at Swindon in 1954. These were used exclusively in the North East and Scotland initially, but this example was transferred to Guildford shed in March 1966. It came down from LMR Northwich shed and saw a lot of use until withdrawn at the end of Southern steam in July 1967 and was used on several railtours.

It is seen at Windsor & Eton Riverside having just come off SPL 100. This is believed to have been the last class on BR to have remained intact, until No 77001 was withdrawn in January 1966, but none survived into preservation. The chimney of No 77014 still exists though, and is to be fitted on new-build Class 3 2-6-2T No 82045 at the Severn Valley Railway.

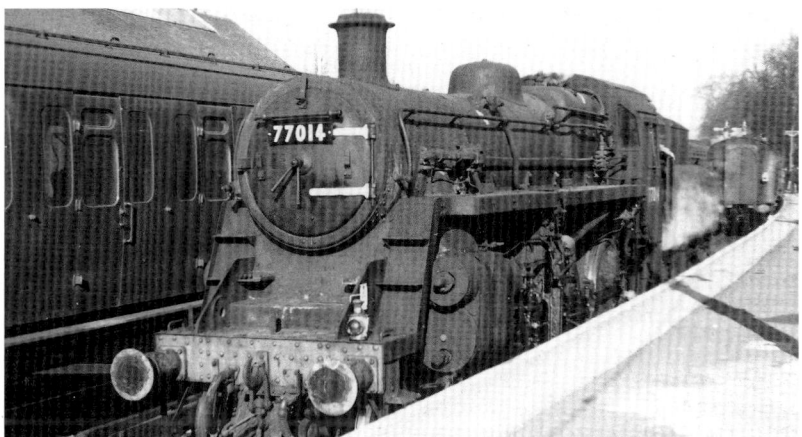

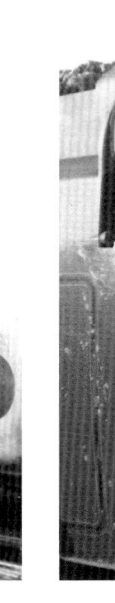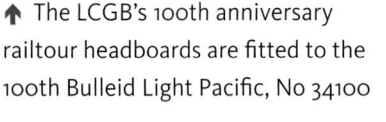

↓ BR Standard Class 4MT 2-6-0 No 76058 runs round at Reading Central Goods after the train's sixth change of engine, in order to take the LCGB's 100th train on to Virginia Water.

↑ The LCGB's 100th anniversary railtour headboards are fitted to the 100th Bulleid Light Pacific, No 34100

Appledore, at Shepperton on the LCGB's 'South Western Suburban Rail Tour' on 5 February 1967.

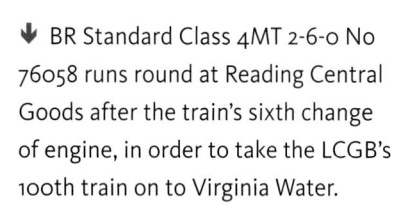

LCGB 'Surrey Downsman Rail Tour',

5 MARCH 1967

A Surrey and South London trip on which I did not travel, but went out to see passing at a few places. It left Waterloo behind rebuilt Bulleid Pacific No 34087 *145 Squadron* and ran all the way to Clapham Junction station (less than four miles from Waterloo), but went via Clapham Junction, Twickenham, Feltham Junction, Virginia Water, Weybridge, Hampton Court Junction, Wimbledon, East Putney, Weybridge and Point Pleasant Junction, a distance of 45 miles.

The train reached many points of the Southern in the South East, with engine changes at Oxted, Norwood Junction, Kensington (Olympia), Tulse Hill and London Bridge. These were, in order: Nos 34087, 34102 *Lapford*, 75077, 34087, 75077, 34102 and 75077, covering a total of 171 miles, without a destination as such. Great fun though, and probably something only an enthusiast would understand.

↓ Rebuilt 'Battle of Britain' No 34087 *145 Squadron* arrives at Clapham Junction with the first leg of the 'Surrey Downsman Rail Tour' having made a journey of less than four miles into a 45-mile one. When at school, I could never remember things like poetry or the words to hymns, but could easily recite all 140 Bulleid Pacific names and numbers – except for those squadrons!

← Waiting to take over the 'Surrey Downsman' at Clapham Junction on 5 March 1967 was original-condition (I have never accepted that dreadful 'unrebuilt' expression) 'West Country' No 34102 *Lapford*, by now minus its nameplates.

↙ The highlight of the day spent observing the 'Surrey Downsman' at various locations was, for me, the fourth leg, behind No 34087 again, when it passed through my local station of Ewell West at about 14.55. I only recall three other occasions of seeing steam at this station and this one was storming through much faster than anything else I ever saw there. It burst under the footbridge I had used literally hundreds of times when travelling to the Capital. This part of the railtour was running from Norwood Junction to Kensington (Olympia) so was obviously on a rather circuitous route, as it had been all day, as Ewell West is on the Epsom to Waterloo line. However, at this point, it was only about four minutes late, which was pretty good time-keeping for such a complex journey with numerous engine changes.

Locomotive Preservation (Sussex) Ltd, 'The Marquess Goes South South West' 12 MARCH 1967

This train was run to give the privately preserved ex-LNER K4 class 2-6-0 No 3442 (61994) *The Great Marquess* the opportunity to be seen in territory alien to the type. The class had spent its working life mainly on the West Highland Line between Inverness and the Kyle of Lochalsh. For the sections of this train covered by the Mogul see Chapter 10, but here are those worked by BR Standard 2-6-4T No 80151. Other sections, such as Chichester to Lavant and back, saw 'Crompton' diesel haulage (No D6544), for which the organisers apologised.

↑ The empty stock for *The Great Marquess* special on 12 March 1967 was brought into London Victoria station by BR Standard Class 5 4-6-0 No 73037 of 70A Nine Elms.

↓ The Standard tank took the train from Southampton to Brockenhurst, and then down the Lymington Pier branch, where it ran round. The weather was not getting any better.

↑ BR Standard Class 4MT 2-6-4T No 80151 took over the train from No 3442 at Southampton Central where it is seen 'dolled up' for the occasion. This is one of 15 members of the class that have survived into preservation, and is now based on the Bluebell Railway.

Southern Counties Touring Society 'Southern Rambler 19 MARCH 1967

Another circuitous route of Southern lines, this time on the Central Section, working out from and returning to Victoria, this being billed as the 'last steam train to Brighton and Eastbourne'. The booked loco was No 34089 *602 Squadron* but this was declared a failure and a very grubby No 34108 *Wincanton* was a last-minute substitute. This loco worked the train all day except for when 'ED' No E6016 took the train from the photographic stop at Selsdon on to East Croydon, and 350hp 0-6-0DE shunter No D3219, which headed the train from Brighton Upper Goods into the station while the Bulleid went off to turn on Hove triangle.

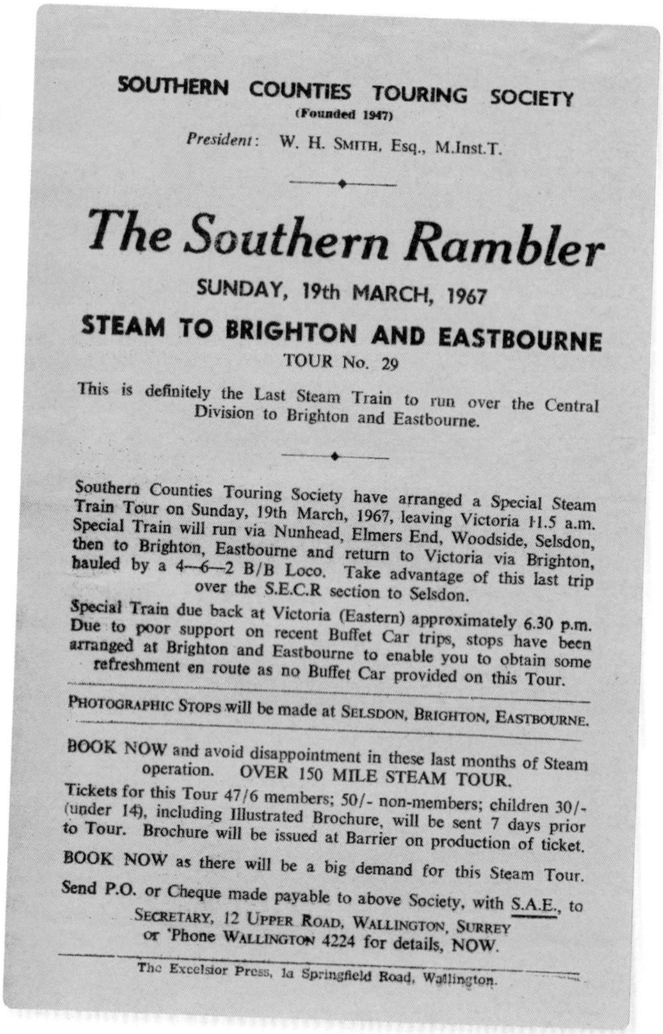

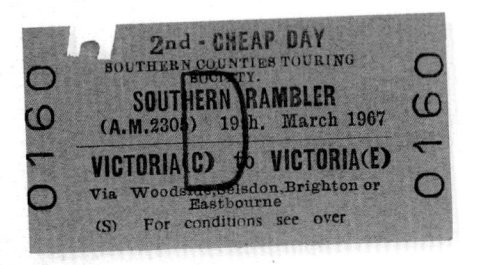

↓ A photo stop at Selsdon provided the opportunity to see rebuilt 'West Country' No 34108 *Wincanton* running round, it being replaced by the electro-diesel as far as East Croydon, where the Bulleid took the train on to Brighton. The presence of conductor rails did not appear to pose a problem to photographers as they seemed to realise these were something best avoided.

SOUTHERN COUNTIES TOURING SOCIETY
(Founded 1947)

President : W. H. SMITH, Esq., M.Inst.T.

The Southern Rambler
SUNDAY, 19th MARCH, 1967
STEAM TO BRIGHTON AND EASTBOURNE
TOUR No. 29

This is definitely the Last Steam Train to run over the Central Division to Brighton and Eastbourne.

Southern Counties Touring Society have arranged a Special Steam Train Tour on Sunday, 19th March, 1967, leaving Victoria 11.5 a.m. Special Train will run via Nunhead, Elmers End, Woodside, Selsdon, then to Brighton, Eastbourne and return to Victoria via Brighton, hauled by a 4—6—2 B/B Loco. Take advantage of this last trip over the S.E.C.R section to Selsdon.

Special Train due back at Victoria (Eastern) approximately 6.30 p.m. Due to poor support on recent Buffet Car trips, stops have been arranged at Brighton and Eastbourne to enable you to obtain some refreshment en route as no Buffet Car provided on this Tour.

PHOTOGRAPHIC STOPS will be made at SELSDON, BRIGHTON, EASTBOURNE.

BOOK NOW and avoid disappointment in these last months of Steam operation.   OVER 150 MILE STEAM TOUR.

Tickets for this Tour 47/6 members; 50/- non-members; children 30/- (under 14), including Illustrated Brochure, will be sent 7 days prior to Tour. Brochure will be issued at Barrier on production of ticket.

BOOK NOW as there will be a big demand for this Steam Tour.

Send P.O. or Cheque made payable to above Society, with S.A.E., to
SECRETARY, 12 UPPER ROAD, WALLINGTON, SURREY
or 'Phone WALLINGTON 4224 for details, NOW.

The Excelsior Press, 1a Springfield Road, Wallington.

⬇ In the typical external condition of the time, No 34108 *Wincanton* pulls forward at Eastbourne to run round, before travelling light engine to Polegate to turn on the triangle via Stonecross Junction and Pevensey & Westham. Arrival back at Victoria was at 17.25, just 13 minutes late, after not too long a day out.

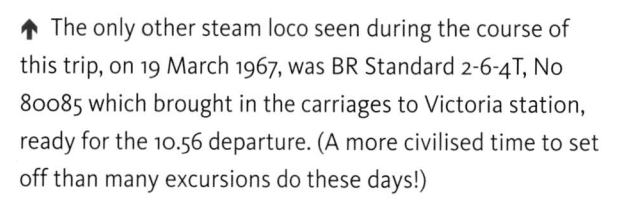

⬆ The only other steam loco seen during the course of this trip, on 19 March 1967, was BR Standard 2-6-4T, No 80085 which brought in the carriages to Victoria station, ready for the 10.56 departure. (A more civilised time to set off than many excursions do these days!)

Epsom Railway Society, the 'Mercian' 16 APRIL 1967

It was advertised as the 'LNER Preservation Tour', but the headboard was the 'Mercian'. This was another special organised by future career railwayman Adrian Shooter and his colleagues G.D.N. Miller and P.G. Thompson. See also Chapters 6 and 10, as it visited a preserved railway (KWVR) and used preserved locos on the main line. These were the two privately preserved LNER locos Nos 3442 and 4472, which were used throughout apart from when 'Black Five' No 45377 piloted the K4 from Stockport Edgeley to Keighley.

⬇ Travelling on a train usually means photography of the locos involved can be quite difficult, apart from during any specific photo or watering stops. In this case, the only opportunity to photograph the sole BR loco used, No 45377, appears to have been during a ten-minute booked stop at Blackburn, which was actually 14 minutes, possibly as a result of trying to get everyone back on the train afterwards. Passengers had more freedom in 1967 than today!

LCGB 'Dorset Coast Express' 7 MAY 1967

This was a particularly memorable railtour, running from London Waterloo to Swanage, Weymouth and Bournemouth. This was my only trip over the Swanage branch in BR days, which is a line I visit regularly now it is a heritage railway. Also, motive power included another subsequent preservation success, 'West Country' class 4-6-2 No 34023 *Blackmore Vale*. I was not alone in remembering this as a notable tour as it was recreated, in part at least, by the Swanage Railway, 30 years later to the day. Resident sister loco No 34072 *257 Squadron* masqueraded as No 34023 and ran two return trips on the Purbeck line, complete with the original headboard, on 7 May 1997. (Gosh, how time flies – even that was now 16 years ago!)

← I must have been quick off the mark in booking this one!

2nd - CHEAP DAY
The Locomotive Club of Great Britain
The Dorset Coast Express Rail Tour
AM3 2413, Sunday, 7th May, 1967

Waterloo-Guildford-Fareham-Southampton
Wareham-Swanage-Wareham-Weymouth-
Bournemouth-Basingstoke-Waterloo

(S) (S)

For conditions see over For conditions see over

← Rebuilt 'West Country' No 34021 *Dartmoor* displays the distinctive 'Dorset Coast Express' headboard at Waterloo prior to the 09.13 departure, running to Wareham via Havant.

⬇ An unrepeatable scene – *Blackmore Vale* at Corfe Castle for a photographic stop en route to Swanage, with the 'Dorset Coast Express' on 7 May 1967. Well, not exactly, as this scene was remarkably well recreated by the Swanage Railway on 7 May 1997 using resident No 34072 *257 Squadron* disguised as No 34023 – déjà vu indeed.

← The real No 34023 *Blackmore Vale* at the Swanage terminus in 1967. Two return runs were made between Wareham and Swanage with a photo stop at Corfe Castle each way. In theory, such a scene could be recreated precisely, as both loco and station are preserved. The loco was later saved by the Bulleid Society and is now based on the Bluebell Railway but awaits funding for a very expensive boiler and firebox overhaul, so its return to steam will be many years hence.

← The 'Dorset Coast Express' was top-and-tailed from Wareham to Swanage and return by No 34023 with BR Standard Class 4MT 2-6-0 No 76026 on the first run. The Mogul is seen waiting to head the train back from the seaside terminus, running tender first.

This was to be my last railtour behind BR Southern Region steam. The next trip was exploratory for me, the LCGB's 'Calais–Lille Rail Tour' on 14 May 1967, but I found that all the locos were, well, 'foreign'. At least it made me realise why I had become so enthusiastic about *British* steam locos – they look so good – and also, that my interest was in Britain's railways as a whole, not just steam engines. It is the fascinating history of the lines, the iconic railway companies of the past, the people who built the railways and designed the

locos and rolling stock, the wonderful architecture, the infrastructure, the workshops and the huge variety of rolling stock that I had studied since early childhood which all means so much to me.

I did go on one more Southern Region tour in BR steam days, on 4 June, but this was worked by a former Eastern Region engine that had found a new life beyond its BR career. This was A4 Pacific No 4498 *Sir Nigel Gresley* which took the train from London Waterloo to Weymouth and return. Being a preserved loco, this train is covered in Chapter 10.

↓ BR Standard tank No 80011 ready to depart Corfe Castle for the last time on 7 May 1967, returning the train to Wareham from where it proceeded to Weymouth behind No 34023.

↓ The second run over the Swanage branch by the Dorset Coast Express saw the Mogul replaced by BR Standard Class 4MT 2-6-4T No 80011. It is seen here at Wareham before the train made its return to Swanage.

CHAPTER 9

BARRY AND OTHER SCRAPYARDS

The end for some, a new
beginning for others

WHEN TRACKING DOWN locos, having to go and see them awaiting their fate in a scrapyard is usually the last resort. Traditionally, locomotives have been scrapped on the railways' own premises, at sheds or main works. This was invariably after the loco had been stored out of use in a shed yard or at the back of the works, often for quite some while following withdrawal, before the final decision was made.

As the number of steam locomotives being disposed of by BR increased dramatically in the 1960s it became necessary to sell them to private scrap merchants to clear them out of the way fast enough. They were sold by competitive tender, which meant many private breakers became involved, some taking just a handful of locos, while others 'processed' many hundreds. In most cases, once the loco had entered the yard it was soon dealt with, reduced to a pile of components within a

few days, ready for sending off to a steelworks for melting down.

Therefore, once a loco had left BR's tracks there was not much time to go and see it as it would soon be gone. This was not always the case, and some engines were allowed to linger on death row for weeks, months and at one yard in particular, for years and even decades!

J BUTTIGIEG, NEWPORT

Bulleid Pacifics a speciality – first and last – was a claim that could be made for this yard which broke up many locomotives between 1960 and 1968. My visit was on 2 July 1967 and there were certainly no locos I had not seen before, but I was interested to see some old friends for the last time. They had already despatched six 'Merchant Navys', but many of the 18 Light Pacifics they dealt with were still present, awaiting the chop. This included the first 'West Country' to have been rebuilt, but I didn't know that day that the last Bulleid Pacific to be lost was also one of those seen and photographed.

← Bulleids as far as the eye can see. Nearest the camera is rebuilt 'West Country' No 34032 *Camelford* with No 34005 behind. No 34032 was withdrawn in October 1966 and broken up here in October 1967.

➜ 'West Country' class No 34005 *Barnstaple* was the first Bulleid Light Pacific to be rebuilt, emerging from Eastleigh Works in its new guise in June 1957. Withdrawn in October 1966 after just nine years' work, it was broken up in October 1967. To the left is No 34009 *Lyme Regis*.

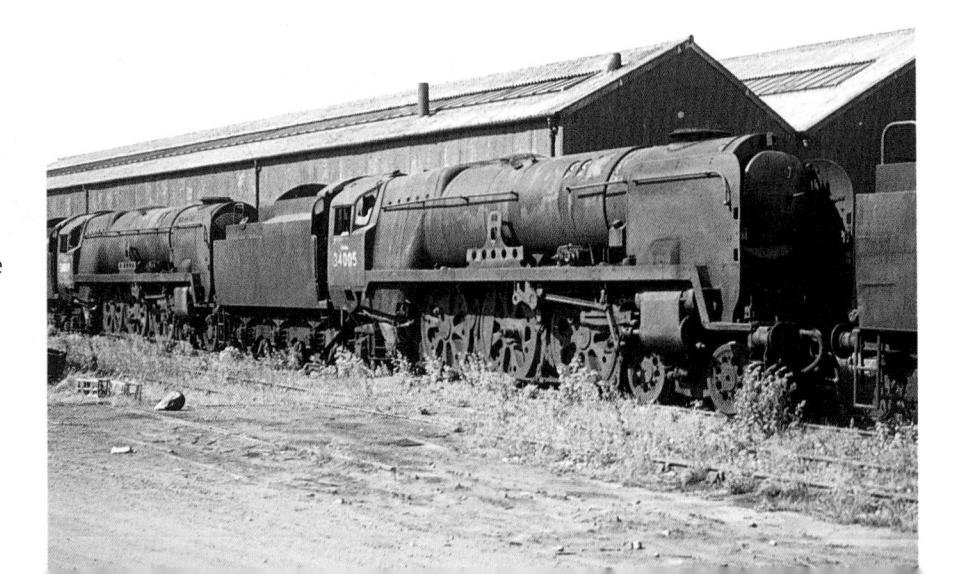

→ Rebuilt 'West Country' No 34017 *Ilfracombe* has the dubious distinction of having been the last Bulleid Pacific to be cut up, anywhere. Withdrawn in October 1966, it was not broken up at Buttigieg's until December 1968. No Bulleids have succumbed since, the two which did not survive at Barry were the 'dreaded' No 34094 *Mortehoe* (see Chapter 8), which was finally laid to rest in January 1965, and No 34045 *Ottery St. Mary*, scrapped in March 1965. Also, the National Railway Museum later carried out a partial cutting-up job of 'Merchant Navy' No 35029 *Ellerman Lines* to show the public the internals of an atypical steam loco.

JOHN CASHMORE, NEWPORT

Cashmore's was probably the biggest of the private yards to break up main line locos, with premises in Great Bridge, Tipton, Staffordshire and at Newport, which was then in Monmouthshire but was not classified as being in Wales until the Local Government Act of 1972. The Newport yard was on the site of the old Western Dry Dock and claimed the lives of more than 1,000 steam engines between April 1959 and 1969.

Locos entering this yard were soon dealt with and components piled up awaiting final disposal, creating some iconic scenes of steam loco destruction in the late 1960s. These views date from my visit on 2 July 1967.

← BR Class 3MT 2-6-2T No 82031 awaited the torch at Cashmore's along with Nos 82003 and 82034, the last BR Standard tanks to be withdrawn. This is a type of which none of the 45 examples built from 1952 to 1955 was to survive, but a new-build, to be No 82045, is taking shape at the Severn Valley Railway.

→ ↗ A couple of views showing piles of loco parts at Cashmore's, including complete smokebox sections and cylinder blocks in Cashmore's Newport yard, July 1967.

↓ Fireboxes are lined up at Cashmore's awaiting further dismantling.

↑ The smokebox and chimney of BR Standard Class 5MT 4-6-0 No 73087 *Linette*, no doubt to be unceremoniously chucked on the heap a few moments later in the Newport yard.

← Fairburn 2-6-4T No 42102, built by BR at Brighton in 1950, has little time left before being reduced to a pile of mangled parts at Cashmore's.

→ One of the distinctive Southern Railway USA class 0-6-0Ts, its time soon to be up at Cashmore's. Numbered DS234 in departmental stock like five others of the type, it was previously SR No 62/BR No 30062. Acquired after the Second World War for shunting in Southampton Docks, it later found further use at BR's Meldon Quarry, following replacement by Class 07 Ruston & Hornsby 0-6-0DE dock shunters.

G COHEN LTD (600 GROUP), COBURN WORKS, KETTERING

Located on the site of the former Cransley Iron Works, Cohen was part of the 600 Group which broke up hundreds of locos in different yards, from South Wales to the North East.

← Among the first locos dealt with at Kettering was 'Schools' class 4-4-0 No 30935 *Sevenoaks*, which was part of a consignment of Southern engines purchased. It was one of three members of the class to meet their end in this Midlands yard and it is seen awaiting the torch, on 14 June 1964. The other two were Nos 30902 *Wellington* and 30921 *Shrewsbury*.

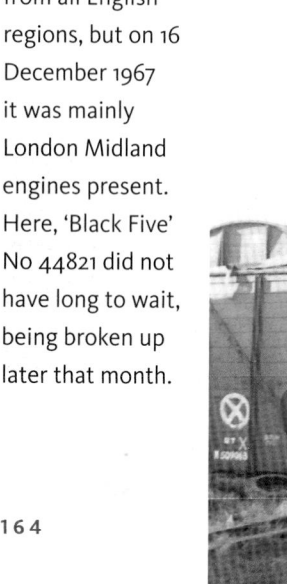

→ Cohen's took in locos from all English regions, but on 16 December 1967 it was mainly London Midland engines present. Here, 'Black Five' No 44821 did not have long to wait, being broken up later that month.

WOODHAM BROS, BARRY

The most famous of them all, and a story that does not need retelling in detail here. My first visit was virtually by chance, while on a London Railfans' Club bash of South Wales sheds in January 1964. We knew there were a good number of stored locos at Barry, but found they were not at the shed itself but a few hundred yards away, mainly in a long line in one of the dockyard sidings. My notes and photo records of the time do not even record the site as being Woodham Bros.

This was a sunny Sunday afternoon and to this day, I remember the sound of distant church bells ringing as we walked along the line of ex-GWR tank engines, trying to identify them. Many of those there that day were scrapped, while others we thought we were seeing for the last time are well-known engines today.

I was to visit this yard many times later and got to know Dai Woodham well when involved with the extrication of locos in the late 1970s and early 1980s. Many friendships were forged through the Barry connection, not least with the late Robert Adley MP, and Francis Blake whose now-historic letter to *The Railway Magazine* passionately pleaded for more to be done to save these locos. It included the classic words: 'some engines are too young to die, others too old'. From this was founded the Barry Steam Locomotive Action Group which coordinated very many rescues, putting practical people together with those with finances available.

It is hard to imagine what the heritage railway scene would be like today without the 200 locos that survived thanks to Woodham Bros. It would not just mean fewer locomotives to maintain interest in the subject, but also far fewer heritage railways as there simply would not be enough motive power available.

The reasoning behind BSLAG was not just to provide locos for working heritage railways at that time, but to give future generations the opportunity of undertaking the challenge of bringing a steam loco back to life from scrapyard condition. Subsequent restorations, although very important, do not generate quite the same pioneering spirit or feeling of achievement. It was never thought practical or even desirable for all to be restored within the first few years of their departure from the yard.

The fact that there are locos still awaiting restoration is therefore in no way a failing of the group's ambitions, quite the opposite in fact. However, what was not anticipated or foreseen by those involved was the destruction of some of these locos in order to obtain a few small components for incorporation in so-called 'new-build' projects. This would appear to be a short-term, corner-cutting exercise, especially after the A1 Steam Locomotive Trust has shown the way in how a new-build should be undertaken in the 21st century – with all-new parts specially produced for the purpose.

The illustrations here are confined to the period before the official end of steam in August 1968. This, therefore, covers just three visits to the Barry yard, in 1964, 1966 and 1967.

First visit 26 JANUARY 1964

⬇ I have often wondered who the lone spotter was, a fellow member of the London Railfans' Club. Right to left in this row of Prairie tanks and pannier tanks are Nos 4561, 5521, 4566, 5539, 5572, 5538, 5542, 5553, 5552, 5557, 5794, 9468, 7722, 5558, 9462, 5510, 8419 and 9491. The first nine Prairies will be familiar numbers to today's enthusiasts, the others beyond that will not be, as they were among the 84 locos broken up at Barry by Woodham Bros between 1959 and 1980.

↓ A much earlier departure was No 4588, which was the 11th, going to the Dart Valley Railway, Buckfastleigh in November 1970, where it was soon restored. Named *Trojan,* it took up duties on the Paignton–Kingswear branch. This is the only surviving member of the Collett 4575 class numbered in the 4500 series, the other ten all being in the 5500 series. Behind No 4588 is No 5532, now safely on the Llangollen Railway.

↑ GWR Churchward Class 4200 2-8-0T No 4253 was withdrawn in April 1963, and it was the 190th departure from the yard, in August 1987, so it saw many other locos come and go in that time. Here, it still carries its smokebox door and cab side number plates, which it did not have when acquired for preservation. It is only now being restored, a quarter of a century since leaving the yard. Perhaps surprisingly, this is on the Kent & East Sussex Railway, so it is fortunate for them that Terry Rippingale had the foresight to save it when he did.

← One that did not make it, and this was the only time I ever saw this loco, No 9449, a 9400 class 0-6-0PT which was broken up by March 1965. Disposal was still not as quick as in most other yards though, it having arrived in late 1960.

Second visit 2 SEPTEMBER 1966

By now it was obvious that Woodham's was not just another loco graveyard and a special detour was made during the course of our Rail Rover holiday, as described in Chapter 5. However, we still thought it was something we had to see before they were all suddenly broken up. There was even a rumour that they would be shipped complete to South America for breaking up, even though

➜ The scene that greeted us as we approached the yard. Perhaps hard to understand today, but the site was completely open and used by local children as a playground. I refrained from taking photos on several occasions as children were ruining the view by running along the tops of the locos, pulling faces and making un-childlike gestures at me! It was not just the obvious hazard of loose metal parts with sharp edges and a danger of falling off, but asbestos boiler lagging was either still in place on the locos, often exposed to the elements where cladding had come adrift, or was simply piled up in an old box van body when removed. The dangers of this harmless-looking material were so little understood

➜ But for Barry there would be no SR Maunsell Moguls today. Fortunately, five found their way to Woodham's yard and all are now in preservation, on the Bluebell and Mid-Hants railways. Four are U class with 6ft diameter driving wheels and there is just the one N class with 5ft 6in wheels, No 31874. Seen here on 2 September 1966 it was moved to the MHR in March 1974 and hauled the railway's opening train on 30 April 1977. Today, it is in the queue at Ropley, awaiting overhaul again.

Woodham Bros had signed a clause in the purchase contract that locos could not be sold in a complete state. It was to be another year before this clause could be circumvented to allow the sale of the first engine for preservation, which was 4F 0-6-0 No 43924 going to the Keighley & Worth Valley Railway. So this appeared to be the last opportunity of photographing these locos, with many more still to come for which space would be required.

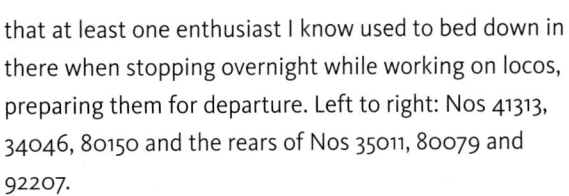

that at least one enthusiast I know used to bed down in there when stopping overnight while working on locos, preparing them for departure. Left to right: Nos 41313, 34046, 80150 and the rears of Nos 35011, 80079 and 92207.

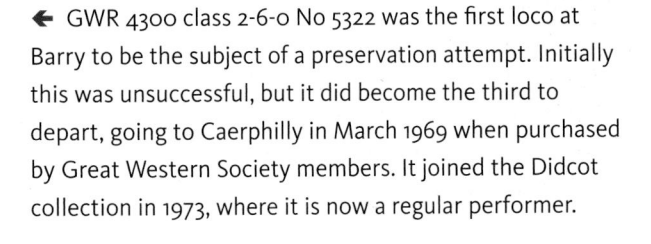

← GWR 4300 class 2-6-0 No 5322 was the first loco at Barry to be the subject of a preservation attempt. Initially this was unsuccessful, but it did become the third to depart, going to Caerphilly in March 1969 when purchased by Great Western Society members. It joined the Didcot collection in 1973, where it is now a regular performer.

Third visit 2 JULY 1967

Well, another year has passed and they're still here, and even more of them! A more leisurely visit to the Woodham Bros' loco emporium this time, but with the locos now so tightly packed together in the main yard there were many that could not be photographed satisfactorily. Here is just a very small selection from that day's visit.

→ Yes, I think we will save this lot... a general view across the West Pond site on 2 July 1967.

← It looks better today – 'air-smoothed' 'Battle of Britain' class No 34070 *Manston*, the last steam loco built by the Southern Railway, in 1947. I well remember meeting the Pryor brothers, Bill and Bob, at the Gravesend model railway exhibition in May 1978 and was impressed by their Manston Preservation Group stand which was raising funds for its purchase, as they had a large-scale cardboard model of a Bulleid Pacific on show. I wonder if that survives? *Manston* left Barry in June 1983, bought by the MPG, going to Kent for restoration. Now owned by Southern Locomotives Ltd, this magnificent locomotive entered service on the Swanage Railway in 2008, 42 years after this photo was taken.

↓ Rebuilt 'Battle of Britain' No 34059 *Sir Archibald Sinclair;* withdrawn in May 1966, arrived at Barry in October, and departed for the Bluebell Railway in October 1979. It entered service following restoration in 2009, but was withdrawn in late 2011 as it requires extensive boiler and firebox repairs, for which funding was being successfully raised at the time of writing in early 2013.

↑ A third of all 'Merchant Navys' built have survived, thanks to Barry. The only one of these not to have served time in the Barry yard was No 35028 *Clan Line,* which was bought direct from BR for preservation. One that has still to return to service is No 35022 *Holland-America Line* which was the 170th of the 213 Barry departures, going to the Swanage Railway in March 1986. Now part of the Jeremy Hosking's collection of locos, it is at Riley's works, Bury, in a dismantled state awaiting restoration.

→ The accumulation of locos spread over a wide area, including the sidings alongside Hood Road, now the site of the Barry Tourist Railway's Waterfront station. I actually remarked when there, jokingly of course: 'Once all these locos have been removed, someone will come up with the bright idea of starting a heritage railway here...'

Leading the roadside line-up in 1967 was BR Standard Class 2 No 78018, now on the Great Central Railway with No 78019. Four members of this once 65-strong class of 2-6-0s survive thanks to their stint at Barry. The other two are Nos 78022 on the KWVR, and 78059 on the Bluebell Railway, in the process of being rebuilt to become No 84030 of the extinct sister class of 2-6-2Ts. With the lack of a tender and the similarity of the basic design this, to me, is a logical and worthwhile project.

↓ One that did not escape. BR Standard 9F class 2-10-0 No 92085 awaits its fate in July 1967. A lull in wagon arrivals in summer 1980 gave Dai Woodham an opportunity to start on loco cutting-up as the workforce had to be kept employed. Also, it was a wake-up call to enthusiasts as sales had been dropping off about that time. He thought this was due to complacency that the locos would all be kept here at his expense, until required sometime in the future.

The locos nearest the cutting-up area of the yard in July 1980 were GWR 2-8-0 No 2807 and 2-8-0T No 4277 and were therefore the first in line to go, when loco cutting recommenced. The author made a special trip to Barry, and over a pub lunch with Mr Woodham, persuaded him to sacrifice the locos on the second row leading to the cutting area first as they were not so historic. When

it was pointed out that 2807 was the oldest loco in the yard and a newly-launched group was actively raising funds for its purchase, that clinched it.

It was not known then how many locos would be lost before more wagons arrived, but in the event, single-chimney No 92085 and GWR 2-6-2T No 4156 were scrapped, although Dai said he thought all in that row would have to go. No 2807 was subsequently purchased by Cotswold Steam Preservation Ltd, becoming the oldest GWR loco in private ownership. No 4277 was also later bought by CSP but had to be sold in order to raise additional funds for the restoration of 2807, which is today, an important member of the Gloucestershire Warwickshire Railway's operational roster.

↑ All the locos at Woodhams could so easily have ended up like this: 9F 2-10-0 No 92085 was one of two locos that were sacrificed in July 1980; the other was GWR 2-6-2T No 4156.

CHAPTER 10

PRESERVED STEAM ON THE MAIN LINE

Privately owned locomotives

before the 'steam ban'

I SUSPECT MANY TODAY look back on railway preservation history, believing that prior to the lifting of the BR 'steam ban' in 1971, A3 class 4-6-2 No 4472 *Flying Scotsman* had been the only privately owned steam loco to have worked on the national network.

For a short while that was the case, following the end of main line steam in August 1968, because owner Alan Pegler had negotiated a contract with BR to run on the national network until 1972. However, in 1969 the loco went on a tour of North America, leaving the UK without any steam locomotives permitted on the main line. This resulted in the formation of the Return to Steam campaign led by a committee of high-profile enthusiasts.

Meanwhile, Peter Prior, managing director of the Bulmer cider company at Hereford, was negotiating with BR to be allowed to run the company's exhibition train of five Pullman cars, to be hauled by GWR 'King' class 4-6-0 No 6000 *King George V.* The company had sponsored the full restoration of this officially preserved loco. BR relented, agreeing to a series of trial excursions being run in October 1971.

These were deemed a success and satisfactory as BR then agreed to further trains, with other privately owned locomotives being run in 1972. This has subsequently grown to today's virtually daily steam operations. The period covered here is that before the end of steam and the introduction of the ban, when many privately owned locos were able to run on BR, an episode perhaps now largely forgotten.

As the last days of steam approached various groups and individuals were determined to secure operational steam locos for the future, but there were next to no preserved railways on which to run them, and those that had opened were relatively short. These lines were more suited to small tank engines rather than running express passenger locos such as 4-6-0s and 4-6-2s. If such engines were to run, as their owners desired, this had to be on the national network. Also, at this time, the infrastructure for operating steam locos was still in place in many parts of the country, although this was being reduced as lines, areas and regions turned exclusively to diesel and electric traction.

There were countless railtours and excursions being run in the 1960s for different reasons (see Chapter 8), but increasingly these were beginning to make use of preserved locos working alongside BR ones. While some were run specifically to showcase the loco by their owners, including No 4498 *Sir Nigel Gresley* by the A4 Locomotive Society and No 3442 *The Great Marquess* by Viscount Garnock, on other occasions the choice of motive power seemed almost incidental to the route and destination of the train. One such was the Epsom Railway Society's tour I booked on to because it was a very cheap and easy way for me in the south to visit the embryonic Keighley & Worth Valley Railway. It was only after I had ordered my ticket that I learnt haulage included Nos 3442 and 4472, so this was something of a bonus!

The photos featured in this chapter were taken in two different situations. There are those where I went out to see the loco in question, finding a suitable lineside spot, and those on which I travelled. There used to be far more photo stops, sometimes with run-pasts and generally more opportunities and freedom to wander around the tracks than for today's main line steam-hauled passengers. They are now kept so isolated from the loco heading their train that I am sometimes puzzled by the appeal of such outings. Neither can they be regarded as a cheap means to get to places by rail as they used to be.

This is a selection of preserved locomotives that ventured on to the main line in the period prior to the BR ban of 1968. It includes officially preserved locos as well as those bought privately from BR. While some locomotives were familiar from their BR operational days, others were certainly not. A prime example of the latter was Caledonian Railway single No 123, which was an exciting 'cop' when it headed as far south as Brighton on the south coast, when working a special to the Bluebell Railway.

CALEDONIAN SINGLE NO 123 AND LSWR GREYHOUND NO 120

The 'Scottish Belle' 15 SEPTEMBER 1963

Caledonian Railway 4-2-2 No 123 was one of the four historic locos returned to steam by BR Scottish Region in 1958. It was designed and built by Scottish loco builders Neilson & Co in 1886 primarily for display at the Edinburgh International Exhibition that year. Always a one-off, it was taken into CR stock, passing to the LMSR and was not withdrawn until 1935. It had become the last single-wheeler in regular operation on Britain's railways, although GNR No 1 was turned out for specials by the LNER in 1938.

Following No 123's return to the main line as a preserved loco, it was withdrawn again in 1965 and placed on static display in the Glasgow Museum of Transport.

The Bluebell Railway's announcement for the train that appeared in *Trains Illustrated* in July 1963 did not mention it by name, but said a train would be running from London Victoria to Sheffield Park on 15 September 1963, departing at 11.15am and returning at 6.30pm and calling at East Croydon. It stated that at 42s 6d (£2.12), the inclusive fare was 'higher than normal for a Bluebell excursion because of the cost of bringing the Caledonian engine from Scotland'.

↑ This ticket is not what it seems, as it is dated 22 September 1963. There was no mention in the announcement of a second train being run, or of one being rescheduled. Perhaps it was printed too far in advance, before the date had been confirmed. Disposal of these tickets was made through the Transport Ticket Society to its members, and it is probably more common than a ticket from the train which did run the weekend before on the 15th.

↓ CR No 123 and LSWR T9 class 4-4-0 No 120 headed the 'Scottish Belle' from London Victoria to Haywards Heath on 15 September 1963. They passed through Balcombe station far faster than I had expected – an amazing and unforgettable sight! The headboard carried was the 'Blue Belle' as used by a number of excursions destined for the Bluebell Railway via Haywards Heath and Ardingly to Horsted Keynes in the early 1960s. One of these trains, on 1 April 1962, had been headed by the first privately preserved loco to run on the main line, Captain Bill Smith's ex-GNR J52 0-6-0ST No 1247.

↘ The 'Scottish Belle' was handed over to two Bluebell Railway engines at Haywards Heath while Nos 120 and 123 ran light down to Brighton shed for servicing. This was one of the few occasions when Bluebell locos worked over the national network, heading the train from Haywards Heath to Horsted Keynes via the since-lifted electrified Ardingly line.

LSWR Adams Radial tank, 4-4-2T No 488 and LBSCR E4 0-6-2T No 473 *Birch Grove* pass through Ardingly en route to Horsted Keynes.

↑↗ I seem to remember not being too sure, but a lot of people were waiting around at Horsted Keynes in anticipation of the arrival of Nos 120 and 123, as it was being said they were going to put in an appearance after servicing at Brighton. I well remember the excitement of seeing them approaching the station from the Ardingly line, coming right out of the bright sun, making a photo of their arrival impossible from where I was standing, but a truly unforgettable sight. They were then parked up on the platform at Horsted Keynes for inspection and photography as these views show. This was probably the first time I had seen whitewashed coal! The whole affair was worth an unprecedented number of shots!

↘ Double heading with No 123 on the 'Scottish Belle' from London Victoria to Haywards Heath and return was T9 class 4-4-0 No 120. This had been retained for working specials and repainted in LSWR apple green in 1962, but was still in BR capital stock. It was officially withdrawn in July 1963 when it was declared 'preserved', and was retired from main line use by the end of the year. It is seen on show at Horsted Keynes in between working the train to and from Haywards Heath and London Victoria.

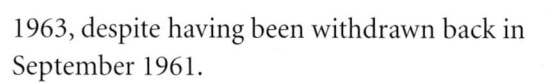

LNER B12 CLASS 4-6-0 NO 61572

The Wandering 1500 5 OCTOBER 1963

When I heard about this tour it was a 'must see' event. Although B12 class No 61572 had outlived the other members of the class by two years I had still not seen it and was thinking I might never do so. There was an appeal to secure it for preservation, but success for such things was never assured and many similar schemes failed to obtain the loco they wished to save. I was therefore delighted and surprised to hear it was to work a special from London Broad Street on 5 October

1963, despite having been withdrawn back in September 1961.

What I did not know was that the 4-6-0 had been bought by the Midland & Great Northern Joint Railway Society and was therefore already preserved at this time. Perhaps it was not so surprising that as a young enthusiast I was not aware of this fact, as it appears not everyone on BR knew either that this was now a privately owned steam loco, or it might not have been permitted to work on the network that day. It was generally

thought it was simply being taken out of store at Devons Road shed where, in fact, a lot of work had been undertaken on it by its new owners.

This trip was so notable that as this chapter was being written there was talk of the train being 're-enacted' on 5 October 2013 to mark its 50th anniversary, albeit with different locos on a different route, but hopefully using the B12 with the train routed on to the North Norfolk Railway.

↗ I only saw the 'Wandering 1500' with No 61572 when departing from Broad Street, but it did wander far and wide, well away from the area frequented by the class when in service. This took in Bedford, Northampton, Stratford upon Avon, Leamington Spa, Rugby, Bletchley, Willesden and back to Broad Street via Dalston Junction; a distance of 223½ miles.

It is seen pounding away from Broad Street – past the impressive signalbox, where the enthusiasts appear to have wandered off the end of the platform. This turned out to be my only photographic visit to this now long-gone London terminus.

LNER K4 CLASS 2-6-0 NO 3442 *THE GREAT MARQUESS*

'The Marquess Goes South South West' 12 MARCH 1967

Another 'new' loco to me in the South was ex-LNER K4 class 2-6-0 No 3442 *The Great Marquess.* Withdrawn as BR No 61994 in 1961, the Mogul was bought by David Lindsay, Viscount Garnock and restored to working order at Cowlairs Works, finished in apple green livery.

Organised by Locomotive Preservation (Sussex) Ltd, this train was worked by No 3442 on several legs, with BR Class 33 diesels and an 'ED' Class 73 on others, taking the train from London Victoria to Brighton, Lavant, Southampton Central, and Eastleigh, Brighton and back to Victoria.

The K4 worked Victoria–Brighton; Preston Park–Chichester; Chichester–Southampton Central; Eastleigh–Preston Park; and Brighton–East Croydon. A track circuit failure at Preston Park on the return delayed the train, with many passengers electing to return to London by means of a service train EMU in preference to continuing behind steam, albeit over an hour late. The author remained on board, with arrival at Victoria at 22.30 rather than the booked 21.02, but in plenty of time for the last train home.

↓ K4 class 2-6-0 No 3442 *The Great Marquess* awaits departure from London Victoria on 12 March 1967.

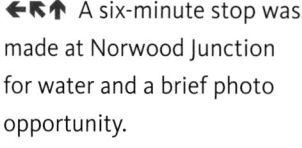

← ↖ ↑ A six-minute stop was made at Norwood Junction for water and a brief photo opportunity.

→ The Gresley Mogul is seen on arrival at Brighton, for the first time that day. The jaunty angle of the headboard became a notable feature of this working.

↓ The train was taken out from Brighton behind 'ED' No E6009 to Preston Park, from where No 3442 took it on the next leg to Chichester. There were plenty of photo opportunities throughout the day of this complex schedule.

The 'Mercian' 16 APRIL 1967

This was organised by the Epsom Railway Society, one of the team being a young Adrian Shooter (as mentioned in Chapter 8) who came along to the Epsom & Ewell Model Railway Club one evening to promote this tour, for which I immediately made a booking. This included haulage by *The Great Marquess* a month after the previous excursion, but this time heading in the opposite direction.

Running from Euston behind ac electric loco No E3103, the 2-6-0 came on the train at Stockport Edgeley for the run through to Keighley via Bolton, where 'Black Five' No 45377 was put on the front as pilot.

After a visit to the yet-to-be-opened Keighley & Worth Valley Railway (see Chapter 6) the train continued to Leeds Central where another privately owned ex-LNER loco took over. This was A3 4-6-2 No 4472 *Flying Scotsman*, which worked the train all the way back to King's Cross, arriving almost dead on time, at 21.56.

➜ No 3442 is seen during a ten-minute stop at Blackburn on 16 April 1967 with the 'Mercian'. This view almost gives the impression that the photographer was standing on the main line track, but it must be the effect of a wide-angled lens...

LNER A4 4-6-2 NO 4498 *SIR NIGEL GRESLEY*

On tour on the Southern 4 JUNE 1967

There was no shortage of railtours in 1967, and the next I went on with a preserved loco was organised by the A4 Locomotive Society, on 4 June. At this time, there was a definite bias in the preservation of LNER locos on the main line, there being the GNR J52 0-6-0ST, K4 2-6-0 No 3442, A3 4-6-2 No 4472, and now A4 class 4-6-2 No 4498 *Sir Nigel Gresley*. Withdrawn in February 1966 as No 60007, it was acquired by the A4 Locomotive Society Ltd and restored at Crewe Works, turned out in LNER garter blue, but without the original side valances and retaining the BR double chimney.

The inaugural run of the restored loco was on 1 April 1967 when it worked from Crewe to Carlisle and return. This was followed by two excursions on the Southern, the first on 3 June, from Waterloo, but only to Bournemouth and Southampton and back.

I therefore booked on the Sunday trip which included a stop at Eastleigh for a shed visit and then on to Weymouth for another shed visit. All that for a fare of £3 10s (£3.50) for us non-members of the society. It turned out to be a particularly memorable day with wonderful photo opportunities.

⬅ Making its Southern debut, A4 No 4498 *Sir Nigel Gresley* rushes through Raynes Park on 3 June 1967, heading for Bournemouth. After this, I nipped over to the narrow gauge Brockham Museum near Dorking to assist with the off-loading of 2ft gauge Bagnall 2-4-0T *Polar Bear*, which had just arrived from the Isle of Man. The narrow gauge bug was biting!

↑ The next day, 4 June, it was back to the 'big railway' for *Sir Nigel Gresley*'s second Southern outing. On the way up to Waterloo I got one of my luckiest ever shots. The A4 was just running down to the main line from Nine Elms shed as we passed, and I was able to capture the moment from the passing 4-SUB EMU. Despite the many times of passing this spot, I was never so lucky in photographing any of the usual locos coming off shed like this.

↑ No 4498 a few minutes later, backing down on to the train ready for departure from Waterloo.

←→ We had an hour at Eastleigh to visit the shed (see Chapter 2) and to get some detail shots of our motive power. Yes, garter blue and double chimney. Only four A4s had the double chimney and Kylchap blastpipe in LNER days: No 4468 *Mallard* and the last three built in 1938, Nos 4901–4903. The rest of the class were so equipped between May 1957 and November 1958.

→ No 4498 takes on water at Wareham.

↓ The Streak arrives at Weymouth station.

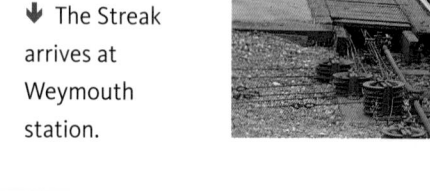

↓ The view from the coaling stage shows smartly turned out 'Warship' No D830 *Majestic* in the background, receiving little attention from the enthusiasts.

↑ ↓ A visit to Weymouth shed provided a marvellous opportunity to see the Gresley Pacific being serviced.

GWR CASTLE CLASS 4-6-0 NO 7029 *CLUN CASTLE*

Ian Allan special train King's Cross to Leeds

17 SEPTEMBER 1967

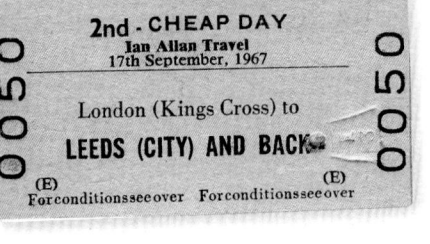

2nd - CHEAP DAY
Ian Allan Travel
17th September, 1967

London (Kings Cross) to

LEEDS (CITY) AND BACK

(E) (E)
For conditions see over For conditions see over

0050

Described as 'an historic occasion' by Ian Allan Travel on the information sheet handed out on the train, this excursion does not appear to have had a name. The headboard carried was simply 'Ian Allan Rail Tour'. It was of great interest however because, as the sheet stated, it was the first time a GWR 'Castle' class 4-6-0 had 'followed in the footsteps of her illustrious sister *Pendennis Castle* in 1925, with far-reaching results'.

The loco this time was No 7029 *Clun Castle* which had been acquired for preservation the previous year. In 1965, it was the last member of the class in BR service when it headed 'Farewell to Steam', the last official Western Region steam-hauled train, the 4.15pm from Paddington to Banbury, on 11 June.

It was an obvious candidate for preservation, but for the fact that two 'Castles' had already been saved: No 4073 *Caerphilly Castle*, then on static display in the London Science Museum, and No 4079 *Pendennis Castle*, owned by William McAlpine and John Gretton. A private fund was set up and sufficient money was raised, helped by Patrick Whitehouse, and No 7029 was secured for Tyseley,

from where it would work railtours.

Having had LNER haulage from Victoria and Waterloo stations earlier in the year it was good to have the opportunity to have GWR power from King's Cross and down the East Coast Main Line. The destination was the Middleton Railway, as described in Chapter 6.

⬆ GWR 'Castle' class 4-6-0 No 7029 *Clun Castle* poses under the arches of King's Cross before backing down on to its train, destined for Leeds, on 17 September 1967.

⬅ There was a half-hour water stop at Peterborough which also served as a photo opportunity. Presumably the note on the bottom of the information sheet requesting participants not to leave the platform had not been noticed. Oops... but this was 1967.

BR STANDARD 9F CLASS 2-10-0 NO 92203 AND 4MT CLASS 4-6-0 NO 75029

With the end of steam fast approaching, and already eliminated the previous year on the Southern Region, the prospect of seeing a couple of locos steaming down the South Western main line in April 1968 was an exciting prospect. This came about when artist David Shepherd bought two BR Standard locos, 9F 2-10-0 No 92203 and Class 4MT 4-6-0 No 75029, direct from BR. David persuaded BR that the best way to move them south from Crewe to their new home on the Longmoor Military Railway in Hampshire was in steam.

LNER A3 4-6-2 NO 4472 *FLYING SCOTSMAN* – THE WORLD'S MOST INFAMOUS LOCOMOTIVE

When the late Alan Pegler bought Gresley A3 class Pacific No 60103 *Flying Scotsman* from BR in April 1963, he introduced a new approach to railway preservation. He wanted this to be high-profile, coined the phrase 'the world's most famous locomotive' and employed a PR company to ensure that is what it became.

An agreement was made with BR that it could continue running on the main line, even after steam was eliminated in August 1968, and for a while after

↑↗ I had a tip-off that Nos 75029 and 92203 had arrived for an overnight stop at Cricklewood depot on 6 April, so nipped up to London to find them sizzling away, basking in the late evening sun – quite an amazing sight.

Apparently, BR had expected them to be moved south by road, but the owner insisted they travel by rail. BR then offered and expected this to be behind a diesel, but David was more determined than that and was eventually given permission for them to travel down under their own steam. What a memorable journey it must have been for the owner.

↙↓ The next day, 7 April 1968, I went to West Byfleet station to see the two locos passing through en route to the Longmoor Military Railway. First through was the 9F, followed a few minutes later by the 4-6-0. They were named *Black Prince* and *The Green Knight* a couple of months after arrival in Hampshire.

← Organised by Locomotive Preservation (Sussex) Ltd, the 'Flying Scotsman Goes South' railtour on 17 September 1966 used No 4472 throughout, apart from Eastleigh–Salisbury–Eastleigh behind BR Standard 2-6-4Ts Nos 80016 and 80152. Departing London Victoria the train travelled to Salisbury via Brighton and Eastleigh, returning to London via Fareham, Havant, Hove and Preston Park. Here, *Flying Scotsman* arrives at East Croydon station where a large crowd was waiting to greet it and where a stop was made.

that it was indeed the only steam loco to be seen running on the national network. Through this unique contract, Alan Pegler had demonstrated that it was possible to operate a steam loco on BR with servicing facilities removed, and others were inspired and encouraged to work towards further locos being granted similar status. It was a long and hard task, but it was achieved in the end. The rest, as they say, is history regarding the return of steam to the main line in the 1970s and into the present day.

It has become all too well-known that this iconic engine was eventually acquired for the National Collection at great expense. It had been turned down when the original list of officially preserved locos was drawn up, when it would have been available free of charge. Restoration for use on the main line is still ongoing in early 2013. Many reasons for the delay were quoted in an official report published in late 2012, with completion predicted for 2015.

Having gained the moniker 'the peoples' engine', due to having been bought and much of the overhaul paid for by public subscription, all its troubles have been in the spotlight with much media attention.

However, it should perhaps be added that other main line steam locos being restored have also suffered considerable setbacks, but less publicly, such as GWR 'King' class 4-6-0 No 6023 *King Edward I*, rebuilt Bulleid Pacific No 34046 *Braunton*, and LMSR No 46100 *Royal Scot*. So, each of the 'Big Four' has had a 'star' loco with expensive restoration problems, and at the time of writing, January 2013, none of these locos had made a successful return to main line operation, despite receiving attention over many years at considerable expense.

↑ A quick run round to the down side of the station caught the famous Gresley Pacific pulling out a few minutes later. It was only in the time of Alan Pegler's ownership that the loco carried red-backed nameplates.

↓ Just two weeks after I had been hauled from Leeds to King's Cross by No 4472 *Flying Scotsman* it was heading north from there, on 30 April. Haulage and photography do not always go together and having only secured one head-on shot of it at Leeds, I went for another attempt, as an observer only, on this occasion. It is seen being prepared with flags, prior to departure with the 'Michelangelo Tour', organised by the Anglo-Norse Society.

The destination was Chesterfield for brake van rides worked by a pair of J94 class 0-6-0STs, Nos 68006 and 68012, to mark the closure of the Cromford & High Peak Railway between Middleton Top and Friden via Hopton Incline.

CHAPTER 11

MAIN LINE IN INDUSTRY

A second lease of life for

some small locos

ONE AREA OF RAILWAYS that was a total mystery to me in my early BR loco spotting days was industrial locomotives. Occasional glimpses of nondescript, anonymous locos working in factory sidings or colliery yards would be glimpsed from a passing train. I would wonder what they were, and wanted to find out more.

I started to make enquiries, especially as it was clear there were a number of ex-BR and earlier main line locos to be found at industrial railway sites. These were beginning to find their way into preservation and so I was intrigued to find out what else could be seen. Types I thought had passed into history were in fact still in existence, so perhaps I should just track those down, and leave the rest.

However, things did not quite work out like that. I met up with a small group of very knowledgeable industrial railway enthusiasts and soon realised it was an incredibly fascinating subject in its own right, and not just about steam, or standard gauge. When I was taken to a peat works in Somerset swarming with tiny diesel locos on 2ft gauge tracks it was a life-changing experience! But that is another story.

The passing of locos into industry has extended the working lives of many over the years and has been responsible for the salvation of quite a few now in preservation. At a rough count there are something like 30 main line railway company steam locos preserved today, which would otherwise have been lost had they not been used in industry following withdrawal.

These are of course smaller, shunting type locos, but they include some rare and interesting survivors. Some are of main line design and construction while others were typical industrial saddle tanks that had been used by a main line company and were therefore easily sold off to an industrial concern when finished with. Examples of pre-Grouping company locos which can be seen today, having passed through industry, include G&SWR, Taff Vale, Port Talbot, Lancashire & Yorkshire, and North Staffordshire railways.

Illustrated here is as small selection of ex-main line locos I was able to see when in industrial ownership. Most, but not all, are still with us. This is by no means a comprehensive survey and for that one is recommended to refer to Frank Jones's book *Mainline to Industry*.

⬇ This is a classic example of an ex-main line loco surviving in industry, former Burry Port & Gwendraeth Valley Railway 0-6-0ST No 2 *Pontyberem*. Built by Avonside in 1900 as their No 1421, it was sold into industry as far back as 1914, but was still extant at NCB Penrhiwceiber Colliery in South Wales, when I visited on 2 July 1969, carrying the number 11. Today, it is undergoing restoration on the Pontypool & Blaenavon Railway for the Gwendraeth Railway Project. This is the only surviving loco from the BPGVR, which was absorbed by the GWR in 1922, eight years after this loco had been sold to the coal industry.

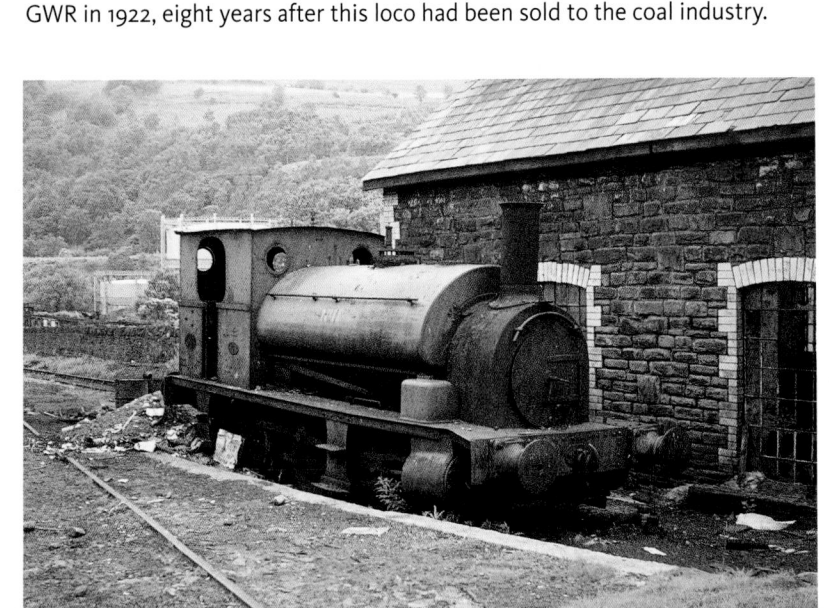

⬆ Several GWR 0-6-0 pannier tanks were to be found at work at South Wales collieries. Here, No 9600, built at Swindon in 1945, is seen at NCB Merthyr Vale Colliery on 2 July 1969. This 5700 class loco had been sold by BR for further use in October 1965 and is now preserved at Tyseley.

⬆ Ex-GWR 5700 class 0-6-0PT No 9792 was sold by BR in March 1964 to the NCB. It is seen at Mardy Colliery in South Wales on 2 July 1969, but it did not survive, being broken up in 1973.

⬆ The 70 members of the Hawksworth-design 1600 class 0-6-0PT were all built by BR at Swindon, between 1949 and 1955. Two were sold to the NCB for colliery service, Nos 1600 and 1607. The latter is shown at Cynheidre Colliery on 5 July 1969. It only survived a couple of months afterwards, being broken up in September. Only one member of the class exists today, No 1638 at the Kent & East Sussex Railway. Also in view, behind No 1607, are 0-4-0ST *Tony* (Hawthorn Leslie 3457 of 1920) and Sentinel 9569 of 1954, a four-wheel, geared, vertical boiler loco. Both were later scrapped.

⬆ GWR 0-6-0PT No 9642 was sold by BR in January 1965 to R S Hayes, scrap metal merchants of Bridgend. However, it was not broken up but was retained for use as the yard shunter and is seen taking water on 2 July 1969. This resulted in its survival and it is today undergoing restoration at a private site in the West Midlands. It is one of about 11 locos from the GW group of companies to survive, having spent a period in industry following disposal by the main line operator.

⬇ One of the delightful P class 0-6-0Ts of the South Eastern & Chatham Railway was sold by BR to Bowaters at Sittingbourne in June 1958, where I saw it in May 1969. Painted in an approximation of SECR lined-green livery it was un-numbered, but carried the name *Pioneer II*. BR No 31178 was acquired by the Bluebell Railway in 1969, joining two other members of the class bought direct from BR, Nos 31027 and 31323.

⬇ Ex-SECR P class 0-6-0T, BR No 31556 was used by James Hodson (Millers) Ltd at their Robertsbridge flour mill, where it was named *Pride of Sussex,* following withdrawal by BR in 1961. It is seen there on 23 March 1968 when the embryonic Kent & East Sussex Railway was using the sidings as a base. It was acquired by the KESR the following year. To the right is the KESR's unique ex-Ford Motor Co Metro-Vick Bo-BoDE of 1932.

⬆ At least five locos from the Southern Railway constituent companies are around today having spent time in industry, including ex-LSWR B4 class 0-4-0T No 30096. It was built by the LSWR at Nine Elms Works in 1893 to William Adams's design for dock shunting. This was one of the last to remain in industrial use, not being secured for preservation until 1972. It had been withdrawn by BR in October 1963 and sold to Corralls, fuel merchants, for use at Dible's Wharf, Southampton, where seen on a fateful day, 11 August 1968. While there it gained the name *Corrall Queen,* but retained its smokebox numberplate and 71A (Eastleigh) shedcode plate.

No 30096 was moved to the Bluebell Railway in December 1972 and restored to working order and original appearance as No 96 *Normandy.* Now owned by the Bulleid Society, it awaits an overhaul. BR had sold 11 other members of the class into industry in 1949, but all were subsequently scrapped.

The green 0-4-0ST in front of the B4 is *Bonnie Prince Charlie* (Robert Stephenson & Hawthorns 7544 of 1949) which passed into preservation in 1969, acquired by the Salisbury Locomotive Society, later a Trust, and was based at the Didcot Railway Centre. It was presented to Great Western Preservations on behalf of the Great Western Society in 2012. It is one of very few non-GWR locos in the collection.

⬆ About a dozen preserved LMS-group locos are extant today courtesy of a stay of execution due to industrial service. This is about the same as the GWR and its absorbed companies, but the LMS has a greater variety of rarities, starting with Stephenson's *Rocket.*

When in industrial ownership even the most interesting of locos could quickly blend in with their stablemates. One such was the ex-North Staffordshire Railway New L class 0-6-2Ts, six of which were sold, mainly to Manchester Collieries, in 1937. NSR No 72 (LMSR No 2262) became *Sir Robert* in colliery service and was seen in a line of locos awaiting their fate at NCB Walkden on 9 July 1968. Despite its suitability for preserved line use and historical pedigree, it was broken up in September 1969.

Ex-NSR No 2 of the same type was more fortunate and by this time was in store at Shugborough Hall, Staffordshire. Obviously one such loco was thought enough. This is now in the National Collection and is currently on display at Locomotion, Shildon. These were the only NSR steam locos I ever saw.

⬅ Although many former LNER and constituent company locos were sold off for further use in industry, there appear to be only three in existence today, excluding the Stockton & Darlington duo, *Locomotion No 1* and *Derwent.* There are two LNER Y7 class 0-4-0Ts, and this great rarity and remarkable survivor, which when tracked down was far from cared for and had an uncertain future.

It is former Great Eastern Railway 'ogee' saddle tank No 229 which was sold off in 1917. It went west, to the National Shipyard at Chepstow. It is Neilson 2119 of 1876 and was seen disappearing in undergrowth at successors Fairfield-Mabey Ltd on 28 June 1969, so had already out-lived most of BR's steam locos. Glad to say, it was saved for preservation and restored for static display. Following a period at the now-closed North Woolwich Station Museum, 1984-2008, it is now at Bill Parker's Flour Mill restoration workshops in the Forest of Dean, from where it will eventually emerge in immaculate, full working condition, with restoration due to start in 2013.

CHAPTER 12

THE
LAST RITES

BR steam in 1968

ALTHOUGH THE END OF STEAM seemed to come quite quickly, its demise across the network was spread out, region by region, area by area, providing time to get used to the idea of a non-steam railway. Southern steam had gone in July 1967 leaving just the North West (Manchester and Preston District areas) to linger on for another year, until August 1968.

I was 'pursuing other interests' by this time, namely non-BR railways in the British Isles – standard gauge, narrow gauge, and even miniature railways. With so much to find out about and to explore there was plenty to maintain my railway interest. Strangely, because steam was ending on BR I had looked elsewhere and in doing so, found that non-steam locos were in fact equally interesting and fascinating after all!

However, I had still not really developed any great interest in BR diesel and electrics at this time. I jotted down any I saw, but they were rarely something I photographed. It is not possible to do everything all at once, so had I been more interested in BR diesels then, I would probably have missed an awful lot of non-BR railway motive power, which I am so pleased to have experienced. I have visited many places that have either passed into history or would today be totally out of bounds to an enthusiast, such as vast steelworks including the blast furnaces, coking ovens, collieries, going down the mines of all sorts, visiting contractors' tunnels, brickworks, quarries, military establishments, chemical plants, town gas works, power stations and some delightful sewage works. Many of my photos, particularly some of those of the industrial narrow gauge railway systems, which have now all gone, are much rarer than those of any main line diesel loco could ever be.

From mid-1967 onwards I rarely visited any BR installations, apart from a fairly comprehensive 'shed bash' in August (see Chapter 2). Even by 1968, I had failed to track down all the surviving BR steam locos, but was able to pick up these during a 16-day north of England tour in July, as detailed in the coming pages. Obviously, many locos were missed through attrition over the years, but I had

seen all those left in stock on the last day before then, along with thousands of other locos that had also gone for scrap since I had started spotting.

The July 1968 tour by road visited every known location with locos right across the north of England. This was with A.D. 'Doug' Semmens and Stan Robinson of the Industrial Railway Society, and Rich Morris of the Narrow Gauge Railway Society. Although our primary aim was visiting industrial and narrow gauge sites and any public miniature railways in the region, we decided to include the remaining BR steam sheds as these were within the area we covered during the first week. We realised this would be our final opportunity to visit such establishments, all of us having started loco spotting with main line steam, so it was very much a nostalgic trip for us.

Although I took a large number of photos during the fortnight, hardly any were of what turned out to be short-lived diesel classes such as the MetroVick D5700s and Clayton D8500s which we encountered on our travels. We also saw English Electric Type 4s (later TOPS Class 50) under construction at English Electric, Vulcan Foundry, but again, took no photos regrettably. This was partly due to the unofficial and therefore hurried nature of our visit which did not permit much time for photography in the vast erecting shop. When we called in the office seeking permission for a quick look round, we were informed a visit could not be permitted at that time. Doug never liked to take 'no' for an answer when wishing to visit a railway establishment and so came up with an alternative idea to gain entry.

We mingled with the staff as they were at that moment clocking off for lunch, and we even joined them in their canteen for a very cheap, subsidised meal. We then casually chatted to some chaps as they filed back into the works, enabling us to walk in amongst them unnoticed by the security staff. During our scoot round we saw EE Type 5s Nos D434 to D446 in various stages of construction plus No D405 in for repair, as well as the crash-damaged prototype, No DP2, awaiting its fate. There were also East African Railways Nos 9111 to

9114, together with a number of industrial locos for the UK market being built.

As the end of BR steam approached I decided I could not let it all go now without having a final fling, and so as August approached I booked to go on one of the BR steam farewell tours.

I travelled with my by then regular narrow gauge companion Rich Morris, as he too did not want to miss this end of an era. It was a strange experience, as the narrow gauge and industrial scene had become so important in our lives that it was already like going back in time to be witnessing BR steam in action.

We purposely chose to go on one of the 4 August trains rather than the following weekend's 1T57 'Fifteen Guinea Special', as this was the real last day of BR steam as far as we were concerned. The latter train, although organised by BR, was being run a week after the official withdrawal of BR steam and so was purely an enthusiasts' special and not part of the real thing. Despite talk of the 'steam ban' we could see no reason why such a train could

not be run time and time again for enthusiasts on BR in the future, once the dust had settled. *Flying Scotsman* was still going to be running so why not other privately preserved steam locos? Although our train featured three locos that were later preserved, Nos 45025, 48773 and 70013, they were part of BR capital stock on that day, as were Nos 45390 and 44781, which were not so fortunate.

Looking back 45 years later, I am convinced we did the right thing as you can still travel behind steam on the national network but none use BR capital stock. A gleaming loco of today is only a representation of the past, attempting to re-enact the days of steam and those who were there in the 1960s will be fully aware of the differences between the two scenes. I know there was historical significance to 1T57, but No 70013 can still be seen today on occasions, heading a train on the Settle & Carlisle route, just as it did on 11 August 1968. Therefore, it was not the 'unrepeatable and unmissable' scene so many made it out to be.

↓ In the depths of Patricroft shed on 19 May 1968 was one of the only four of the 842 Stanier Class 5MT 'Black Fives' to be named: No 45156 *Ayrshire Yeomanry Earl of Carrick's Own*. The other three were Nos 45154 *Lanarkshire Yeomanry*, 45157 *The Glasgow Highlander* (its badge above the nameplate), and 45158 *Glasgow Yeomanry Field Brigade R.A.T.A.* Despite their celebrity status, none of the named Stanier Class 5s survived into preservation, but other preserved members of the class have since been named.

↓ One of 17 8F class Stanier 2-8-os seen at Patricroft on 19 May included the highest numbered, No 48775. This was one of three 8Fs not taken into BR stock until 1957, bringing the total to 666 of the 852 Stanier 2-8-os built. These late additions included No 48773, the well-known preserved example bought direct from BR and based on the Severn Valley Railway. These three had been returned to Britain in 1952 from the Middle East where they had been in war service, and had continued in military use.

SHED VISITS IN SUMMER 1968

9H Patricroft

VISITED 19 MAY, OFFICIALLY CLOSED 30 JUNE 1968

It was not until May that I went north to see any BR steam in 1968, this being on a trip to the Manchester area mainly to visit 2ft gauge peat works lines, but we included this one shed visit while in the vicinity.

This former LNWR shed at Patricroft opened in 1885. The original building was later reduced in size following construction of a second, ten-road shed in 1904, but it remained in use until the end. The buildings were demolished soon after closure, in August 1968. On shed that day, six weeks before closure, were:

LMS Class 5MT 4-6-0	LMS Class 8F 2-8-0	BR Standard Class 5MT 4-6-0	BR Standard Class 5MT 4-6-0	BR Standard Class 9F 2-10-0
44777	48282	73000	73132	
45055	48325	73010	73133	
45156	48327	73034	73134	
45187	48338	73040	73136	
45287	48374	73050	73138	
	48390	73053	73142	
	48453	73067	73143	
	48467	73069	73155	
	48491	73126	73157	
	48549	73128		
	48553			92218
	48749			
	48775			
48033				
48170				
48212				
48267				

⬆ No fewer than 19 BR Standard Class 5MT 4-6-0s were on Patricroft at the time of our 19 May visit, including nine of the 30 members of the class fitted with Caprotti valve gear (Nos 73125 to 73154). Nicely posed alongside the shed was No 73126, the second of those to be so equipped. Of these, No 73129 is today the only survivor, based at the Midland Railway-Butterley.

⬆ BR Standard 5MT No 73069, centre, was fitted with Walschaerts valve gear as were 142 of the class of 172 4-6-0s. Class 8F No 48775 is on the left. Surviving Walschaerts Class 5MTs are Nos 73050, 73082 *Camelot*, 73096 and 73156.

8F Springs Branch Wigan

VISITED 7 JULY, OFFICIALLY CLOSED TO STEAM 4 DECEMBER 1967

The other remaining BR steam sheds were visited during the 16-day North of England 'grand tour', 6–21 July 1968, starting with Springs Branch. Class 8F 2-8-0 No 48752 was the only steam loco present amongst all the diesels at this former LNWR shed. It was dead, in the yard at the end of a line of diesel shunters, but was not officially withdrawn until the following month.

9D Newton Heath VISITED 9 JULY, OFFICIALLY CLOSED TO STEAM 30 JUNE 1968

This former Lancashire & Yorkshire Railway shed was the largest on the system. Opened in 1876, it had 24 parallel roads within the building.

LMS Class 5MT 4-6-0	45206	48373
	45254	48368
44780	45255	48529
44803	45310	48533
44818	45330	48612
44845	45411	48620
44884	45420	48678
44890		48687
44891	**LMS Class**	48746
44910	**8F 2-8-0**	
44949	48132	**BR Standard**
45076	48321	**Class 9F**
45202	48366	**2-10-0**
45203	48369	92054

↑ Newton Heath shed on 9 July, nine days after official closure to steam, but with 33 locos present. Left to right are 'Black Fives' Nos 44884, 44845 and 45255 and 8F 2-8-0 No 48620.

↓ Another view of the 24-road shed at Newton Heath on 9 July showing Stanier 8F No 48529 and Class 5MT 4-6-0 No 44818 in typical condition and 'livery' of the period.

10F Rose Grove

VISITED 9 JULY, OFFICIALLY CLOSED TO STEAM 5 AUGUST 1968

Along with 10A Carnforth and 10D Lostock Hall, this was one of three sheds to remain open to steam right to the end. Opened by the Lancashire & Yorkshire Railway in 1899, the shed accommodated six roads.

↓ 'Black Eight' No 48519 is seen on the turntable at Rose Grove shed on 9 July. This was one of 26 8Fs that remained in traffic until the last day.

LMS Class 5MT 4-6-0	LMS Class 8F 2-8-0	48385	48665
44690	48115	48389	48666
44781	48167	48393	48727
44809	48257	48400	48730
44816	48278	48410	
45096	48294	48423	**BR**
45110	48323	48448	**Standard**
45397	48340	48451	**Class 4MT**
45407	48360	48493	**4-6-0**
		48519	75027

↓ 'Black Five' No 45110 at Rose Grove on 9 July. This was one of the Stanier 4-6-0s acquired for preservation direct from BR, and one of 46 Stanier 4-6-0s in service until the end of BR steam. Initially, when in preservation, it was named *RAF Biggin Hill* to honour the RAF's Battle of Britain airfield in Kent as Bulleid Pacific No 34057 *Biggin Hill* was unable to be saved.

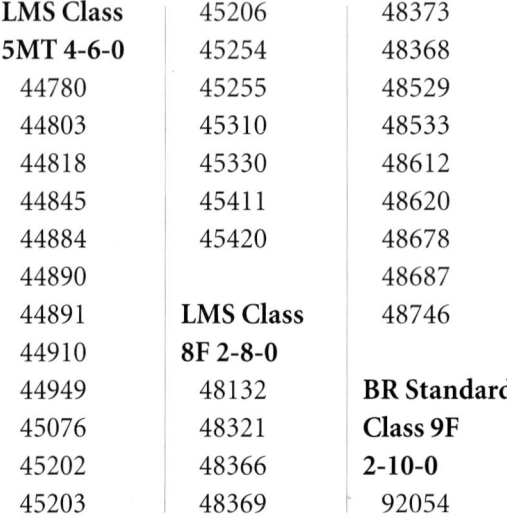

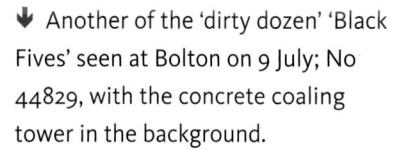

⬆ No 48340, one of 22 8F class 2-8-0s seen during our visit to Rose Grove on 9 July.

⬆ Stanier Class 5 4-6-0 No 44888, on shed at Bolton on 9 July, nine days after official closure.

⬇ Another of the 'dirty dozen' 'Black Fives' seen at Bolton on 9 July; No 44829, with the concrete coaling tower in the background.

9K Bolton

VISITED 9 JULY, OFFICIALLY CLOSED 30 JUNE 1968

This former Lancashire & Yorkshire Railway shed dated back to the 1870s and was later extended to accommodate 12 roads.

LMS Class	45104	48168
5MT 4-6-0	45260	48319
44664	45290	48380
44802	45312	48392
44829	45381	48504
44888		48652
44929	**LMS Class 8F**	48692
44947	**2-8-0**	48702
45046	48026	48720

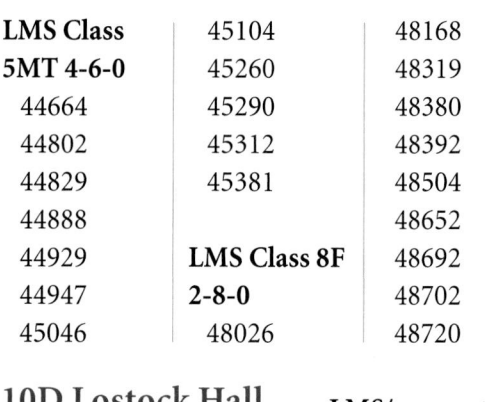

10D Lostock Hall

VISITED 10 JULY, OFFICIALLY CLOSED 5 AUGUST

One of the last three sheds to close to steam, this shed dated from 1881 when opened by the Lancashire & Yorkshire Railway. It accommodated eight roads and was not demolished until 1990, having been used by a BR engineering department in the meantime.

LMS/ BR(LMR) Class 4MT 2-6-0	44950	45444
	44971	
	45149	**LMS Class**
43019	45200	**8F 2-8-0**
43027	45212	48293
43106	45269	48445
	45305	48476
	45318	48546
LMS Class	45345	48646
5MT 4-6-0	45353	48723
44683	45386	48763
44713	45388	48765
44878	45407	48775
44942	45436	

10A Carnforth

VISITED 10 JULY, OFFICIALLY CLOSED TO STEAM 5 AUGUST 1968

This well-known shed was built in 1943–44 on the site of the former Furness Railway shed and was equipped with a turntable, mechanical coaling plant and an ash-elevating tower. It was one of the last three BR steam depots to remain open and was used again after official closure to steam when it serviced the locos used on the 11 August special.

It had become a storage site for a number of privately preserved locos (see Chapter 6) and was itself preserved, becoming Steamtown Carnforth following total closure on 31 March 1969. This was open to the public with a museum display of locos and a 15in gauge miniature railway as well as servicing steam locos for railtours. However, today it is the base of West Coast Railways serving the railtour industry and is most definitely not available for enthusiast access.

LMS/BR (LMR) Class 4MT 2-6-4T	LMS/BR (LMR) Class 2MT 2-6-0	LNER Class B1 4-6-0	Class 4MT 4-6-0
42073	45085	61306	75009
42085	45134		75019
	45209	**BR Standard 'Britannia' class 4-6-2**	75020
LMS Class 5MT 4-6-0	45231		75048
44758	45390	70013 *Oliver Cromwell*	
44809	45435		**BR Standard Class 9F 2-10-0**
44831	45445	**BR Standard Class 5MT 4-6-0**	92077
44877	**LMS/BR (LMR) Class 2MT 2-6-0**	73069	92088
44894	(4)6441		92091
44897		**BR Standard**	92118
44963	**LMS Class 8F 2-8-0**		92160
45025	48247		92167
			92223

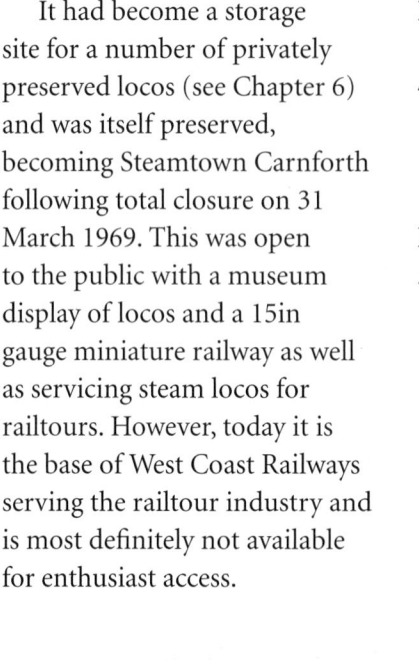

↑ Making a welcome change from the plethora of ex-LMS Class 5s and 8Fs, BR Standard 9F class 2-10-0 No 92091 was nicely posed in the sun at Carnforth on 10 July.

↓ Less than a month before closure to steam and still busy, with five of the six roads occupied by at least one loco in steam on 10 July. A scene partly recreated in 2008 during the one-off *The Railway Magazine*-sponsored open weekend of the WCR depot. The locos were all then facing the camera, smartly turned-out, giving a taste of the atmosphere of a working steam shed.

12A Carlisle Kingmoor 'old shed'

VISITED 13 JULY

Finally, on this epic tour of northern England's industrial railway sites, which would make a book in its own right, my notebook records the last BR steam locos seen as being three 'Black Fives' in the 'old shed': Nos 44767, 44932 and 45262.

1Z74, THE LCGB'S 'FAREWELL TO STEAM RAIL TOUR' 4 AUGUST 1968

This really was the end of witnessing real BR steam operations, as far as I was concerned. Our train had a good variety of motive power from when it left St Pancras at 08.30 behind 'Peak' No D63. The diesel took the train to Manchester Victoria where it handed over to 'Britannia' Pacific No 70013 *Oliver Cromwell* and 'Black Five' No 44781. They worked through to Blackburn where Stanier 8F No 48773 replaced the 'Brit' for the run through Clitheroe,

Hellifield, Settle Junction and Clapham to Carnforth for a shed visit.

Two 'Black Fives', Nos 45390 and 45025, then headed the train back from Carnforth via Clapham for a photographic stop, then to Settle Junction, Hellifield, Clitheroe and Blackburn to Lostock Hall Junction. From there, English Electric Type 4 No D416 took over for the leg to Crewe where it handed over to ac electric loco No E3064 for the return to London Euston. We arrived at 00.13, two hours late, but that was not uppermost in our minds. I missed the last train home and presumably spent the night there, not for the first time, tucked up in the compartment of a 4-SUB EMU waiting for the morning's services.

➜ The end of BR steam meant that tour operators such as the LCGB had to think of different reasons to continue running trains after the sad day, as outlined in the letter passed to all participants of the 'Farewell to Steam Rail Tour'.

THE LOCOMOTIVE CLUB OF GREAT BRITAIN.
THE FAREWELL TO STEAM RAIL TOUR.
SUNDAY, 4th AUGUST, 1968.

Dear Sir/Madam,
Good morning and welcome to our last rail tour using British Railways steam motive power. No doubt many of you will feel a little sad on this occasion and we hope you will enjoy this historic event. B.R. and the L.C.G.B. have given you many enjoyable and interesting rail tours over the years and we regard the future as an interest challenge. We hope all genuine railway enthusiasts will continue to show an interest in railways and support our modern traction and family tours. On this tour we shall be distributing leaflets of forthcoming tours run by the L.C.G.B. and other Clubs. Some of these are experiments and include steam and modern traction, Stately Homes, coach tours, paddle steamer trips, visits to museums, diesel depots and works, visits to preservation lines and model railways. We trust you will support these tours and make them a social and very enjoyable day out.

Providing the tour is near to time at Carnforth, a visit will be made to the motive power depot. You are requested to exercise great care during the visit and obey the instructions of B.R. staff.

Each passenger will be given one copy of the itinerary and if your copy is lost or damaged it cannot be replaced and in your own interests it is suggested you take great care of your itinerary.

You will notice from this letter and your itinerary that a class '5' 4-6-0 will assist the 'Britannia' and the '8F', this has been arranged for two reasons, an extra coach has been added making 12 vehicles and it is hoped that the extra loco will assist timekeeping. A restaurant buffet car has been provided instead of a kitchen car, this will enable a counter buffet service to be provided. This has presented difficulties for the restaurant car staff with a smaller kitchen for cooking meals. They will be working long hours under very difficult conditions and have to serve over 400 meals and your co-operation and understanding would be appreciated.

Members of the publicity department will be conducting a survey on the train and may ask you questions about tours and what you may like in the future and your co-operation would be appreciated.

The formation departing St. Pancras will be:-
BSK - (32 seats) - Two compartments reserved for tape recorders.
SO - (64 seats) - Reserved for Club Members.
SO - (64 seats) - Reserved for Club Members.
SO - (64 seats) - Reserved for St. Albans and Bedford Passengers and Club Officers.
SO - (64 seats) - Reserved for meal service and Club Officers.
SO - (64 seats) - Reserved for meal service only.
RB - (23 seats) - Only to be used for passengers taking light refreshments.
SO - (64 seats) - Unreserved.
SO - (64 seats) - Unreserved.
SO - (64 seats) - Reserved for parties.
SO - (64 seats) - Reserved for parties.
SO - (64 seats) - Reserved for tape recorders.
BSK - (32 seats) - Two compartments reserved for tape recorders.

Passengers are requested not to take seats reserved for parties, officers, tape recorders and passengers joining at St. Albans and Bedford. Please do not sit in the buffet car except when taking light refreshments and vacate their seats in the meal coach after paying their bills to enable the car staff to clear up and lay the tables for the next sitting.

We trust you will have enjoyable, interesting and memorable day.

M. BURTON.
Club Chairman.
for the Rail Tours Committee.
4th August, 1968.

⬆ The LCGB's 'Farewell to Steam Rail Tour' was run on the last official day of BR steam traction, 4 August 1968. 'Britannia' No 70013 *Oliver Cromwell* is seen at Manchester Victoria, with wooden nameplates, before taking the train on to Blackburn with 'Black Five' No 44781.

➜ No 70013 is ready to depart from Manchester Victoria, with a wreath attached to the smokebox door. It worked the train to Blackburn where it was replaced by 8F No 48773 so that it could be released to work another train, 1L50, the RCTS's 'End of Steam Commemorative Railtour'. That train encountered various problems throughout the day, becoming even more delayed than ours. Even though a section from Manchester to Liverpool Docks was dropped it was still more than four hours late by the time the 'Britannia' was attached at Lostock Hall Junction. The eventual late arrival back at London Euston resulted in compensation being paid to the 600 passengers! It was a day none of us there will ever forget.

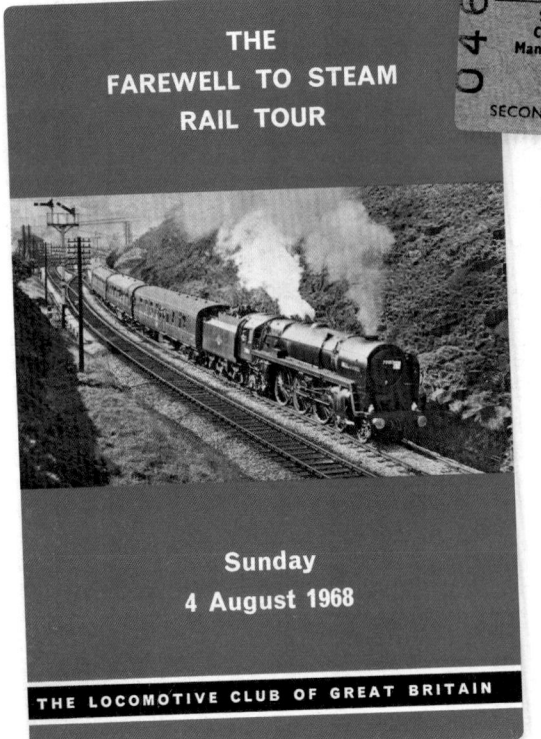

THE FAREWELL TO STEAM RAIL TOUR

British Railways Board (M)
The Locomotive Club of Great Britain
LAST DAY OF STEAM RAIL TOUR
Sunday 4th August, 1968

0464 0464

St. Pancras, Bedford Midland Road, Chesterfield, Edale, Chinley, Romiley, Manchester Victoria, Blackburn, Hellifield, Carnforth, Hellifield, Lostock Hall, Crewe, Euston

SECOND CLASS   For conditions see over

Sunday 4 August 1968

THE LOCOMOTIVE CLUB OF GREAT BRITAIN

→ 'Black Five' No 45156, now minus its *Ayrshire Yeomanry* nameplates, waits under the mechanical coaling plant at Carnforth. Seen during our shed visit, this 4-6-0 was working one of six commemorative railtours run that day using steam in the Manchester and Preston Divisional areas. It headed 1T80, GC Enterprises' train from Stockport (Edgeley) to Carnforth and return, out via Manchester Victoria, Bolton, Blackburn and Hellifield.

↑ 'Black Five' No 45390 with No 45025 behind, being prepared at Carnforth to take our train from there to Lostock Hall Junction.

↑ The end is nigh. Nos 45390 and 45025 now coupled up to 1Z74 at Carnforth and ready to leave on the final steam section of the LCGB's steam farewell train to Lostock Hall Junction. No 45025 is now preserved, but No 45390 was cut up in October 1968.

← A quarter-hour photo stop at Clapham provided a final opportunity to see and photograph our locos from the lineside. This was the last occasion we would be steam hauled on BR prior to the withdrawal of all remaining steam locos. Nos 45390 and 45025 catch the sun at about 18.00.

→ One last sighting of BR steam locos in regular BR traffic. These were seen from our farewell train as we passed 'Black Fives' No 44781 and No 44894 at Lostock Hall Junction at about 19.45 on 4 August 1968. They had worked 1Z78, the Stephenson Locomotive Society's 'Farewell to Steam Railtour No 1'. This train originated from Birmingham and was steam hauled by the two 4-6-0s from Manchester Victoria to Huddersfield, Blackburn (via Bolton avoiding line), Wigan Wallgate, Bootle, Rainhill and Manchester Victoria to Stockport.

THE VERY LAST ONE?

At the end of BR steam there were still a few outstanding ex-main line locos I had not yet tracked down. These were all in preservation, so hopefully safe, and I no longer made urgent efforts to go after them, certain I would pick them up in due course. Among these was LNWR 0-4-0ST No 1439, which had survived by passing into industry. Built at Crewe in 1865, it was presented to the BTC in 1954 by ICI Ltd. It was stored in various locations, including the mysterious Shugborough Hall, and I did not catch up with it until 1990 when it appeared at the National Railway Museum on Tour exhibition at Swindon. It is now on loan to the Ribble Steam Railway collection, Preston.

However, one main line steam loco remained outstanding long after all the others, ex-GWR No 921. The only surviving steam loco in the UK built by Brush (314 of 1906), it was Powlesland & Mason No 6, used for shunting at Swansea docks, and absorbed by the GWR at the Grouping. This 0-4-0ST was sold to Berry Wiggins & Co Ltd, oil refiners at Kingsnorth, North Kent in 1931. It passed to Leicester Corporation Museum of Technology and was housed at Stoneygate Museum, Leicester from 1968, but I never got to see it there. In fact, it was not until it arrived at its present home at Snibston Discovery Museum, Coalville, which opened in 1992, that I was able to catch up with it; job done.

I saw it again on 23 June 2012, as here. What I like is that it has been preserved and displayed in as-withdrawn industrial condition and has not been unduly cleaned up, repainted and presented in an unrealistic, pristine 'museum display' finish. It is the genuine article, and was worth the wait to see.

But was it really the 'last one'? Well, now that the Duke of Sutherland's Sharp Stewart 0-4-4T *Dunrobin* has returned to the UK from Canada, and at the time of writing is undergoing restoration at the Severn Valley Railway for Beamish, there is now another one for me to 'cop'. I shall have the chance to see this lovely little loco after all. I previously dismissed this as a private rather than an ex-main line loco (when it was out of reach). I now concede that perhaps it does have such a main line pedigree as it was used on the Highland Railway on passenger trains, albeit in private use. Having another engine to look forward to keeps the fascinating and addictive locospotting hobby alive.

When I see it, hopefully later this year, I think that really will be the last true British main line steam loco for me, nearly 60 years after I started the quest. On the other hand, I hope to live long enough to see the real new-build locos now under construction, when they are completed and steamed. There is always something to look forward to for the railway enthusiast.

APPENDIX I

RAIL ROVER JOURNEYS, 30 AUGUST TO 5 SEPTEMBER 1966

Details taken from log book compiled en route and notes made at the time. Unfortunately, identities of DMUs and some EMUs were not recorded as it was a time when the interest was in steam. Also, cross-London journeys by London Underground were not recorded as they were not covered by the BR Rail Rover ticket.

Day 1 TUESDAY, 30 AUGUST 1966

		timetable	actual	miles*

TRAIN 1 (SR)
Eight-car EMU (2 x 4-SUB) with set No 4673 leading. Brian and John had joined the train at Leatherhead.

		timetable	actual	miles*
Ewell West	*dep*	07.37	07.40	13
London Waterloo	*arr*	08.03	08.05	**13**

TRAIN 2 (LMR – GC)
DMU

London Marylebone	*dep*	08.38	08.38	121.5
Nottingham Victoria	*arr*	11.35	11.35	**134.5**

TRAIN 3 (LMR)
BR Sulzer Type 4 'Peak' No D75 on the 'Thames-Clyde Express'; mainly blue and light grey stock

Nottingham Midland	*dep*	12.00	12.13	35
Sheffield Midland	*arr*	13.00	13.14	**179.5**

TRAIN 4 (NER)
Four-car DMU

Sheffield Midland	*dep*	13.25	13.28	27
Wakefield Kirkgate	*arr*	14.21	14.21	**206.5**

TRAIN 5 (NER)
B1 class 4-6-0 No 61173; train comprised four coaches detached from London train

Wakefield Westgate	*dep*	16.32	16.32	18
Bradford Exchange	*arr*	17.09	17.10	**224.5**

TRAIN 6 (NER)
Fairburn 4MT class 2-6-4T No 42073 and two coaches to be attached to London, King's Cross train at Leeds. This loco is today preserved on the Lakeside & Haverthwaite Railway.

Bradford Exchange	*dep*	17.10	17.13	8
Leeds Central	*arr*	17.40	17.40	**232.5**

TRAIN 7 (NER)
Brush Type 4 No D1729.

Leeds Central	*dep*	17.40	17.43	10
Wakefield Westgate	*arr*	17.56	17.57	**242.5**

TRAIN 8 (NER/ER)
Brush Type 4 No D1534 on a mainly parcels train.

Wakefield Kirkgate	*dep*	22.33	22.35	175
London King's Cross	*arr*	03.26	03.20	**417.5**

Day 2 WEDNESDAY, 31 AUGUST 1966

TRAIN 9 (ER/NER)
Brush Type 4 on a parcels train with three passenger coaches

London King's Cross	*dep*	04.00	04.10	175.75
Wakefield Westgate	*arr*	08.17	08.17	**588.25**

TRAIN 10 (NER)
Class 5MT 4-6-0 No 44896 on ten-coach train

Wakefield Kirkgate	*dep*	09.12	09.12	69.5
Scarborough	*arr*	11.01	11.00	**657.75**

TRAIN 11 (NER)
Four-car DMU

Scarborough	*dep*	11.05	11.06	42
York	*arr*	12.00	11.59	**699.75**

TRAIN 12 (NER/LMR)
Six-car DMU

York	*dep*	14.07	14.07	75.25
Manchester Victoria	*arr*	16.05	16.05	**775**

TRAIN 13 (LMR)
Class 5MT 4-6-0 No 73157 on seven-coach train

Manchester Victoria	*dep*	16.30	16.30	84.25
Llandudno Junction	*arr*	18.34	18.30	**859.25**

*Figures in bold show cumulative miles travelled

TRAIN 14 (LMR)
Two-car DMU

Llandudno Junction	dep	18.40	18.40	40.25
Holyhead	arr	19.42	19.44	**899.5**

TRAIN 15 (LMR)
EE Type 4 No D333 on ten-coach train, with two TPOs.

Holyhead	dep	19.55	19.55	105.75
Crewe	arr	23.35	23.40	**1,005.25**

Day 3 THURSDAY, 1 SEPTEMBER 1966

TRAIN 16 (LMR/ScR)
Brush Type 4 No D1853 on 12-coach train of blue and light grey stock, with 'Royal Scot' nameboards. Arrival at Crewe delayed by late departure of the 'Irish Mail' on the same platform, due to a loco failure.

Crewe	dep	00.30	00.50	243.5
Glasgow Central	arr	05.45	05.45	**1,248.75**

TRAIN 17 (ScR)
NBL Type 2 No D6123 on six-coach the 'Grampian'.

Glasgow Buchanan St	dep	08.25	08.25	63.25
Perth	arr	09.39	09.39	**1,312**

TRAIN 18 (ScR)
BR Sulzer Type 2 No D7614 on ten-coach train

Perth	dep	10.50	10.51	20.75
Dundee Tay Bridge	arr	11.19	11.16	**1,332.75**

TRAIN 19 (ScR/NER/ER)
EE Type 4 No D290 Dundee to Edinburgh Waverley, where it became the 'Heart of Midlothian' for London King's Cross. Our through coaches were attached at Waverley by 350hp 0-6-0DE shunter No D3889. Hauled from Waverley to London King's Cross by EE 'Deltic' No D9016 Gordon Highlander – today owned by Martin Walker.

Dundee Tay Bridge	dep	12.04	12.05	452.25
London King's Cross	arr	20.30	20.32	**1,785**

TRAIN 20 (SR)
Waterloo & City Railway car No S84. The W&C was then part of BR on which we understood our Rover ticket was valid. The ticket inspector on our arrival at Waterloo disagreed, as we had expected, and asked us to pay the 6d fare, or whatever it was. We stood our ground and more senior members of staff were called. It was eventually agreed that we were correct and allowed to proceed, but the delay was of course much longer than the journey time.

Bank	dep	-	20.53	1.5
Waterloo W&C	arr	-	21.00	**1,786.5**

TRAIN 21 (SR)
Four-car EMU, 4-SUB set No 4362

London Waterloo	dep	21.30	21.30	13
Ewell West	arr	21.56	21.56	**1,799.5**

Day 4 FRIDAY, 2 SEPTEMBER 1966

TRAIN 22 (SR)
Four-car EMU, 4-SUB

Ewell West	dep	10.38	10.38	13
London Waterloo	arr	11.06	11.11	**1,812.5**

TRAIN 23 (WR)
Brush Type 4 No D1637 on nine-coach train. Delayed departure due to removal of defective coach.

London Paddington	dep	12.00	12.25	145.5
Cardiff General	arr	14.28	14.55	**1,958**

TRAIN 24 (WR)
Three-car DMU

Cardiff General	dep	15.10	15.10	11
Barry	arr	15.36	15.36	**1,969**

TRAIN 25 (WR)
Three-car DMU. Departure delayed due to several members of staff insisting we should alight from the train as we had not bought valid tickets, and we were told we would be questioned by the police, who were being called to the station. Upon refusal to leave the train, they entered the carriage and demanded to see our tickets, which we were pleased to produce, but they were not what they were expecting to see.

Before boarding, I had quickly bought a platform ticket for my collection and they thought this was the only ticket we three were holding. After reluctant apologies the train was allowed to depart with us on board, and waving, as we drew out from the platform.

Barry	dep	18.35	18.49	11
Cardiff General	arr	18.59	18.59	**1,980**

Exhibit 'A' – the offending platform ticket that caused a bit of bother.

TRAIN 26 (WR)

Three-car DMU

Cardiff General	*dep*	19.15	19.15	11.75
Newport	*arr*	19.30	19.30	**1,991.75**

TRAIN 27 (WR/LMR)

Brush Type 4 No D1790 (?) on eleven-coach train

Newport	*dep*	20.15	20.15	123.25
Crewe	*arr*	23.11	23.12	**2,115**

Day 5 SATURDAY, 3 SEPTEMBER 1966

TRAIN 28 (LMR)

EE Type 4 No D236 on ten-coach train, banked out of Crewe by Class 4MT 2-6-0 No 43020.

Crewe	*dep*	00.17	00.30	35.75
Wigan North Western	*arr*	00.57	01.05	**2,150.75**

TRAIN 29 (LMR/ScR)

BR Sulzer Type 4 'Peak' No D13 on 13-coach train

Wigan North Western	*dep*	01.50	01.59	207.5
Glasgow Central	*arr*	07.20	07.18	**2,358.25**

TRAIN 30 (ScR)

A4 class 4-6-2 No 60019 *Bittern* on eight-coach the 'Grampian', a special relief being the last A4-hauled train on BR in regular passenger service. No 60019 was subsequently preserved and is today restored for main line operation.

Glasgow Buchan St	*dep*	09.55	09.52	63.25
Perth	*arr*	11.09	11.08	**2,421.5**

TRAIN 31 (ScR)

BRCW Sulzer Type 2 No D5344 on five-coach train

Perth	*dep*	14.12	14.12	63.25
Glasgow Buchanan St	*arr*	15.45	15.43	**2,484.75**

TRAIN 32 (ScR/LMR)

Brush Type 4 No D1939 on nine-coach train

Glasgow Central	*dep*	16.15	16.15	243.25
Crewe	*arr*	20.41	20.41	**2,728**

TRAIN 33 (LMR)

EE Type 4 No D294 on 14-coach 'Emerald Isle Express'. Travelled in loco cab from Chester to Holyhead.

Crewe	*dep*	21.21	21.21	105.75
Holyhead	*arr*	23.18	23.14	**2,833.75**

Day 6 SUNDAY, 4 SEPTEMBER 1966

TRAIN 34 (LMR)

EE Type 4 No D303 on ten-coach train, riding in the cab all the way to Crewe, which was only a signal-check and not a timetable passenger stop. There was an Inspector on the platform, so we had to be unceremoniously ejected from rear cab. Delayed departure from Holyhead caused by faulty loco boiler, after two other locos had failed completely. Travelled for a whole hour at 80mph.

Holyhead	*dep*	00.40	01.00	105.75
Crewe	*arr*	–	02.45	**2,939.5**

TRAIN 35 (LMR)

AL5 class No E3061 on the 'Royal Scot'

Crewe	*dep*	03.22	03.12	158
London Euston	*arr*	05.50	05.45	**3,097.5**

TRAIN 36 (LMR)

AL6 class No E3200 on 13 coaches. North of Bletchley 102.2mph logged, the highest speed of the week.

London Euston	*dep*	10.20	10.20	158
Crewe	*arr*	12.50	13.00	**3,255.5**

TRAIN 37 (LMR)

Brush Type 4 No D1941 on ten-coach train

Crewe	*dep*	15.00	15.23	24
Warrington Bank Quay	*arr*	15.22	15.44	**3,279.5**

TRAIN 38 (LMR)

EE Type 4 No D291 on 13-coach train

Warrington Bank Quay	*dep*	17.43	17.54	24
Crewe	*arr*	18.15	18.17	**3,303.5**

TRAIN 39 (LMR)

Class AM4 four-car EMU set No 015

Crewe	*dep*	22.20	22.23	35.5
Liverpool Lime St	*arr*	23.13	23.15	**3,339**

TRAIN 40 (LMR/NER)

Class 5MT 4-6-0 No 73131 (Caprotti valve gear) on five-coach train to Huddersfield where loco was changed to EE Type 4 No D352, plus four additional coaches. Travelled in ex-LMS coach.

Liverpool Lime St	*dep*	23.38	23.38	74
Leeds City	*arr*	01.50	03.00	**3,413**

Day 7 MONDAY, 5 SEPTEMBER 1966

TRAIN 41 (NER/LMR)
BR Sulzer Type 4 'Peak' No D39 on ten-coach train

Leeds City	*dep*	02.42	03.24	113
Carlisle	*arr*	04.54	05.23	**3,526**

TRAIN 42 (LMR)
Two-car DMU.

Carlisle	*dep*	13.25	13.25	40
Whitehaven (Bransty)	*arr*	14.35	14.36	**3,566**

TRAIN 43 (LMR)
Two-car Derby DMU, including power car No M79009

Whitehaven (Bransty)	*dep*	15.15	15.15	46
Barrow-in-Furness	*arr*	16.50	16.48	**3,612**

TRAIN 44 (LMR)
Four-car DMU.

Barrow-in-Furness	*dep*	17.15	17.15	55.75
Preston	*arr*	18.58	18.58	**3,667.75**

TRAIN 45 (LMR)
Brush Type 4 No D1618 on eleven-coach train to Crewe, from there it was behind AL3 class No E3029

Preston	*dep*	19.44	19.55	209
London Euston	*arr*	22.58	23.09	**3,876.75**

TRAIN 46 (SR)
Four-car, 4-SUB EMU
Brian and John travelled on to Leatherhead

London Waterloo	*dep*	23.45	23.45	13
Ewell West	*arr*	00.13	00.13	**3,889.75**

APPENDIX II

RAIL ROVER SHED VISITS

Loco names are shown, but in many cases were no longer carried.

62B Dundee (Tay Bridge)
VISITED AT ABOUT 11.30 ON THURSDAY, 1 SEPTEMBER.

Number	Name	Class	Wheel arrangement
44720		5MT	4-6-0
44782		5MT	4-6-0
45473		5MT	4-6-0
46464		2MT	2-6-0
60530	*Sayajirao*	A2	4-6-2
60813		V2	2-6-2
60818		V2	2-6-2
60836		V2	2-6-2
60919		V2	2-6-2
61293		B1	4-6-0
61403		B1	4-6-0
64547		J37	0-6-0
64577		J37	0-6-0
64597		J37	0-6-0
64608		J37	0-6-0

63A Perth
VISITED ABOUT MID-DAY ON SATURDAY, 3 SEPTEMBER

Number	Name	Class	Wheel arrangement
42154		4MT	2-6-4T
44698		5MT	4-6-0
44704		5MT	4-6-0
44705		5MT	4-6-0
44727		5MT	4-6-0
44797		5MT	4-6-0
44878		5MT	4-6-0
44954		5MT	4-6-0
44997		5MT	4-6-0
44998		5MT	4-6-0
45461		5MT	4-6-0
45472		5MT	4-6-0
45475		5MT	4-6-0
60026	*Miles Beevor*	A4	4-6-2
60034	*Lord Faringdon*	A4	4-6-2
80028		4MT	2-6-4T
80092		4MT	2-6-4T
80093		4MT	2-6-4T
80126		4MT	2-6-4T

5B Crewe South VISITED ABOUT 13.30 ON SUNDAY, 4 SEPTEMBER.

Number	Name	Class	Wheel arrangement	Number	Name	Class	Wheel arrangement
42548		4MT	2-6-4T	47494		3F	0-6-0T
42942		5MT	2-6-0	47521		3F	0-6-0T
43007		4MT	2-6-0	47530		3F	0-6-0T
43020		4MT	2-6-0	47592		3F	0-6-0T
43024		4MT	2-6-0	48057		8F	2-8-0
43026		4MT	2-6-0	48092		8F	2-8-0
43034		4MT	2-6-0	48186		8F	2-8-0
43052		4MT	2-6-0	48255		8F	2-8-0
43112		4MT	2-6-0	48256		8F	2-8-0
43113		4MT	2-6-0	48338		8F	2-8-0
43151		4MT	2-6-0	48343		8F	2-8-0
44663		5MT	4-6-0	48349		8F	2-8-0
44677		5MT	4-6-0	48526		8F	2-8-0
44681		5MT	4-6-0	48551		8F	2-8-0
44684		5MT	4-6-0	48554		8F	2-8-0
44685		5MT	4-6-0	48559		8F	2-8-0
44759		5MT	4-6-0	48718		8F	2-8-0
44761		5MT	4-6-0	48724		8F	2-8-0
44771		5MT	4-6-0	48749		8F	2-8-0
44774		5MT	4-6-0	48758		8F	2-8-0
44799		5MT	4-6-0	70002	Geoffrey Chaucer	7MT	4-6-2
44819		5MT	4-6-0	70005	John Milton	7MT	4-6-2
44832		5MT	4-6-0	70008	Black Prince	7MT	4-6-2
44833		5MT	4-6-0	70009	Alfred the Great	7MT	4-6-2
44834		5MT	4-6-0	70011	Hotspur	7MT	4-6-2
44897		5MT	4-6-0	70012	John of Gaunt	7MT	4-6-2
44935		5MT	4-6-0	70014	Iron Duke	7MT	4-6-2
44937		5MT	4-6-0	70018	Flying Dutchman	7MT	4-6-2
44993		5MT	4-6-0	70025	Western Star	7MT	4-6-2
45005		5MT	4-6-0	70027	Rising Star	7MT	4-6-2
45021		5MT	4-6-0	70028	Royal Star	7MT	4-6-2
45033		5MT	4-6-0	70041	Sir John Moore	7MT	4-6-2
45060		5MT	4-6-0	70042	Lord Roberts	7MT	4-6-2
45107		5MT	4-6-0	70049	Solway Firth	7MT	4-6-2
45145		5MT	4-6-0	70051	Firth of Forth	7MT	4-6-2
45154	Lanarkshire Yeomanry	5MT	4-6-0	73093		5MT	4-6-0
45203		5MT	4-6-0	73160		5MT	4-6-0
45232		5MT	4-6-0	78018		2MT	2-6-0
45259		5MT	4-6-0	78019		2MT	2-6-0
45261		5MT	4-6-0	78031		2MT	2-6-0
45299		5MT	4-6-0	78036		2MT	2-6-0
45331		5MT	4-6-0	92004		9F	2-10-0
45345		5MT	4-6-0	92019		9F	2-10-0
45352		5MT	4-6-0	92045		9F	2-10-0
45391		5MT	4-6-0	92055		9F	2-10-0
45393		5MT	4-6-0	92086		9F	2-10-0
45421		5MT	4-6-0	92106		9F	2-10-0
45428		5MT	4-6-0	92110		9F	2-10-0
45432		5MT	4-6-0	92111		9F	2-10-0
45446		5MT	4-6-0	92114		9F	2-10-0
46495		2MT	2-6-0	92154		9F	2-10-0
46512		2MT	2-6-0	92161		9F	2-10-0
47482		3F	0-6-0T	92249		9F	2-10-0

8B Warrington Dallam

VISITED ABOUT 15.45 ON SUNDAY, 4 SEPTEMBER

Number	Name	Class	Wheel arrangement
44732		5MT	4-6-0
44819		5MT	4-6-0
44935		5MT	4-6-0
45109		5MT	4-6-0
45129		5MT	4-6-0
45187		5MT	4-6-0
45221		5MT	4-6-0
45232		5MT	4-6-0
45303		5MT	4-6-0
45312		5MT	4-6-0
45424		5MT	4-6-0
48163		8F	2-8-0
48301		8F	2-8-0
48357		8F	2-8-0
48506		8F	2-8-0
70030	*William Wordsworth*	7MT	4-6-2
73142		5MT	4-6-0
92086		9F	2-10-0
92095		9F	2-10-0
92119		9F	2-10-0
92132		9F	2-10-0
92156		9F	2-10-0
92224		9F	2-10-0

Number	Name	Class	Wheel arrangement
45212		5MT	4-6-0
45217		5MT	4-6-0
45228		5MT	4-6-0
45236		5MT	4-6-0
45253		5MT	4-6-0
45254		5MT	4-6-0
45319		5MT	4-6-0
45353		5MT	4-6-0
45432		5MT	4-6-0
45442		5MT	4-6-0
45477		5MT	4-6-0
47471		3F	0-6-0T
47531		3F	0-6-0T
47641		3F	0-6-0T
70001	*Lord Hurcomb*	7MT	4-6-2
70003	*John Bunyan*	7MT	4-6-2
70006	*Robert Burns*	7MT	4-6-2
70037	*Hereward the Wake*	7MT	4-6-2
70040	*Clive of India*	7MT	4-6-2
70046	*ANZAC*	7MT	4-6-2
70047		7MT	4-6-2
70050	*Firth of Clyde*	7MT	4-6-2
92008		9F	2-10-0
92009		9F	2-10-0
92015		9F	2-10-0
92019		9F	2-10-0
92043		9F	2-10-0

12A Carlisle Kingmoor

VISITED ABOUT 07.30 ON MONDAY, 5 SEPTEMBER

Number	Name	Class	Wheel arrangement
43049		4MT	2-6-0
43120		4MT	2-6-0
43121		4MT	2-6-0
43139		4MT	2-6-0
44675		5MT	4-6-0
44726		5MT	4-6-0
44736		5MT	4-6-0
44795		5MT	4-6-0
44854		5MT	4-6-0
44884		5MT	4-6-0
44887		5MT	4-6-0
44900		5MT	4-6-0
44911		5MT	4-6-0
44982		5MT	4-6-0
45002		5MT	4-6-0
45013		5MT	4-6-0
45018		5MT	4-6-0
45065		5MT	4-6-0
45097		5MT	4-6-0
45126		5MT	4-6-0
45135		5MT	4-6-0
45167		5MT	4-6-0
45185		5MT	4-6-0
45195		5MT	4-6-0

12B Carlisle (Upperby)

VISITED LATE-MORNING ON MONDAY, 5 SEPTEMBER

Number	Name	Class	Wheel arrangement
41207		2MT	2-6-2T
41217		2MT	2-6-2T
41285		2MT	2-6-2T
43047		4MT	2-6-0
45019		5MT	4-6-0
45273		5MT	4-6-0
45340		5MT	4-6-0
45371		5MT	4-6-0
46426		2MT	2-6-0
46455		2MT	2-6-0
46458		2MT	2-6-0
46513		2MT	2-6-0
70020	*Mercury*	7MT	4-6-2
70022	*Tornado*	7MT	4-6-2
70024	*Vulcan*	7MT	4-6-2
70031	*Byron*	7MT	4-6-2
70041	*Sir John Moore*	7MT	4-6-2
70048	*The Territorial Army 1908-1958*	7MT	4-6-2
92096		9F	2-10-0

APPENDIX III

LOCOMOTIVES PRESERVED BY THE BTC IN 1960/61

There were various anomalies in the original BTC list, and the one below is based on that published in *The Railway Magazine,* March 1961, but with locations added for the 44 locos already officially preserved at that time. Withdrawal dates of the actual locos preserved have been added to the list of locos then scheduled for preservation.

Great Western Railway

Year	Origin	Type	Number/name	Place of preservation in 1960
1837	GWR	2-2-2	*North Star*	Swindon Museum (non-working replica) (1)
1868	SDR	0-4-0T	*Tiny*	Newton Abbot station (7ft 0in gauge) (1)
1897	GWR	0-6-0	2516	Swindon Museum (4)
1903	GWR	4-4-0	3440 *City of Truro*	Working order (1)
1903	GWR	2-8-0	2800 (2818*)	Withdrawn October 1963 (3)
1907	GWR	4-6-0	4003 *Lode Star*	Swindon Works (2)

Southern Railway and constituents

1880	LBSCR	0-6-0T	82 *Boxhill*	Clapham Museum (1)
1882	LBSCR	2-4-0	214 *Gladstone*	York Museum (5)
1893	LSWR	4-4-0	563	Clapham Museum (1)
1901	SECR	4-4-0	737	Clapham Museum (3)

London Midland & Scottish Railway and constituents

1838	LMR	0-4-2	57 *Lion*	Crewe Works	
1845	GJR	2-2-2	45 *Columbine*	York Museum (1)	
1846	FR	0-4-0	3 *Coppernob*	Horwich Works (1)	
1847	LNWR	2-2-2	173/302 *Cornwall*	Crewe Works (1)	
1857	SPR/LNWR	0-4-0WT	5 *Shannon*	Wantage Road station (1)	
1865	LNWR	0-4-0T	*Pet*	Crewe Works (1ft 6in gauge) (1)	
1865	LNWR	0-4-0ST	1439	Crewe Works (5)	
1866	MR	2-4-0	158A	Derby Works (2)	
1886	CR	4-2-2	123	Working order (1)	
1889	LYR	2-4-2T	1008	Horwich Works (3)	
1892	LNWR	2-4-0	790 *Hardwicke*	Crewe Works (1)	
1894	HR	4-6-0	103	Working order (1)	
1898	HR	4-4-0	54398 *Ben Alder*	Boat of Garten shed** (3)	** Broken up in May 1966
1899	MR	4-2-2	118	Derby Works (1)	
1902	MR	4-4-0	1000	Working order (3)	
1909	LTSR	4-4-2T	80 *Thundersley*	Derby Works (3)	

London & North Eastern Railway and constituents

1825	SDR	0-4-0	*Locomotion* No 1	Bank Top station, Darlington (1)
1845	SDR	0-6-0	No 25 *Derwent*	Bank Top station, Darlington (1)
1869	NER	2-2-4T	66 *Aerolite*	York Museum (1)

1875	NER	2-4-0	910	York Museum (1)
1870	GNR	4-2-2	1	York Museum (1)
1874	NER	0-6-0	1275	York Museum (1)
1885	NER	2-4-0	1463	York Museum (1)
1893	NER	4-4-0	1621	York Museum (1)
1895	GER	2-4-0	490	Clapham Museum (3)
1898	GNR	4-4-2	990 *Henry Oakley*	York Museum (1)
1902	GNR	4-4-2	251	York Museum (1)
1911	GCR	2-8-0	O4 (63601*)	Withdrawn June 1963 (3)
1913	NBR	4-4-0	256 *Glen Douglas*	Working order (4)
1920	GNSR	4-4-0	49 *Gordon Highlander*	Working order (4)

London Transport and constituents

| 1866 | Metropolitan R | 4-4-0T | 23 | Clapham Museum (3) |
| 1872 | Wotton T | 4wWT | | Clapham Museum (5) |

Mersey Railway

| 1885 | Mersey R | 0-6-4T | *Cecil Raikes* | NCB, stored (5) |

Industrial and military

| 1822 | Hetton Colliery | 0-4-0 | - | York Museum (1) |
| 1893 | SMLR | 0-4-2T | *Gazelle* | Longmoor Military Railway (1) |

As published, locos were listed as:

1) Preserved by the Railway Companies before 1948
2) Preserved by the BTC 1951
3) Preserved by the BTC 1953
4) Preserved since 1953
5) Donated since 1953

LOCOMOTIVES SCHEDULED FOR PRESERVATION BY BTC IN 1960

Great Western Railway

Year	Origin	Type	Class	Number/name	Date withdrawn by BR
1923	GWR	4-6-0	4073	4073 *Caerphilly Castle*	May 1960
1927	GWR	4-6-0	6000	6000 *King George V*	December 1962
1947	GWR	0-6-0PT	9400	9400*	December 1959

Southern Railway and constituents

1874	LSWR	2-4-0WT	3298	30587*	December 1962
1897	LSWR	0-4-4T	M7	30245*	November 1962
1899	LSWR	4-4-0	T9	30120*	July 1963
1925	SR	4-6-0	N15	30777 *Sir Lamiel**	October 1961
1926	SR	4-6-0	LN	30850 *Lord Nelson**	August 1962
1934	SR	4-4-0	V	30925 *Cheltenham**	December 1962
1942	SR	0-6-0	Q1	33001*	May 1964
1946	SR	4-6-2	WC/BB	34051 *Winston Churchill**	September 1965

London Midland & Scottish Railway and constituents

1921	LNWR	0-8-0	G2	485 (49395)*	November 1959
1924	LMSR	0-6-0	4F	4027 (44027)*	November 1964
1926	LMSR	2-6-0	5MT	13000 (42700)*	March 1966
1934	LMSR	4-6-0	5MT	5000 (45000)*	October 1967
1934	LMSR	2-6-4T	4MT	2500 (42500)*	June 1962
1937	LMSR	4-6-2	7P	6235 (46235) *City of Birmingham*	September 1964

London & North Eastern Railway and constituents

1891	NER	0-6-0	C (J21)	1576	See note
1904	GER	0-6-0T	S56 (J69)	87 (68633)	November 1960
1919	NER	0-8-0	T3 (Q7)	901 (63460)*	December 1962
1920	GCR	4-4-0	11F (D11)	506 (62660) *Butler-Henderson*	October 1960
1936	LNER	2-6-2	V2	4771 (60800) *Green Arrow**	August 1962
1938	LNER	4-6-2	A4	4468 (60022) *Mallard*	April 1963

British Railways Standard designs

1951	BR	4-6-2	7	70000 *Britannia*	June 1966 See note
1954	BR	4-6-2	8	71000 *Duke of Gloucester*	See note
1956	BR	4-6-0	5		See note
1960	BR	2-10-0	9F	92220 *Evening Star*	March 1965

* These locos were not specified at the time the list was published and only the class details were given, but interestingly, the year quoted turned out to be the correct building date for nearly every example actually chosen, except for the 'Schools' class 4-4-0, given as 1930 and the Bulleid Pacific as 1945, with later examples being finally selected.

NER Class C (LNER Class J21). The loco from this class that was ultimately preserved was No 65033 (NER No 876 of 1889) withdrawn in April 1962. Although reserved for the National Collection it was subsequently removed as it was not considered to be in original enough condition. Fortunately, it was able to be saved after five years languishing in Darlington Works, and taken to the North of England Open Air Museum (then the North Regional Industrial Museum), Beamish. This loco is now owned by the Locomotive Conservation and Learning Trust which is working with the NRM at Shildon to restore it. No 1576 (65099) was scrapped in February 1966 as its main frame was cracked and had been stored at Darlington without a boiler in situ since September 1960. It is understood its boiler was transferred to

No 65033, but this remains to be confirmed.

No 70000 was later replaced as the National Collection example by No 70013 *Oliver Cromwell*, withdrawn at the end of BR steam in August 1968, and No 70000 was then preserved privately.

No 71000 was dropped from the official schedule and after a period in Woodham Bros scrapyard at Barry was acquired for preservation privately. One set of its valve gear had been claimed previously for the Science Museum.

No BR Class 5 was retained by BR although an example with Caprotti valve gear had been listed. No 73129 of this type was eventually secured for preservation privately from Woodham Bros, Barry as well as Nos 73050, 73082 *Camelot*, 73096 and 73156, all bought privately.

The Scottish locomotives, Nos 49, 103, 123 and 256 were passed to the Glasgow Museum of Transport and not the National Collection.

No 46235 *City of Birmingham* is no longer regarded as part of the National Collection. Now preserved in Birmingham as a static exhibit, it was replaced by No 46229 *Duchess of Hamilton* acquired from Butlins.

BIBLIOGRAPHY

Three books were vital when pursuing my loco spotting and photography interests in the 1960s:

Ian Allan *abcs* – regional, combined volumes and Locoshed for various years, 1949–68. These books made it all possible.

The British Locomotive Shed Directory (Ninth edition 1960) by Flt Lt Aidan L.F. Fuller, a 'hero' who I was delighted to meet many years later when attending Birmingham Locomotive Club – Industrial Locomotive Information Section meetings in Birmingham.

British Railways Pre-Grouping Atlas and Gazetteer (Fourth edition) by W. Philip Conolly, who (I only learnt many years later) had lived about half a mile from me in West Ewell. Today's enthusiasts might be puzzled as to why I should have been using a pre-1923 map for my rail travels in the 1960s. The answer is that this was simply the only such book giving a comprehensive mapping coverage of lines, stations, junctions etc. However, it was of course very educational with regard to railway history as one travelled around the country.

Many more-recent publications have been consulted and provided valuable information while compiling this book, including:

A Locomotive History of the Railways of the Isle of Wight D.L. Bradley (RCTS 1982)
An Illustrated History of British Railways' Workshops Edgar Larkin (OPC 1992)
BR Steam Surrender Roger Siviter (Kingfisher Railway Productions 1988)
British Railways Steam Locomotives 1948-1968 Hugh Longworth (Ian Allan 2005)

Crewe Works Narrow Gauge System Second edition Edward Talbot and Clive Taylor (LNWR Society 2005)
Mainline to Industry Frank Jones (Lightmoor Press 1998)
Mile By Mile David Maxey (Peter Watts Publishing 1987)
Nameplates of the Big Four Frank Burridge (OPC 1975)
Preserved Locomotives Second enlarged edition H.C. Casserley (Ian Allan 1969)
Preserved Locomotives of British Railways Thirteenth edition Peter Fox and Robert Pritchard (Platform 5 2009)
Preserved Locomotives in the British Isles M. Swift (Industrial Railway Society and Narrow Gauge Railway Society 1970)
The Barry Locomotive Phenomenon Francis Blake and Peter Nicholson (OPC 1987)
The Barry Story, Includes The Barry List Tenth edition by Martin Beckett and Roger Hardingham (Kingfisher Productions 2010)
Southern Steam Specials 1966/7 John H. Bird (Kingfisher Railway Productions 1987)
Southern Steam Surrender John H. Bird (Kingfisher Railway Productions 1987)
Steam for Scrap The Complete Story by Nigel Trevana and Tony Wakefield (Atlantic Transport Publishers undated)
50 Years of Preserved Steam on the Main Line J.S. Whiteley and G.W. Morrison (OPC 1989)

Magazines: *The Railway Magazine, Modern Railways* and *Trains Illustrated*
Various preserved railways and railway museum stock books and guides
Railtour booklets published by the organisers
Website www.sixbellsjunction.co.uk
The Railtour Files

INDEX

While it seemed every other railway enthusiast we knew had travelled up to Ais Gill to witness the passing of the 'Fifteen Guinea special', BR's farewell-to-steam tour on 11 August 1968, Rich Morris and I went south. We had 'signed-off' BR steam the previous weekend, the actual last day of scheduled BR steam and thereafter, steam-hauled trains on BR were only enthusiasts' specials. Nevertheless, we went to see a main line loco that remained in active service.

This was ex-LSWR B4 class 0-4-0T, still carrying its former BR smokebox door numberplate 30096, and 71A Eastleigh shed code plate. Withdrawn by BR in October 1963 having started life in 1893 at Southampton Docks. It had now returned there, but now operated by fuel merchants Corralls at Dible's Wharf, Northam, where named *Corrall Queen*.

It was sold into preservation in 1972, acquired by members of the Bulleid Society, and is now based on the Bluebell Railway. BR may have dispensed with steam in August 1968, but we were going to continue our interest in the subject regardless!